T
T
fo
s

TRAVELLER'S QUEST

TRAVELLER'S QUEST

Original Contributions towards a
Philosophy of Travel

BY

Henri Bordeaux, Hilton Brown, Rupert Croft-
Cooke, Lord Dunsany, P. T. Etherton, Negley
Farson, Peter Freuchen, John Garstang, Cora J.
Gordon, Frank Illingworth, Ella Maillart, Adrian
Seligman, Freya Stark, Walter Starkie, H. M.
Tomlinson, Alec Waugh.

Edited by
M. A. MICHAEL

London   Edinburgh   Glasgow
WILLIAM HODGE AND COMPANY LIMITED

First published October 1950

The translation of Mr. Henri Bordeaux's essay from the French, and that of Mr. Peter Freuchen from the Danish, has been made by the editor.

PRINTED IN GREAT BRITAIN
SPOTTISWOODE, BALLANTYNE AND CO. LTD.
LONDON AND COLCHESTER

Tou

CONTENTS

v

"I pity the man who can travel from Dan to Beersheba and cry, ' 'Tis all barren!' "

LAURENCE STERNE

"He travels safe, and not unpleasantly, who is guarded by poverty and guided by love."

SIR PHILIP SIDNEY

"Go far—too far you cannot, still the farther
The more experience finds you: And go sparing;—
One meal a week will serve you, and one suit,
Through all your travels; for you'll find it certain,
The poorer and the baser you appear,
The more you look through still."

BEAUMONT AND FLETCHER

"Rester chez soi est une negligence dont, tôt ou tard, on se vera puni."

PAUL MORAND

WHAT IS TRAVEL?

An Introduction

M. A. Michael

PARIS—2½ hours, Istanbul—14 hours, Reykjavik—17 hours, Santiago—41 hours, Cape Town—57 hours! Just pay your money and you may step into the technologist's working model of the magic carpet and be sped to the other end of the world if not in a trice, at any rate in not very much longer.

But what on earth for?

Why does man want to play leap-frog in seven-league boots about the world? I can see that for peddlers it has its commercial uses, but do none of the others who take these giant hops wish to see what lies in between? Something unreasoning within me revolts at the idea of the magic carpet being reduced to a means of public transport. In the same way my mind refuses to accept the implication in a recent advertisement in the daily press offering travel "bargains." Travel is a state of mind and not a commodity to be bought or sold, and all the so-called "travel" bureaux and agencies are falsely named. They are sellers of tickets, forwarders of human beings and dealers in board and lodging, exciting wares I know, but they have nothing to do with real travel.

Travel—you see the word so often in the street and in the newspapers that you might think this was the age of travel. The steam engine and the internal combustion engine have indeed revolutionized the transport of merchandise and made it incredibly easy for man to translate himself to places half the world away and farther still; but, in doing so, they have so compressed time and space that few of us are left with much of either. The guard's whistle and the drone of aeroplanes in the sky are together sounding the death knell of true travel, not proclaiming its heyday.

What is travel? All travel, as Freya Stark says, is a quest, a conscious or unconscious searching for something that is lacking in our lives or in ourselves. This it always has been, though in the days before the world became black with ink it was a more conscious quest for more material things. Now that there are no new markets to be found, no new goods to buy, no new lands with unknown riches to discover, the merchant of Danzig no longer loads his goods on to pack-horses and sets off to sell them in far Cathay. He uses the telephone instead. The traders of Samarkand have exchanged their camels for Bentley's code, and the Doges of Venice have turned themselves into "bears" and "bulls." There may still be romance in business, but there is certainly no travel, just hurried journeying.

The modern traveller travels for himself alone. His reasons for going are purely personal, as are the gains of his travels.

A century or two ago this was by no means the case. In those days in many countries the intending traveller had to obtain the permission of the State before he could leave his country, and on his return he was expected to impart all that he had learned and observed to the authorities. The old books of "hints to travellers" listed the things the traveller was supposed to observe and enquire into. These lists occupy several pages and read like the Intelligence programme of the Secret Service. In those days at least there must have been some justification for the inability of the Russian to understand how anyone could travel for travel's sake alone and not be just a spy. Similarly, the student or academician who ventured beyond his country's boundaries was expected to ferret and fossick after the secrets of nature. Linnaeus in his *Benefits of Travel* enumerates the things to which the person of learning should devote attention in a list that is quite as long as that of the intelligence tasks laid down for the ordinary person. Today, the traveller is in search of different things, things mostly of the spirit, and he leaves the furtherance of the tasks allotted to his predecessors to the specialist. The division of labour and of knowledge have changed the traveller's role from an active to a passive one, except in what concerns his own mental and spiritual growth.

I have always thought that the urges which drove the early travellers out on their wanderings must have been in essence violent, rather than quiet and compelling; that these were men avid for riches, covetous of fame, striving to be the first to visit distant places, craving to know more than their fellows. If that is so, then their motives were those which today make men stay at home imprisoned in their laboratories, libraries and offices, while the impulses that send the modern traveller forth are quite different. Behind his travels there is above all longing. He is no conqueror, no crusader, no knight in armour searching for a holy grail, not even a blazer of trails, but rather a Saracen maid searching for her Gilbert.

It is not only the motives for travel that have changed, but everything about it down to the traveller's equipment. A hundred years ago the traveller was advised to equip himself against every eventuality with articles that ranged from cutlass to catheter. His usual means of travel was some kind of carriage which he either took with him from home or bought in the country he first visited, and it was pulled from stage to stage by post-horses. That was an excellent system that almost precluded hurry and gave constant opportunities for such conversations as Marnier had with the Swedish postmistress "concerning the character of her cat and fecundity of her hens."

That was the true heyday of travel, an age when time was not yet money and no man minded whether it waited for him or not. Those conditions have gone for ever, but I have always felt that if I could ever achieve sufficient independence to be able to wander—not having the courage to set out before—I should follow the example of the arch-traveller, the gypsy, buy one of his caravans and a Suffolk Punch and so travel not with the complete independence of Asclepiades who made the Grand Tour on the back of a cow and lived off her milk, but with the maximum of independence, leisure and comfort possible today. Surely that is the ideal way, especially when your quest is undefined, a complex of longings and hungers all pulling and tugging at once.

Another great change that has come over travel is the shift of interest from man and his works to Nature and her beauties. As Henri Bordeaux reminds us in his essay it is not so long ago since people had no appreciation for natural beauties unless they served as a setting for man, or as he puts it "wore our livery." In those days people travelled chiefly to see their fellows and to learn about and of them, but we have lost some of our conceit since then and have come to see that Nature is the greater artist whose work man defiles more often than he enhances it. Man, being man, has largely driven the things of the spirit from the places in which he dwells; God has withdrawn to the open, and it is there beneath the sky and the stars that many seek Him today.

Certain parts of the world, the high places, the seas and the oceans, have a specific appeal to certain people, they know more or less what they will find there, and to them the railway, the motor car and the aeroplane are covenient means of approach, nothing more. The travel begins where transport stops.

The apologists of the railway have contended that it is a superior form of conveyance to the motor car because from the carriage window you can often catch glimpses of the interiors of homes, see people at work in their shops, or in the fields; that you see the backs of houses and so can gain some insight into the way the people live. That is true, but how little it is. You might as well say you have travelled because you have seen the so-called travelogues that at the cinema sometimes accompany the news film. As Vandal said, when you go by train, you do not travel, you merely arrive—and you arrive in considerable comfort. I am the last to decry the pleasures of the *wagon-lit* or restaurant car, but they are pleasures that have nothing to do with travel. To most of us they represent a sudden rise in our standard of living which gratifies our vanity and gives us a pleasant feeling of importance. For a few hours or days we are waited upon hand and foot and naturally we like it. But that is no part of travel. The fact is that the moment you entrust yourself to a mechanical means of transport you surrender part of your liberty. The machine takes charge of you. A train will only stop at certain specified points. An aeroplane has not even a communication cord. Admittedly, a motor car can be stopped, but because you would have to retrace your steps to look at whatever it was caught your attention, your natural inclination, being human and, so, lazy, is to say: "Never mind!" and on you rush. Then you are always aware that the motor car requires petrol, oil and water which can only be obtained at certain specified points. You will hesitate to turn down some attractive by-road or lane, even though intuition tells you that some enchantment is to be found at the end of it, because you doubt whether the tyres or springs will stand up to its surface. And so you drive along a route planned in advance, going from the expected to the expected, preening yourself because you are

4

abroad and saying to yourself "I'm a traveller now;" but you are nothing of the sort.

Unfortunately, today, when in a three weeks' holiday it is possible to girdle the world three times, it is far from easy to be a true traveller. Travel, indeed, is one of those things of which it is easier to say what it is not, than to define. In the first place, it is necessary to distinguish true travel from going abroad for a holiday, which may be travel, but is usually just a turning-down of the leaf to mark our place in the book of life which we then lay aside for a few weeks and with it our cares and responsibilities. Then there are the journeyings of those whose profession or job takes them abroad. These people may travel, as well as journey, but such travel is subsidiary and so cannot count as true travel. What then is travel? It would be easier, perhaps, to say who is a traveller. At any rate, it should be possible to construct an ideal type.

In my youth I should have described the true traveller as a cross between the Beloved Vagabond and Alain Gerbault. Now, having journeyed in various parts of the world and having read the opinions of such true travellers as Aldous Huxley, C. E. Montague, Norman Douglas and those who have contributed to this book, I should define the "ideal" traveller as one who in the first place has set out in search of something, definite or indefinite. He may have a concrete aim, or just a vague longing, but his journey is a quest. In his travels he must enjoy absolute liberty and independence. The first means that he must not plan his travels more than to set himself a vague goal. He may say: "I shall go to the Puszta and see if I can find it there"—whatever his "it" may be. But he will not be surprised if, instead, he lands up in Lapland. He can never tell, and he should not want to be able to tell. There should be no arbitrary time-limit set to his travels, for true travel can have no time-table. The traveller must have plenty of time, time to stop, to look and to investigate, time to turn aside and follow his nose or his intuition, and, above all, the time to linger where delight is. It is only to the tourist that it really matters to what places he goes. If you set out heading vaguely for Rome, Stockholm or Seville, and end up in some other place at a quite different point of the compass, what does it matter? Rome, Stockholm or Seville will still be there, and so are you, and so is life. All things can wait. Perhaps, as I do, you regret that you never went to Spain before the Civil War, or to Budapest before the Russians destroyed it, and so have missed things of real beauty. That is just one of Fate's tricks and must be accepted. If you rush round trying to see the whole world before another catastrophe destroys still more of its beauties, you will see nothing. To those who hurry the true traveller has the same to say as had the old Border farmer who was driving along the centre of a narrow road in an aged decrepit Ford to the driver of another car ten years its junior. The driver of the other car was an impatient man and he kept blowing his horn, but the old farmer would not budge. Finally the road widened so much that the second car could have passed on either side. As it drew level, the old farmer leaned out and shouted: "I can't see how it can possibly matter to anyone when a man like you gets anywhere."

Complete liberty means that there are no days of the week, just morning and night, rain and sunshine, heat and cold, no worrying about when you must be back. To be completely independent the traveller requires a private and sufficient income, or the knowledge of some craft by the practice of which he can earn money as he goes along, or would be able to but for the restrictions imposed upon him in this age of freedom and democracy. The amount required is not great, for true travel means living among the people mostly on the cheap, seldom putting up at other than modest inns and certainly never at the international luxury hotels frequented by those who are neither travellers nor tourists, but strange beings without perception, who flit from place to place the only difference between which is the currency in which the bill is paid, those whom officialdom might call "Blue-trainees" and "Orient-Expressionists."

The ideal traveller being bound by no considerations of time or space will always be ready to stop, to look, to investigate, to talk. Some people, like Karel Čapek, whose perception was that of true genius, have been able to get the feel of a country and its people through the window of a railway carriage or motor car, but most of us are like a certain business man of my acquaintance whose total knowledge of the cow was that it existed in fields and produced milk. This he knew because he had seen them in fields from his motor car and had drunk milk.

For all but the exception, the genius, it is essential to be able to talk with the people encountered whilst travelling, with the countryman in his cottage, with the townsman in his shop, with all who are abroad on their lawful or unlawful occasions, and so the traveller must be able to speak the language of the country in which he finds himself. In the old days this was not so necessary because educated people the world over spoke Latin and possibly Greek as well, and with them at least the traveller could converse. Today, however, we must go to the pains of learning the languages of the countries we intend to visit, if we are really to travel in them.

The true traveller has in him something of the explorer's urge to discover. It does not matter that there is little scope left for original discovery. The important thing is that he should discover things that are new to him and be able to feel the same thrill and excitement as though they were equally unknown to everyone else. The true traveller is also able to explore. Even in Europe there are still places uninhabited and sufficiently untouched by the works of man for them to be to all intents and purposes virgin territory to the traveller who penetrates into them. There are plenty of uninhabited little islands off the west coast of the British Isles or along the shores of Norway and Sweden, which anyone landing on them today or tomorrow "discovers" as effectively as the person who actually was the first to set foot there. As Freya Stark says, "The tide will see to it that anyone landing on a beach from which it has just retreated shall have the thrill of setting his footprints in virgin sand." In his *Gifts of Fortune* H. M. Tomlinson has written of a Devonshire creek that is still unexplored. The world is full of such places.

The ideal traveller has the " 'satiable curiosity" of Kipling's baby elephant, something of the child's gift of surprise and ability to wonder. He is tolerant and broad-minded, always ready within certain limits of principle to do in Rome as the Romans do. He will naturally prefer a certain degree of comfort and the conveniences of modern plumbing, but he will know how to dispense with them and not mind.

In all true travel there is an element of revelation, and so the ideal traveller possesses what C. E. Montague has called "the knack of seeing visions at the instance of seen things." It is, perhaps, the possession or lack of that knack which is the infallible criterion that distinguishes the true from the bogus traveller.

That, then, is one portrait of the ideal traveller, a being whom modern conditions render all but impossible. Between him and the bogus "traveller," the tourist, there is an endless variety of travellers who are still worthy of the name.

There are those "two-dimensional" travellers who travel both in time and space. Those like Norman Douglas, who to satisfy their craving for antiquity and beauty, go to some place where, along with the visible relics of it, the atmosphere of bygone but still living civilization lingers on, and there, while their physical bodies live in the present, they themselves dwell happily in the past of a thousand years or more ago. There are those semi-precious beings whom C. E. Montague called "aromatists," those, whom Aldous Huxley has described, who travel not to broaden and enrich their minds but in order pleasantly to forget its existence, and his congenital traveller "one of those more fastidious spirits who cannot find the distractions they require in betting, mah jong, drink, golf or fox-trots." But that already brings us to the bogus, for travel is certainly not a search for distraction.

Are sailors travellers? No, or only very seldom and then usually only after they have run away from their ships and the sea. Sailors are voyagers, which is quite different. They are no more entitled to call themselves travellers than are engine-drivers, and few, I think, would ever wish to claim the title. They are not travellers if for no other reason than that they have no time for travel, especially in these days when the time a ship takes to turn round is a matter of prime concern to her owners. Those who most deserve the title are the ones who sail single-handed, but then few of them are sailors. As H. M. Tomlinson and Adrian Seligman have pointed out, sailors do not love the sea. They go to sea for motives that have nothing to do with the sea, motives that are the opposite of those that must have lain behind the voyages of such as Alain Gerbault. They are the true escapists, not the self-deceivers whom Hilton Brown pillories.

Alain Gerbault said that he loved the sea; but did he? Was he not rather in love with boats, the independence they gave him, the sense of power? Did he not revel in the contest of having to strive with the sea, pitting his strength and dexterity against the blind forces of nature as the mountaineer does when he attempts the "impossible" climb. His quest was for the sun, for solitude and simplicity. He must have been a complex character and it is by no means easy to assess his motives. Some, I know, hold the view that he was no sailor, just a disappointed young man turned misanthrope, who enjoyed performing feats of endurance like those who swim the Channel. But, surely, he was in many ways a true traveller. He did set out on a quest and in the end he found, if not what he originally sought, at least what satisfied him, and so his travels came to an end.

Similarly, those who potter about the world in small boats are travellers. Their boats are their caravans, the sea their mountains and deserts. If what you seek is most likely to be found on an island, if the call you answer is that of a siren, you can only go by boat. And the sea is a Golconda of beauty.

These, then, are the travellers. But why do they travel? What is their quest? The essays that follow discuss the major reasons why people travel nowadays, the calls that summon, and the urges that drive them from their homes in the changed circumstances of today. Compare these with the travel books of the late seventeenth and eighteenth centuries. What a difference in the quest! Simplicity, solitude, beauty, instead of riches and fame; knowledge of self instead of self-aggrandisement; fulfilment instead of conquest. Almost the only motives to be found then, as now, are curiosity and the desire for knowledge. Though these are just different expressions of the same urge, a sense of triviality attaches to the very word "curiosity." It is, however, one of the most compelling urges there is. It drove F. R. Holman, invalided out of the Navy because of blindness, to travel round the world. With him he took a companion who had to describe and explain every scent and sound, every impression his four senses received. Holman's quest was in reality a search for sight. He felt that his affliction had robbed him of part of his heritage, but by travelling in the way he did, he was able to "see" it and to enjoy it.

There are other reasons for travel not discussed in the following essays. Some, perhaps, are minor ones, but they are nonetheless compelling.

We are most of us starved of beauty. Above even the ugliest,

9

dirtiest roof there is always the sky, and the sky is beautiful. In most homes there is some lovely relic of a bygone age. But, taking it all in all there is little visible beauty in the lives of the urban dweller. What he has he finds in books, in music, in loving and being loved, in the beautiful things of the spirit, but his eyes are hungry. When he looks up at the sky he is poignantly reminded that the world is crammed with beautiful things and he longs to satisfy the hunger of his eyes. That is what many seek who travel today.

Peace is another of the things for which we long. I do not mean freedom from war, nor the freedom from the restraint of princes that the sailor is promised, but freedom from the incessant clangour of our brazen civilization, from the blare of the wireless, the raucous headlines of the newspapers. We long to get away from those who plan and snoop and from the impertinent takers of polls. So, we seek for peace where man is not, or at any rate where he is still the intruder overshadowed by nature, the child who waits to speak till he is spoken to. How many of us seek for that?

To change one's country is often to change one's century, and it is in this ability of space to give what time cannot that those who find it distasteful, or themselves unable, to conform to the rules and values which govern their part of the world, find a means of relief and release. It is this which encourages the Peter Freuchens in their search for a better life, and although we know that theirs is a hopeless quest, that civilization has left too deep a stamp on their souls for them to be able to content themselves for long with the primitive, it is a comforting thought that there are places where other values prevail and that, if we like, we can go and share them for at least a time. There is, too, a great satisfaction in knowing that there still are places, sterile deserts and empty wastes, that remain safe from the appalling effects of man's activities, and that to these we can go and, as Norman Douglas said, be sure of not finding man.

Today we are not in search of new worlds, but of old. We live in a new world which has deprived us of leisure and we often feel that we would willingly exchange it for an old one where we could have time to stop and think, to contemplate, and to savour. That is another of the great blessings of travel, the knowledge it gives that there are in fact other worlds. To some they are refuges, to others specimens to be examined scientifically; but they are there and if we want to badly enough, we can go to them. These other worlds, too, are part of our heritage. It is to a certain extent true when we say to ourselves: "The world belongs to me," and in a certain sense also it is our duty to acquaint ourselves with this heritage of ours. We can learn much of it from books, but that is not enough. No description, no photograph even, can possibly make us realize what a sandy desert, an icefield, or a range of tall mountains is really like. No one can put into words the light over the sea, the aurora borealis, or the beauty of a wild duck's wing. To get the full value of our heritage we must see it for ourselves. Between us and all but a tiny particle of this world that belongs to us is at least one horizon that must be crossed, and that means travel. Having crossed it and seen, we find that we have three pictures: that of our anticipations which was based on what we had read or heard, that of the actual vision, and the remembered. And so we pass from horizon to horizon enriching our experience immeasurably. Travellers are in many ways like hamsters storing up moments of delight for the stiff-jointed winter that lies ahead of us all.

H. M. Tomlinson once questioned the right of most of us to travel on the grounds of ignorance, and quoted the example of the late Lord Bryce as the traveller *par excellence* who knew all about what he was going to see and so his appreciation was immeasurably enhanced. Admittedly most of us are not suffidiently educated to be able to say that we have come of age in this respect, and so perhaps we have no proper right to insist now upon being given our heritage. All the same, I cannot help feeling that the important thing is that we should have the desire, the thirst for knowledge and the sight and understanding of what our inheritance contains. It is surely the urge to discover for ourselves that counts. However ignorant we may be, if we have the intelligence and the enquiring mind we can get as great, possibly greater, pleasure out of our "discoveries" than those to whom most things are already known. We lose the pleasures of anticipation, but gain the delight of the unexpected.

There is a tremendous thrill in discovering a bird or plant that is new to us, a Viking grave, or a pagan altar which we had not realized existed, that is perhaps worth more to the individual than the pleasure of recognition of something already known from books and study with the completer understanding the sight of the actual object gives.

Supposing someone completely ignorant of the history and culture of ancient Greece were to come one moonlight night upon the Parthenon when tramping into Athens. What a thrill that discovery would be. And it would be a true discovery as far as that person was concerned. And what pleasure he would get from finding out all about the Parthenon.

Though there may be few discoveries to be made that can be communicated to the world and that would be new to everybody, yet everyone can make endless discoveries for himself alone that will provide him with as much of a thrill as Columbus, Linnaeus, Hudson, or Humboldt ever got. We can all still stand in such men's shoes. We can have the same thrills, acquire the same riches of beauty and experience, only not the fame, the thing least worth having of all, especially in these days when fame brings with it an intolerable invasion of one's privacy.

And privacy is another of the things that the modern traveller seeks.

One of the main causes for the flood of applications for passports pouring into the Passport Control Office, is surely the fact that the great majority of us are forced to live in large communities. Beyond a certain number of individuals we do not really like our fellow men, but we are artificially thrust one upon the other and sooner or later this becomes intolerable and we must seek relief. That is one reason why the speed of modern means of communication, excellent as it may be for a variety of purposes, will never do what is so often claimed for it and lead to increased international understanding and lasting peace between the peoples. Even if it would, it will probably never be permitted to do so. Sooner or later, as the aeroplane spreads disease and introduces Eastern plagues into the West and *vice versa*, all travel will be restricted to journeys of necessity, as C. E. Montague foretold. We shall not be permitted to go abroad until we have been inoculated, injected, vaccinated and passed through a lengthy period of quarantine, and the same may well be required of us at the other end.

We tolerate, rather than like our fellows. Those who suffer the daily degradation of riding in the underground railways of London often find themselves even loathing their fellows. The majority of urban dwellers have had their natures warped by modern civilization. At any rate, true hospitality, kindliness, unselfishness, helpfulness and simplicity are more likely to be found among those who live on the land or gain their livelihood working with nature. Such people are, on the whole, decent and likeable. The unpleasant character is the exception among them rather than the rule. What fools we are to live as most of us do, in huge cities under artificial conditions that sour our souls and sap our fundamental virtues!

Some years ago, on a warm summer's night, my wife and I were on a great slab of rock out in the Åland Sea picnicking with a Swedish author and his wife and the island farmer with whom we were staying. We lay or squatted on sheepskin rugs laid round a wood fire built on the pink rock two inches above the gently lapping waters of the Baltic. It was dark, but not proper night, for the sky was reflecting light from the sun that was moving along just below the horizon beneath a strip of pink sky that was both sunset and dawn. A few yards away some baby sandpipers were bustling about, their dark shapes and peeping squeaky voices like those of mice. We talked intermittently, with long silences that let one enjoy the utter peace that dwells in those parts. Then Emil, the farmer, began speaking: How dreadful it must be, he said, to live in London. Why did we do it? Why not come and live in the islands where all that we seemed to value was there just for the enjoying of it. Why come all that way just to stay a few weeks and then voluntarily go back to what we seemed to consider a prison.

The *ädelbrännvin* we had been drinking had loosened his tongue and filled him with missionary zeal, for every conviction he had told him that he was right and we were wrong. Had he but known it, he was preaching to the converted, whose only fault was that they lacked the guts to put their convictions into action.

Were we escapists? No, not in the sense that we were pursuing the fiction which Hilton Brown has exposed. We had not escaped and we knew it. But we had retreated, withdrawn awhile from the battle for our daily bread and butter. The great and essential difference between us and the Hilton Brown escapist was that we would have been prepared to make a considerable sacrifice to attain what we wanted. That that attainment was then beyond us was not because we were stupidly and futilely trying to flee from ourselves, but because we lacked the training to earn our keep in those circumstances. Emil was a farmer and a fisherman and a forester. He could build a boat or a house, shoe a horse, repair a binder, mend his boots, mill his corn, milk a cow, fell a tree, and shear his sheep, whose wool his women folk could spin and weave and knit into all the garments he required. He and his small family were an almost self-sufficient community; but had we changed places with him we should have been reduced to the level of cave-dwellers, perhaps starved.

Escapism has been called the occupational disease of the twentieth century. A lot of it is as futile and stupid as Hilton Brown describes it, but in much of it too there is a religious element. It is a retreat, not a flight, a mass retreat of square pegs from the round holes of their uncongenial occupations to the square holes in which the best that is in them comes uppermost. Each goes for a while to the place that to him is "God's ante-chamber" knowing full well that he cannot stay but for a certain limited time. But whether he is in the mountains, the desert, or among the eternal ice, he does listen for some few days or weeks or months to God's voice through "the party-wall of creation" and so his soul increases in stature.

The mountains, the high places of this world, seem to attract more travellers than any other parts. This is not surprising, such is their grandeur and sublimity, their beauty that is at once ethereal and, as Prince William of Sweden and others have found, reminiscent of the architecture of ancient Greece, but it is in part also because it is the mountains which, after the deserts, have best resisted man. They are the nearest, most accessible spots, in which we can really get away from our fellows.

Solitude and leisure for contemplation are two of the vital needs of any thinking person, but the so-called welfare state does not recognize them, and we must seek them for ourselves. Solitude, thank goodness, is still comparatively easy to find. There are plenty of lonely places left even in our British Isles, and in the last resort there is the foreign crowd. If you do not speak the language there is real solitude to be found in the crowded streets, or beaches, of some foreign place. The welter of strange meaningless sounds are no more than a background of noise, like the roar of breakers. Your untrained ear cannot shrink at harsh or vulgar voices, nor your mind at the futility of the chatter.

Ella Maillart rightly points out that at the end of any road, however long, it is ourselves that we find. Man, however, is a very complex being and not all of his fundamental qualities necessarily find expression in the life he is forced to live. Our characters may easily have components that circumstances keep dormant and it is one of the benefits of travel that it enables us to know ourselves in a way that is often otherwise impossible, unless during wars which are the travels of nations.

The telephone, wireless and all our means of summoning speedy help are, happily, not yet omnipresent, so that the traveller who keeps off the beaten track is still to a large extent the man of his faculties. His titles, position, income, are unknown and, if he is abroad, would probably not impress even if they were known. What he is depends entirely upon the qualities of his mind and heart; what he does upon the strength, endurance and skill of his hands and feet. He must rely upon himself alone. Help may be forthcoming, but it will be fortuitous and to count upon it would be stupid. Travelling will often reveal to a person for the first time his true stature. Rough going is intolerable to feet of clay, and mountains as well as desert-lands have produced Admirable Crichtons. It is this search for knowledge of one's true self, that has sent many people out travelling. If it sometimes takes the exaggerated form of pitting one's strength against the dumb forces of nature, as in the mountaineer and those like him, it is nevertheless still in that limited respect a quest.

Those who voluntarily undergo ordeals of this kind in order to prove their manhood or their right to be, know too the intoxication of success. The reward for achievement is instantaneous and automatic, and the duration of the struggle is counted in hours or days, at the most in months, but rarely, if ever, in years.

What else does travel give? Perhaps above all a healthy mind, if only because it is an excellent purgative of prejudice and a cure for many of our discontents. Aldous Huxley has said that "to travel is to discover that everybody is wrong." Travel does at any rate disabuse us of many of our preconceptions and shows up our hasty judgments for what they are. To travel is to live life at first hand—and there is no getting away from that; so, travelling we discover that many of our rosy pictures of life elsewhere are not so lovely after all; our pet theories are apt to explode by a foreign wayside, and our prejudices to dissolve in the face of reality. You cannot travel and remain rabid.

To those whose outlook and opinion of their fellows is jaundiced by having dwelt too long in cities, one of the great comforts travel has to offer is the realization that there are decent people left in the world. Rupert Croft-Cooke relates how by being stranded in Buenos Aires he discovered that human beings are not really ill-disposed or ungenerous, but ready enough to help one another when they *see* the need. The traveller's need is always obvious, the moment it is realized that he is a traveller and so away from home and support. Hospitality to the traveller is enjoined by many religions, especially in the east. Primitive peoples extend it to include even the provision of a companion for the traveller's bed. Off the beaten track the obligation of hospitality is still acknowledged and acted upon. Naturally, hospitality is a quality that can be strained. The greater the degree of civilization in the giver, the sooner it is likely to wear thin. It is easy to take someone to your bosom, when you know that his stay is inevitably restricted by the length of time for which his visa is valid. The political refugees of today could tell us much about the comparative elasticity and sincerity of European hospitality.

Once when we were in the Ålands my wife and I were going early one morning to a house where lived some friends who had invited us for the day. Uncertain of the way, we went up to a farmhouse to ask for directions. We found the family at breakfast. We made our request and immediately the elder of the farmer's two daughters jumped to her feet and came outside with us, we thought to show us the way from the porch. However, she ran down the steps, disappeared into a shed and came out a moment later wheeling a bicycle. Despite our protests she insisted on walking with us a full mile down the road till we reached the turning in the woods which would lead us to our destination. Then she mounted her bicycle and rode back home, assuring us that her breakfast would taste all the better for having had to wait. To ourselves we had to admit that had we been disturbed at our breakfast in London with a similar request for help, we would have given the intruder a very different reception. It was humiliating.

Travel inevitably has such moments. There is always a harsh side to it: the occasional loneliness, the boredom, the sudden panics when a feeling of despair and helplessness overcomes you when faced with a mentality that is completely foreign and uncomprehending, the discomforts of bad weather and mean accommodation, of midges, mosquitoes and the things that bite in the night, the utter weariness of an exhausted body, the dangers that still await the traveller. These things are the shadows of travel. Physical fatigue, however, has its light side as well, an intoxication of its own. After some exceptional physical exertion comfort, or just ease, can go to the head. The gratitude of a chilled body and numbed extremities for the warmth of a well-heated room, or of a hot body for the coolness of a stone-flagged kitchen; the wonderful relief of being able to stretch out and relax, the beatitude of the nose when it can convey promises of appeasement to the belly, those are delights that have to be earned. After considerable exertion the senses seem to indulge in an orgy of voluptuous enjoyment that intoxicates the whole body, but those who journey by motor car, aeroplane or train will never experience that. A sore stiff bottom is no substitute for the fatigue of a well-trained body.

Another of the shades of travel is danger. It is still there for the traveller, even though robber barons are now nationalized and called customs officials, and footpads and highwaymen have abandoned the mask for the dinner jacket and the lonely road for the night club and American Bar. In the Amazon basin and a few other parts of the world there are still tribes of so-called savages who may kill you for the inadvertent violation of some taboo, or to avenge the offences of some previous white visitor, or merely because they do not like the look of you, but as H. M. Tomlinson has said "Tigers, snakes, lovely but indignant nymphs, and head hunters are not the dangers. What kills men in the wilderness is anxiety, under-nourishment, and mosquitoes." The only real danger the traveller encounters is himself. His ineptitudes and clumsiness, his lack of knowledge or his inexperience, some act of rashness or foolhardiness, are much more likely to prove fatal than any beast ravening or otherwise. The trouble is that after centuries of civilization our bodies require so much. We no longer know the herbs and plants that have the power to heal; even food we often fail to recognize if it is not surrounded by tin and a gaudy label. Wander a few miles away from the beaten track and it requires but some slight accident to send you hurtling back through the centuries to the status of primitive man, but without his knowledge or his powers of endurance: space and time are curiously linked.

There may be danger too in getting to the starting point for your travels. The railway is not always safe, the motor car is a lethal weapon, the aeroplane a challenge to providence. Use them, if you care to take the risk, as a means of getting quickly to the place from which you intend to set out; but your travel, if it is true travel, will be a matter of feet: your own, the hooves of the horse that you ride or drive behind, or those of the dogs that draw your sleigh; or it may be a matter of muscle or skill, if you sail a boat or paddle a canoe; but never can a means of travel be mechanical. The one concession is, perhaps, the bicycle. It depends upon man for its motive power, its restrictions upon his liberty are not extensive and, being a thing of little value, it can be abandoned without great loss.

There is only one thing to be said for the aeroplane: it allows you to gain a truer idea of the immensity of space. The greater breadth added to the horizon from the air puts grandeur in a truer proportion to its setting, lets you grasp the full magnitude of the labour it would be to traverse desolation step by step. It gives perspective, but no detail, an impression, but no more.

It may sound excessive, perhaps be judged mere sentimentalizing, to renounce all mechanical aids when travelling, to hold that if you are truly to travel in the meaning of that word such as those who have contributed to this book understand it, that you must go on foot or employ the services of dog or horse, or boat. But I believe that this is true. All other travel is more or less bogus, in essence just touring. The speed and noise of mechanical means of locomotion prohibit their use. To get the true feel of a city or town you take to your feet, for how can you perceive and discover unless you rub shoulders with the crowd, unless you are able to peer into windows, dive down strange alleyways, climb steps that lead you know not where, giving immediate obedience to every prompting of intuition and curiosity? It is the same everywhere. How can you travel if you cannot hear the songs of the birds, the ripple and chatter of water, the music and wild poetry of the wind, the barking of geese or the hot cooing of wood-pigeons? How can you travel if you cannot stop when a hare or fox lollops out of the hedge, or when you see a bird or animal freeze a few yards away? How can you travel if you cannot smell the scent of the hedge-rows and trees, the fragrance that comes on the air, or if you cannot feel the weather? How can you travel if there is no silence and no solitude? You cannot.

OUTWARD BOUND

H. M. Tomlinson

THE boy's gaze, from his corner seat in the train, was fixed on England flowing past. He was too shy to look round at the rest of us, or else he was day-dreaming and had forgotten we were there. I don't think he saw, except absently, the telegraph posts and wires undulating along, and the distant sunny fields and hills in slow retreat. Occasionally he glanced quickly overhead at the luggage rack. His treasure was still there. I guessed he and his baggage, so new, were outward bound. That canvas bolster had not been aired before. This was the first time. So it was for hours. Then someone exclaimed at what had come into view from the opposite window. There were signs of the sea. The boy rose, one of our betters in a moment, and over our feet he went, ever regardless of our presence, to gaze out. As he stood with his back to us, and as the masts and funnels grew higher, he began to sing to himself.

I could have sung with him, had I known the song. The music of the spheres, harmony in the poise of universal fettle, is not for the likes of us. It would be a *continuo* too deep for our ears, as inaudible as the dance of generative heat and light over rocks in summer. That boy's humming might have been a faint echo of it. I wish I could recall the tune. I used to know an air of its kind, life rejoicing because it knows no better, but it is as far away as the hour—eight bells, midnight—and I was watching from a ship's bridge the coast-lights of England fade astern. I was bound south to the foreign, for the first time. She was a collier, from Barry Dock. A bright eye was winking at us from shorewards. Then a small voice came at my side. "The Longships!" I hadn't heard the ship's master come up the ladder. It was a dark night, clear and calm. The ship's wash was the only sound. The Longships was winking at us. The port-light of a schooner was abeam.

The schooner was a trim black silhouette in luminous night, with a red spark in her middle. I don't know her name, but she has not yet completed that voyage, for me. The Longships!

How telling a name is, if heard in the due moment! There was nothing of consequence about my ship, nor in her business, and there would be no romance in her destination. She was deep with fuel for France, no more than an item in the old traditional economy, now lost, of coal out, and corn and wine home, but it is as if she moved briefly into a position where, for the lucky, there is a glimpse of a truth which endures beyond routine and duties, and departures and arrivals. She was soon out of it, of course. In another minute I was in the chart-room, and the master was getting a bottle and glasses out of a cupboard; and even he didn't know what unverifiable dimension his ship had appeared to reveal a moment ago, and I didn't tell him. For his part, he said he hoped the barometer was lying, but he supposed we were in for a dusting; and we had that dusting the next evening.

I don't say there was anything peculiar about that evocation off Cornwall. That there was none may be the remarkable thing about it. Nothing rum was there, though Cornwall and its waters have their riddles. It was only as if that instant of night was not of the clock, but was from the beginning, world without end. For a moment I stood at the ship's rail myself, and there it was. If I were off the Longships next week I should not see it. Still, there is no need to try again, for those moments do not pass. They are rare, but they come without warning, we have them, and they sum up to all the eternity we can reason about; and who would believe us? No matter; occasionally we are not only aware of existence, but above it, and are content.

Ought we to round Land's End, bound south, on watch for a predicate? We might as well go to a London tube station. It will not show. If we see it at all, it is when we are looking the other way. Its bearings are no more exact than Ariel's. When the mind is idle, and the occasion is only the end of one more day in the garden, it can meet us then. Sometimes there comes a brief incidence of midsummer twilight when common flowers may be strangely prominent and apparitional. Legendary peace might have come, or at least respite. It does not appear to be our patch of ground. It has another import. Those shapes and colours are not of our asking. Though the hour is dim, they are more individual and shining, in a momentary translation of their kind, than they were this morning. Queerly bright in obscurity, they are a little disturbing, and our confidence in a proper knowledge of circumstance is shaken. A material explanation of the odd communication may be easy, as usual, but is no help. It would not account for the way we saw it. Besides, we have learned that though knowledge may take us far, understanding remains as distant as ever. On that road there can be no end, though we never cease from travel. There, I suppose, is the fun in discovery; we must keep on.

Sailors in the days of sail, when the horizon about them was unbroken for months, seldom had much to show for solitude but a new becket or knot, or a ship in a bottle, just as another man, in the loneliness of his soul, has nothing to prove his interest in existence except a nice collection of investments, or a row of books he wrote, once on a time, but long out of print. It is not easy to count our valuables, if we are foolish enough to try. It would be difficult to name them, to say nothing of selling them. They are inevident. There is no proof. I remember reading of an explorer who had suffered the rigours of a voyage to the ice-barrier of the Antarctic. He noted in his log one day his fear that the ship would not clear the floes before winter caught her. He added to the entry that at daybreak the world of ice changed colour from bronze to light apple-green, from pink to crimson, in an ominous quiet, and was surprised that the dogs peered overside with him, fixed by they didn't know what; no more did he. Afterwards, home in London, the thought of it would come over him and he had to leave his family and a comfortable fire-side to go out, without saying why, to be alone in the wind and the rain.

I don't know, but I fancy he went out, on his lonesome, to look again at the sum of all his voyaging. That sort of impulse will come over a man. It is the only thing to do, if the rest of the company is settled, cheerful, and satisfied. He had a matter to think about, but what was it? Of course, his friends would have seen nothing there. Had he explained it, they might have concluded that his past trials in a latitude well to the south of warm human fellowship had touched him somewhat. Silence in outer darkness had worked into his head.

So not a word to them about it, yet he could not make sense of it himself. Out he goes, then, into the wind and rain of London streets after dark, broody over that momentary half-assurance, or challenge, that chanced in an Antarctic sunrise, while he was stuck in his navigation; as though he had glimpsed an unexpected enlargement of the world, an existence not yet explored. It was gone while he looked, and left no clue. No more light on it yet, either. What a pity it is that thought cannot inveigle a way into that seclusion! Still, he felt fairly sure, it seems, at that juncture of the voyage, of something beyond confinement in a ship with universal ice on guard about. There seemed to be a more serious disability. Was it likely that consciousness, however wide-awake one may be, is not quite good enough? That a man himself is kept within bonds more obdurate than are the ribs of a ship beset by ice and no way on her? And he could not get out; in that he was as the dogs beside him. Verities exist without ascertained aids to their navigation.

That sort of thing must be left to the poets—the old-fashioned sort, of course—and they can make nothing better of it than the beauty of the earth and the glory of the skies; which leaves us where we were. The expectation of hitting on the whereabouts of such a surmise is never in our itinerary, when we board a ship. Instead, very likely it is a wet day, and the ship still taking in cargo. That's how it usually is with me, and in winter, and I like it. The pungent smells are friendly; we have met before. You only get them on a wet deck, the hatches open, and the winches in use, on a heavy November day. The sounds and cries outside the cabin—which is cold and raw as yet—are immemorial to the act of departure. It must have been much the same with Tudor voyagers. Time slows down. But there is nothing in our itinerary concerning Xanadu. What fools we should look, if we wrote it down plain! Constraint might be put upon us by our friends, and they would be right. Still, it is the hope we always carry with us, added to the antiseptics and carminatives, though it is so far from being a buoyant hope that it sinks out of sight.

Better let it go and accept what comes, with good grace. We know quite well that it is not worth while going round the world to count the cats in Zanzibar, as Thoreau needlessly pointed out. Still, we wish he had tried it. He would have counted more than cats. We miss the book he would have made. Anywhere on earth, with any professed object, and to it by any mode of travel, will suit some eyes; and there another regret forms that we shall have no book on the American scene —what a book it could have been!—by the author of *Old Calabria*. Yet speculations as to what this famous author and traveller, and that one, would have made of other lands—instead of France, Henry James in Patagonia, Santayana among the Dyaks making his way across Borneo?—will delay us. While stowing things in the cabin, the idea comes that a whole book could be made of them; it would not be worth writing. The ship has fallen quiet. The winches have stopped. It sounds as if the hatches are going on.

It is necessary, now and then, to find a clear and uninterrupted horizon, and to let a long silence fall between self and the multitude, for the sake of sanity. God knows what nonsense would infect us with a moral and patriotic conviction if we did not move off till too late; the danger won't bear thinking about. The acclamation of the majority is never wrong, even on the steep place, and one might be there in full accord, quite unaware of a crisis. Consider but one of the minor appalling facts of our civility revealed faithfully in that popular newspaper on the cabin floor—I mean its wide display of the advertisements of film plays, the new art; for since we are used to it, who remarks the inane horror of it? Money is in it; the multitude's. A great industrial city, in this age when scientific materialism is our mystical faith, and nothing is celestial except engines at supersonic speeds, makes the continued cunning of an Evil One supererogatory; the job is all but finished. A great city is in the right geographical point, becomes bearable, and can be regarded with calm, only when the tide has turned seaward, the wide glare of neon and other lights sinks down in the night astern, and the only sound at last is the monody of unseen waters. A space opens in the smoke and fudge to let out the stars, and there the constellations are, seen by a townsman even in unbelief, but with the comfort of memory. That each appears at its appointed place restores faith, which may have become a little shaky, in the reality of what in the innocence of childhood and youth was thought to be immortal good. One can turn in tonight with assurance. To hear the hours being made on the ship's bell has no warning of the passing time. Exemption has come. This calling is merely for the convenience of the ship; it is only the journey of the sun being measured. A fixed idea of time is already working loose. We must be passing the Girdler light by now.

The names of our coastwise lights—those traditional lights, too, will go out presently, when the marvellous wireless beacon is in general use—almost rank with those of the stars. I do not regret that I shall have done with the sea in the year when the coasts of our island will be lightless, all one with darkness itself, whatever the weather; when the lamps of home on headland and outlying rock and shoal will be doused. Revisiting the glimpses, coming in from the outer, this ghost won't know his own place when Skerryvore, Pendeen, Lundy, the Eddystone, the Foreland, and the rest, are not keeping watch with characteristic bright eyes for wanderers in the night. No more the Smalls, Fastnet, Pladda, and Ushant? Perhaps the very names will be changed to numbers. Progress, progress! But I cannot yet declare, with that Cabinet Minister whose office it is to plan our towns and countryside, and who had to explain why he allowed the defilement of the surroundings of a glorious old cathedral; "Progress, not sentiment." Yes, that is what he said.

Well, what is progress? Doesn't that depend on the way we are going, and what we want to do? I am all for sentiment while our destiny is uncertain; the earth would turn to ashes without memory and affection. If to make a mechanistic desert of our planet, and that at present is what we are doing, is not to blast from it the reason for our continued existence, then life must be in a void, so of course is without purpose, and we are free to please ourselves while we have time for it, which may not be long. Some people, the sentimentalists, are not yet persuaded that this conclusion need be accepted, though it is a belief natural to the mental climate of our age. It affects the arts as well as science. Without useless sentiment, without affection which never counts the cost, without magnanimity, then nihilism. No more the making of music; mystery has been dismissed from the universe, and instead of awe men feel the pride of conquest. Human aspiration has risen to something more reasonable than nobility, reverence, and joy. The heart is fly-blown, though the brain, cleaned by thorough knowledge of all superstitious nonsense, has its mathematics, and can measure the means to access of power. The admonition of the best that men have thought and done is given to the deaf and blind. The mental climate of our age is pestilential.

In the first morning at sea, little of this is remembered. It all goes down wind like the coils of the ship's vapours, a dream of the night too vague and inconsequential to be noticed. While in the city, you cannot doubt that the future of man is of first importance, and that he seems, poor fellow, to be confidently indifferent to the omens; but with a first look round on heaven and the life of the waters, when outward bound, it is possible to believe than an absolute sanity exists apart; we may share it or leave it, just as we please. With the coming of the sun the English coast is reposeful, as if near neighbour to the splendid east, and its equal, whatever may be the time spirit. The splendour is taken by cliff and upland as its right; the home we are leaving has an aspect we had forgotten. It is still in its prime. History might not have begun. England, we see, keeps an inherency untouched by the zeal of many generations, and could survive the prolonged residence of the most destructive of common convictions. The radiance of England, elevated in the beginning of another day, is not contemporary, nor a promise for the future, but is the sign of an existence not altogether subject to us and our aims. It is worth making a journey to be assured of that, and it was not charged for in the passage money. Our present mental climate, in a distant view, is a patch of cold fog, and will last only while there is no change of wind.

The world has been too much with us. Without a clear space around, to get our bearings, we are lost. There is no feeling that one is lost when right off the map, quite literally off, or at best having but sketchy direction in a wild country, with no security, and no neighbours except natives who remain concealed until they decide to show themselves. We know where we are, then, for a change. There is retrieval of a mislaid identity. The traveller must keep his own feet, and the doubt that he may not get safely out of it, if he isn't up to the mark, tells him what he is; a fact worth having, if there is a purpose to which it can be put.

There is much to be said for a spell of silence in isolation, if one does not go into retreat with too many dogmas, for the unknown gods sport with fixed ideas without mercy; at least we have learned that much of the gods. And why go into retreat, unless it is to test knowledge and faith in the light of discovery, should that good fortune attend on patience? And discovery, a view of things from a new vantage, one is sure to have, unless there is a demand for signs and wonders. There are plenty of recorded wonders, for instance, in Piddington's *Sailor's Horn Book*, while that authority is establishing the law of storms with all the evidence from an abundance of the logs of mariners over many years; but reading about these wonders is all I want. It is not worth while voyaging to the Indian Ocean in the cyclone season to witness the warning that heaven and earth are about to roll up. This threat might be fulfilled, as far as we are concerned. Nobody who has suffered the ocean in a rage would go out of his way to have that experience twice. It may be magnificent, but usually darkness hides it, and anyhow, you can't keep still. Give me fair weather, and as much of it as is going. Only a fool would want to glimpse again mountains of water moving fast under a black ceiling lowered to the foam. After the truth has been rubbed in that bodily survival is not of first importance to anyone but the self, nothing is gained merely by looking doom in the face day after day; though I have always relished observing the way shipmates faced it. You may change completely an opinion of the spirit of a man when with him in an affair of that sort. These dramatic occasions are better when in books.

It is the little things of travel that matter. Early in the first morning out, the cabin is heavy with the residue of departure, and of the claims of the shore. Release comes with the first glance from a port-light that looks forward. An unfamiliar deck is wet with spray or rain, and the glazed hatch tarpaulins might be of Argo herself; they are of gold in a new light, and quivering in the wind with expectancy. The ship's head is alive against bright clouds, and the look-out in his oilskins is high enough in the morning to be on the ramparts of an outpost of earth, watching for a new planet to swim into his ken.

That first peep should content any traveller with his time and place. The steward will be in soon with some tea, and is sure to pause to pass a word or two. He will want to get an inkling of your drift. This is not a liner; and, if you are of no importance, at any rate you are one of a small company, and that is of importance to those who will have to bear with you. You will get to know a few of your fellows in a way that rarely happens in a city street; small steel compartments are echoing, and there is no hiding between bulwarks. The person is bared at sea, and communication must be distinct, direct, and cut to the bone. The sea makes short work of pretence. I remember a ship's master—he was a reader of metaphysics and philosophy—delivering an opinion of a book while in the act of rising from the mess table. He began as he gathered his feet under him, and the criticism was over by the time he had snatched up his cap and clapped it on. I cannot report what he said for a sufficient reason, but he condensed to a line and a half all that my knowledge had been fumbling silently to put into proper shape for a week.

There are moments in a journey that are as if we saw a world science has never measured and cannot explain. If you like, put this down to personal emotion of no consequence, and so save learned argument. We will not argue it. Since *Hamlet* can be psycho-analysed till the play comes down to a bare page from a book of medical cases, what could be made of us? But all the analyses cannot remove the simple impression of the beauty of the earth, and the glory of the skies, as the sun rises on a first approach to a tropical land of the rains; or when night falls there, for that matter. Though a traveller is aware of his brief nature, yet he shares in this triumph of existence, which may be the reflection of a reality of which nothing yet is known.

THE CALL OF HIGH PLACES

Henri Bordeaux

1. *The Discovery of the Mountains*

THE mountains have not been discovered so very long. They have been loved for a bare century and a half. The praises that in former times used to be lavished on Nature were only addressed to her rich pasture lands, her gardens, parks and groves, places in which she wore our livery, to the making of whose charm we ourselves had contributed. In her we were able to love ourselves with a love that was not disinterested. That is the reason why old country houses are almost all built alongside roads, in hollows: they have no view, are not isolated; but they are placed where they are sheltered from the winds and inclemencies of the weather, in the vicinity of refreshing springs and trees which, though they contract the horizon, have ample shade to shed. Easily accessible, these old houses have all kinds of comforts and amenities to make the visitor linger. The new houses of today seek first and foremost a view.

In the days of antiquity mountains were held in no esteem. "For the Greeks and for the Romans," said Humbolt, "a place had no attraction unless it was a pleasant one in which to live; they had no liking for the situations that we call wild and romantic." That is the notion of a society which places man and his dealings above nature. It is the classic idea. Nature should be decorative and pleasing; what is asked of it is a happy stay, the appeasement it can bring to the mind and heart, and if away on the horizon there should be visible a misty line of mountains bathed in light, that is merely one more thing to rest the eyes whose gaze it halts so gently.

When the celebrated traveller Tavernier visited the shore of Lake of Geneva in the neighbourhood of Montreux, he was filled with admiration for its country seats, its orchards and vineyards, and said: "Nowhere have I come across a more beautiful countryside."

And saying that, he turned his back on the Dent du Midi. In those days a lovely countryside was one that man used, to be

29

beautiful it had to have its villas, its terraces, its topiary work, its avenues laid out among lawns and clumps of flowers and trees, and at times even its artificial rocks. When Montaigne visited the falls on the Rhine at Schaffhausen, all he found to write about them in his notebook was: "Above Schaffhausen the Rhine meets a bed filled with great rocks, where it breaks, and below this among these rocks, it comes to a slope and makes a great leap foaming and breaking most strangely." This spectacle in which Ruskin saw a symbol of youth and its tumultuous strength merely drew from Montaigne the prosaic comment: "This stops the progress of the boats and interrupts the navigation of the said river."

La Fontaine was another who required nature to be smiling before he could love it, and if he evokes a countryside that is bare and sterile, it is in order to punish Psyche. In 1701 Addison crossed the Apennines between Florence and Bologna, and declared the journey deadly boring. Some years later President de Brosses went by the Corniche from Nice to Gênes and found the trip intolerable. Buffon told a student audience: "Nature in the raw is hideous and moribund." And Voltaire who from the country of his *Délices* could view the chain of the Alps, saw in it nothing but a barrier separating the different peoples. And did not Madame de Staël say that she would rather travel a hundred leagues to visit a great man than walk a hundred paces to see a lovely setting?

Nor can it be said that the mountains were held in any better regard by those whose sensibilities were less cultured. In them they inspired little other than dread: in olden days the *massif* of Mont Blanc bore the significant name of "The Accursed Mountains." Popular credulity had peopled it with evil spirits at whose door it was laid when, as occasionally happened, a glacier would descend as far as the dwellings of man, invading his fields and pastures. There is even a popular tradition that at the end of the seventeenth century the bishop of Geneva, Monseignor Jean d'Arenthon, while in Chamonix on a pastoral tour, after blessing the kneeling population as he passed, walked right up to the foot of the glaciers and duly exorcised them.

Their final exorcism is generally attributed to Jean-Jacques Rousseau. However, there were others before him who had his taste for solitude and high retreats. Such were all those hermits

who, clearing forests and cutting roads through unknown valleys, built the monasteries of La Chartreuse d'Aillon, of Porte,
of Reposoir, of Grande Chartreuse, and so many others. The
desert retreats before such men when they are fortified by such
spiritual strength as that developed by the Middle Ages. There
where it was difficult to go, they halted to await eternity, forgotten and surrounded by silence, with a few acres of ground
wrested from nature. Into these places of wild desolation they
brought serenity.

Jean-Jacques had another predecessor, St. François de Sales.
Taken by his ministry to Chamonix in 1606, he wrote on
August 18 to Mme de Chantal : "I have found God in all His
gentleness and sweetness even among the highest and most
rugged of our mountains where many a simple soul adores Him
in truth and sincerity, where goats and chamois leap about the
fearful ice to proclaim His praises. Through lack of piety I
understood only a few words of their language, but it seemed to
me that they were saying the most beautiful things." Far from
shrinking from the "accursed mountains," the holy bishop felt
attracted by them and there among them he heard a new hymn of
adoration. Might not this St. François de Sales be the true father
of Alpine literature? Be that as it may, he has other titles to fame.

Jean-Jacques was to push this sentiment of adoration to the
extreme. He turned his back on nature under surveillance, preferring it wild and desert. "People know," he said, "what I
mean by beautiful country. I must have mountain torrents,
rocks, pines, black woods, mountains, uneven roads to climb
and descend, and on every side precipices that make me feel
afraid." And when, after a long absence, he went to revisit Les
Charmettes and see Mme de Warens again, what did he do but
halt at the Echelles where the road is cut out of the rock and
there his all-powerful mistress, Nature, made him forget everything, including even his love. "I spent hours there leaning on
the parapet and catching occasional glimpses of the foam and
blue water whose dull roar I could hear through the cries of the
crows and of the birds of prey that were flying from rock to
rock, from one clump of bushes to the other, a hundred fathoms
below me."

In this sphere Rousseau's influence was as tremendous as in
so many others. He started, or at least developed, the taste for

nature not because of its vegetation, its charm and tranquillity—it has always been loved for those things—but because of the fillip it gives to our sensations, the exaltation it provides for our sensibilities. He used its changing forms as his own passions dictated and he left to the romantics the legacy of the secret of his art. He expanded our feeling for nature by introducing into it our own humanity. In a word, he made nature a friend, a confidant, a living being.

About this period M. de Saussure made his ascent of Mont Blanc (August 1, 1787). This feat acquired the proportions of an historic event. People spoke of it as of a battle won; the conquest of such a mountain set imaginations afire. M. de Saussure was indeed a scientific conqueror. To begin with Mont Blanc was to him nothing more than an elevated place in which to conduct his experiments. The difficulties of the undertaking gradually led him to treat it as an enemy, and when he reached the summit, he trampled its snows in mingled pride and anger, which is not the act of a savant.

The mountain had been conquered and out of its defeat was born its power of attraction. In it the romantics saw a goddess of solitude and of lyrical exaltation. Lord Byron extolled it in *Manfred* and to those who expressed disapproval of its being climbed, insolently replied that the slothful, no doubt, were surprised to see people abandon their comfortable carriages and broad highways to climb dangerous and difficult mountains, but there was in that great mountain a suavity and a source of life of which puffy ease could not hope to partake and that sloth would never know. A *suavity* and a *source of life*, that surely is what those who love the mountains go to them to seek.

Prevented from climbing by his lameness, Byron had to remain a wistful alpinist, but he interpreted exactly that mixture of pride, violence, obstinacy and methodicalness which was the state of mind of the kind of person who delighted in struggling with recalcitrant peaks, such as was Whymper, the first to master the Matterhorn. For a long time the people of Chamonix when speaking of the tourists just called them "the English" and left it at that. A mountain, tackled in this spirit, ceases to be part of the landscape, or a decorative motive. It becomes an opportunity for getting to know oneself both physically and morally, for measuring one's strength, for harmonizing and prolonging one's powers; it is a school of energy; yet if it were no more than that would it be able to inspire the artist?

One of the finest powers of love is its ability to throw fresh light on our sensibility, so that to our surprise and delight we discover depths of feeling of which we had no previous knowledge and which we had never plumbed. It is a gift we like to proclaim to the world which seems suddenly to have grown much wider. Solitude has the same power. It invites us to step into ourselves and to inspect our inner life. What if one's solitude is the deserts of ice where the silence is broken only by the voice of water in labour, the water that will nourish the soil, or, higher still, that immaculate immobility which gives the impression of appeasing and dominating at the same time? It is then that being on a mountain becomes an occasion for self-interpretation, for exalting and extolling ourselves. So, when a Pierre Loti describes the sea, it is still himself that he confides to us, with his desires and longings and sadnesses; and it is the music of his writing, more than the indefinite words he uses, that suggests the pictures to which he gives no definite outline.

At Guiers' death-bed Lamartine found the savage peace that society does not give. Victor Hugo filled his lungs with pure air in the circus of Gavarni; and Balzac, when he could be torn away from Paris which strained his nerves, used to feast on isolation in the *massif* of la Chartreuse. Do you remember in *Brand*, the young girl, Gerd, who lived on the packed snows and who discovered on the peaks the roofless temple where her soul liked to lavish itself in prayer? This spirit of the peaks is best given in the poetry of Lamartine. Let me remind you of the famous invocation in *Jocelyn*:

"Oh, those mountain peaks, the pure air and floods of light,
Deep-toned winds from the woods, the surging heather

I thought that God was thumping there upon my heart."[1]

and farther on

"Those nights on the mountain, when all things keep silence ..."[2]

---

[1] *O sommets de montagne, air pur, flots de lumière*
Vents sonores des bois, vagues de la bruyère

Je croyais sur mon coeur sentir Dieu palpiter ...

[2] *O nuits de la montagne, heure où tout fait silence ...*

And in his *Cours de littérature* he takes up the song again in prose and extols the Alps "whose violent snows stand outlined in the evening against a firmament as deep as an ocean."

There is no denying that Jean-Jacques and the Romantics did much to spread the taste for uncultivated nature and a love of mountains. And the mountains have become a sport for those who like the thrills of warfare, a sanatorium for the sick, a refuge for the broken-hearted and a platform for the lyrist. Having had their heroes, they now have their snobs; after their Christopher Columbuses they today have their Tartarins. Having once been feared as a Divinity of death, they have now become a fashion.

2. *The Conquest of the Mountains*

Ever since then the mountains have been visited, besieged, invaded, conquered, arranged, pierced, and banalized. The English were the first to conquer the Grandes Alpes. But though Whymper may have mastered the Matterhorn, Byron and poetry have stayed down below. Climbers' accounts of their ascents read like reports. These Kiplings of the rocks, the Coolidges, Mummerys, Tyndalls, Tucketts, have no use for the flowery. They leave that to old Ruskin prophesying at Chamonix, and to the German-Swiss novelists, the Hiers, Feyderers and Ernest Zahns, who wax sentimental over the idyllic peace of the upper valleys. Personally, I prefer the furious course of Richard Wagner pursuing the Valkyries across the Bernese Alps. As for the Italians, with their incomparable virtuosity, they have been politic enough to mix lyrism with guide-book information. Guido Rey's *Mont Cervin* is in this sense a marvel of dosage: you set out on the warpath, you exalt; but you know what the weather is and the time you will take; and you will not lose your way.

In the chapter on the Cervin[1] in his book *Les Conquérants* Guido Rey writes admiringly of the great Whymper, but while he does him homage, he cannot refrain from emphasizing his mistake, like one reproaching a general for the needless sacrifice of his regiments. This grim history of the Matterhorn is, perhaps, too well known to need repeating, yet for those who are not "of the Alps" I must just mention that the siege of the

[1] The Matterhorn.

Matterhorn lasted several years and that its capitulation cost four lives. It was assaulted from the Swiss and from the Italian side, from Zermatt and Goimein. On July 19, 1805, Whymper, an Englishman who had shown heroic obstinacy in attacking it despite grave setbacks, snatched victory from under the very nose of the Italians who were within six hundred and fifty feet[1] of the summit. He had set out from Zermatt with a chance company whom he had whipped into a state of exaltation and submission: three compatriots of his, the Rev. Hudson, Lord Francis Douglas and young Hadow who at nineteen was making his first ascent, two guides: Michel Croz of Chamonix and old Taugwalder from Zermatt, and one porter, Peter Taugwalder, son of the old guide. Michel Croz was one of those men who do not know what fatigue or danger are, and on whom you can rely in the worst predicament: he had conquered the Grande Casse and Mont Pourri. Taugwalder, however, was no longer young and also jealous of the better reputation of the younger man. Whymper did not know the three Englishmen, but he had enlisted them for the expedition because they had engaged Michel Croz whose help he greatly wished to have. When you think of the difficulties such an undertaking presented in those days, to have only two guides for four climbers of whom two were untried, was foolish, if not crazy. They conquered the Cervin, but its revenge was swift. On the way down, Hadow slipped and fell on Croz who was in the lead. Michel Croz was taken by surprise and had no time to fasten on. The weight of the two men was on the point of sweeping away the entire string. Whymper and the Taugwalders, who were at the other end of the rope, heard Michel Croz's shout and fastened on to the rock. Could they hold the others who were already falling? And then the rope broke and the four bodies hurtled down the precipice. The three survivors were unjustly accused of having cut the rope. Taugwalder went before the guides' council, that tribunal for professional mistakes from which there is no appeal, and was acquitted. Nevertheless, he was still shunned at Zermatt, like a mangy dog. As for Whymper, his frankness and his fame were eventually able to silence the strictures on his conduct that had accompanied the news of his victory, the most daring yet of Alpine conquests. He never denied his respon-

[1] In his own own account Whymper says 1,200 ft.—ED.

sibility. His tragic account of the accident ends with this ex-hortation: "Climb if you will, but remember that courage and strength are nought without prudence, and that a momentary negligence may destroy the happiness of a lifetime. Do nothing in haste; look well to each step; and from the beginning think what may be the end."

Guido Rey has told us how he met Whymper: "I was coming down from the Théodule: halfway between the *col* and the Goimein, I saw coming towards me a fine-looking old man, tall, his gaze clear, his cheeks red and clean-shaven, his head crowned with very white hair. He was climbing slowly. His whole body bore the stamp of a strong will; his back, straight for all his years, told of enduring vigour, and his long rhythmic stride of familiarity with mountains. As I passed close to him, I gave him the salute that the polite usage of those who meet in high places demands. He returned it and walked on. My guide had stopped to exchange a few words with his. When he re-joined me, he asked: 'Do you know who that gentleman is?' I replied that I did not. He said: 'It is M. Whymper.' And he spoke the name in a tone of respect. Then, I felt as agitated as though I had been faced with an apparition. I had never seen Whymper except in portraits; and I turned at once to look at him. He, too, had halted and was gazing at the Cervin of which you get a wonderful impressive view from this point. I cannot explain the impression I received from meeting that man in such a spot. It was no longer the man I saw, but the idealized image of the greatest of all alpinists whom I and others have so often dreamed of imitating."

Guido Rey found a new route up the Matterhorn by the *arête* of the Furggen. This involves being suspended for at least six hours over an abyss some 10,000 feet deep, and so is not a route you can recommend to everyone. I once met Guido Rey, as he met Whymper. I was coming down a *col* of the Mishabel making for Zermatt. After traversing a precipitous ridge we had reached a cairn and there saw coming towards us two men, a guide and a traveller, the latter an Italian, thin, muscular, with elongated features, as though his face had been struck like a medal. It was not the face of a young man, though at the first glance, what with the shadow thrown by his tyrolean hat and the clean line of his neck, I might well have taken it for one, especially having seen the way he walked. When he came closer and had uncovered, no! That face bore the traces of a life that was already long, though the burden of it was borne lightly. The thin lips beneath that moustache of stiff hair turning up slightly at the point, those hollow cheeks, almost what Saint Simon has called "swallowed," and the straight nose, lent a certain severity to the face, the ruggedness of the practical person accustomed to dealing with men and affairs, yet the high shining forehead and above all the deep-set eyes from which flashed a bright merry flame that seemed to originate far away, deep within him, these changed the whole expression of his face and gave it an indefinable air of repose and at the same time of exaltation, the gladness of the peace that is to be found on the summits of mountains. His was the true look that *always seeks the distance, a gaze as limpid as that of the sailor, a gaze that reflects the expanse of vast horizons.* Forty years and more, perhaps fifty, had passed across those features, giving them the patina of life but without having been able to deprive them of youthfulness. And the youth that still was his had been enhanced in beauty by the stamp set there on his face by life, whose burden he had borne so lightly. Life, too, is an ascent. The higher you go, the better you see, the better you breathe, and the greater your mastery. And at the top there is the serenity of evening.

We drank a goblet of champagne in honour of our countries, Italy and France, and so went our ways. The Italians passed on upwards in our path, which they later left to strike off towards the Adler Pass, while we made for the interminable Gorner glacier. When the Italians were out of hearing, my guide, Zurbringen of Saas, turned to me and asked:

"Do you know that gentleman?"

"I? No. How should I know him?"

"It was M. Guido Rey."

At once I turned and my eyes sought him for another look. But though the dark silhouettes were as sharp as Chinese shadows against the whiteness of the snow, his was no longer distinguishable from that of his companion.

The history of the conquests of the mountains has been written many times. The Chamonix Alps: Mont Blanc, Aiguille Verte, Dent du Géant, Grandes-Jorasses, Aiguilles du Dru, etc.; the Valais Alps: Monte Rosa, Matterhorn, Dent

Blanche, etc.; The Bernese Alps: Jungfrau, Eiger, Monsch, etc., Mischabel and the Alps of Engadine; the Alps of Dauphiné; la Meige, la Barre des Ecrins, all have had their explorers and their heroes. There is not one missing from the lists of the conquered. All these mountains have been discovered. Thus there are special reasons why they today exercise an attraction that is not that of novelty, an attraction that is both of the mind and of the spirit.

3. *Mountain Sickness*

Sometimes, on the slopes of Mont Blanc, among the rocks of the Grands Mulets, or, higher still, on the snows of the Grand Plateau, you will find the little bodies of frozen bees or butterflies. Impelled by the wind or their own fantasy they had embarked upon the glacier, and then, when they realized how they had gone astray, they had flown on upwards instead of down. Some mysterious delusive instinct tells them that they must climb, so up and up they go as long as their feeble wings can beat, until they fall to die. In the same way the alpinist seems to have the soul of a butterfly or bee. Some mysterious instinct impels him too to ascend—it is the mountain sickness. I know that that is the name usually given to the dizziness, difficulty in breathing, and heaviness in the head, that overcome even the most robust at certain heights; but I prefer to keep it for the fascination, the spell that the mountains cast over certain sensibilities.

The symptoms of this sickness resemble those of love. Let me give some examples. In the middle of the eighteenth century there lived at Geneva a certain painter of miniatures, Théodore Bourrit. He was a gentle, peaceable man. He scarcely ever left his studio and his day passed in perfect tranquillity. One day, some friends made him go with them up to the top of a neighbouring mountain, les Voirons. It is an easy climb, and from the top you can see the whole *massif* of Mont Blanc. The moment he saw that, our Bourrit experienced a change of heart. His friends knew him as a calm and balanced person, but he returned down the mountain in a state of exaltation and mild inebriation. This holy intoxication never left him. He gave up his miniatures, his stay-at-home life, and learned to open his eyes and to walk. He had loved his comforts and a life of ease, now he learned to suffer. In order to learn how to paint all over again—for he wanted to paint the object of his passion and was poor—he became a chorister in the cathedral at Geneva, and in the intervals between services he would rush to the mountains one hand grasping his walking-stick, the other his brushes. Even his painting, however, was just a pretext: what he adored was the air of the peaks, their liberty, the solitude, the play of light on the snow, on the rocks and on the valleys seen from above. He was a lover who had received a *coup de foudre*.

There was a certain madness too in the sedate and solemn de Saussure, however much he tried to disguise his lasting passion for Mont Blanc under the cloak of scientific interest. A thirst for knowledge is not in itself by any means enough to explain his furious gesture when at last he made his conquest after twenty-five years of covetousness: "The length of the struggle," he has told us, "the memory and the still poignant sense of the difficulties and hardships this victory had cost me, made me feel a sort of irritation. The moment I reached the highest point of the snow which crowns the peak, I trampled it under foot in what was almost a rage." That is a strange emotion to find in a man of learning.

Women, as they should be, have been even more impassioned. Mlle Henriette d'Angeville was the first foreign woman to reach the summit of Mont Blanc (1838). She too had become obsessed after having seen it from Chamonix. She had to overcome fierce opposition from her family. It was as though she were wanting to marry for love. But in the end she was able to attempt the climb. Her strength betrayed her when she was near her goal, but not her will. Half suffocated, her heart thumping, her eyes closed, she was forced to halt. But her determination persisted.

"If I die before reaching the summit," she said to her guides, "promise me that you will carry my body up to the top and bury it there."

And her guides, because they understood her feelings, being all in love with their mountain, promised her that. It was quite a solemn moment.

"Do not worry, Mademoiselle," said Joseph-Marie Couttet, who was the most experienced and already famous for his nine ascents, "you will go there dead or alive."

She did reach the top, and alive. Once there she indulged in a last piece of childishness, and had her guides lift her up above their heads, so that she had mounted higher still.

These proofs of love should suffice. They could be multiplied. There was Colonel Baufoy, an Englishman, newly married to a charming girl of nineteen. Leaving his young wife in Chamonix, he set out to climb Mont Blanc.

Bourrit, who made the Alps his business, asked him whether he had thought of his wife when he was at the top. "Indeed, no," said the Colonel frankly, "for the mountain wants to be loved exclusively."

What is it that irresistibly attracts the alpinist? The pleasure of the view? Without doubt the magnificent sights they discover at the top are a recompense for so much effort. But the eyes of most tourists are useless for seeing. They live in the snow, as their fellows in motor cars in their dust, without paying heed to the diversity of the universe. Often all that they can find to say about what they have seen is the description reluctantly given by Maria Paradis, a young girl of Chamonix, whom some guides had taken as a joke right up to the top of Mont Blanc.

"I can remember," she said seriously as she served some travellers with milk, "that everything was white near where I was, and black down below; but that's all."

And that is enough for them.

Or is it, then, vanity, snobbery? In the Alps you can certainly meet plenty of Tartarins armed to the teeth who will make you shudder with their accounts of their adventures; yet the silent mountaineer who disappears suddenly without telling anyone his intention, and who, like all true Don Juans, guards the secret of his conquests, is by no means rare. It is he, who risks his life for his pleasure, who is the true victim of the mountain sickness.

He knows and savours the harsh poetry of the mountain, the sense of life being more healthy and free that the mountain gives when it makes you forget your fellow men and the worries of every day, the changing scene that offers your eyes one moment a narrow gorge in which a mountain torrent leaps and roars, and the next a limitless expanse stretching away to distant confines, away beyond yet other mountains, where sky and plain come together again in airy colour; he knows and savours all the signs of daring afforded by the lacework of the peaks, and how the vegetation flees from beneath his feet, beginning with the retreat of the rhododendrons that beflag the rocky slopes, then that more reluctant of the blue gentians, forget-me-nots, wild pansies and other anonymous little pink flowers that are like minute stars fixed in a firmament of pale green moss; he knows and savours, too, the magnificence of the snowfields in which the sun kindles innumerable stars, the virginal beauty of the little lakes of glaucous water that you suddenly come across in the hearts of glaciers, and the glittering glaciers themselves, those deathly solitudes to which the light gives a sort of strange vertiginous beauty like that of the sirens who used to draw sailors down to the bottom of the sea. . . .

Yet it is not that which has him by the shoulders, urging him on. Mountain sickness is really love of danger. Love of danger is at the bottom of all passion. People love in order the better to feel and experience life, and you cannot do that with real force unless there is the contrast of death in the air. Though death may not be immediately visible in the mountains, you can always sense its invisible presence. The rocks, the snow, the ice all belong to it. It is there waiting for its prey, like those snow-flake flowers or the snow-finches to whom the wind brings flocks of butterflies or bees deluded by that mysterious instinct that impels them to ascend.

He would be a poor lover, who was afraid to risk his life for his love. But how much more disinterested and daring is he who risks his days merely to give them spice! Fewer and fewer people believe in a future life, yet instead of taking every precaution to hold on to this life which has to pass, which will pass, is passing, never before has man invented so many new risks to run. The more important life becomes to him, the more willing he is to stake it. He breaks his neck on the ice, he hurtles down from up in the air, he crushes himself, or what is worse, others beneath his motor car. His feverish love of life could almost be taken for hatred of it. He flings himself upon it with as much fury, as though he wished to destroy it. He no longer creates in calm and serenity, but instead dashes frenziedly to his ruin. He requires that joy shall be less insipid than he usually finds the worldly pleasures and women to be. Poor Don Quixote, he is reduced to substituting undertakings from which prudence is absent for the opportunities for heroism that today are so rare.

41

But does he not expend the same amount of energy? He imitates the hero of *Triomphe de la Mort* who found the height of voluptuousness in suicide. It is, to borrow one of Barrès' favourite phrases: "the eternal motive of death through excessive love of life."

The cover of a Munich periodical, *Alpine Majestäten und ihr Gefolge,* devoted to the beauty of mountains, depicts a young alpinist, ice-axe in hand, with a roll of rope round his shoulders, saluting the symbolic majesty of the Alps. Mont Blanc is personified as an old king, crowned and bearded with snow, his right hand resting on the Rochers Rouges; Monte Rosa is an august, almost regal old man, and the Jungfrau a virgin who with a bashful movement is pulling a white gown over a bare and sensitive shoulder.

To those who love them the mountains are indeed living beings. Considered as motionless as a corpse, they are yet animated by glorious life. They hold converse with the clouds, yield to the caresses of the light, their glaciers are on the move—and are they not the reservoir of the universe, they who feed the rivers and with their pure waters make the earth fertile?

4. *The Call of the Mountains*

I have been, and still am, a passionate lover of mountains. For me their attraction has been progressive. At first, it was that of the gentle wooded slopes, all green with pastures and fir-woods, with their herds of cows and echoing bells, the mountain that lulls and refreshes, that rests and soothes, where you delight to stretch out softly after picking strawberries, raspberries and myrtles, with their gory mark still on your lips. I was born at the foot of the mountains. I was still quite a child when I first proudly set my foot on them, and the enchantment of my first ascent has not gone from my memory. There was a little chapel at the top to which people made pilgrimage. I was surprised to see how from that height our country house looked small and half hidden among the greenery, and at that moment I despised the plain. Yet I came down from there.

Later, I attacked the rocks. That is the most exciting of all sports. Once you are sure that you have successfully rebelled against vertigo, to attempt the most hazardous climbs is just a matter of developing your muscles and your skill. I remember one climb I made with two well-known alpinists, Commandant Godefroy and Lieutenant du Verger. We had to cross an *arête* of rock sitting astride it with a chasm on either side. At such times you do not worry about the chasm; you are too preoccupied placing your hands and feet. However, these old exploits are but trifles compared with the unheard-of audacities of the new generation of climbers. In Grenoble there are two or three groups of young people who have successfully made climbs hitherto reputed to be impossible. It is true that these climbs claim their victims. Indeed, too many lives are sacrificed. These young people are too enthusiastic and should learn patience and prudence. Love of the mountains is a noble passion, but it is not an end in life. It should lead to health of mind and body, not to death. It has risks and dangers of its own and there is no need to multiply them or to make new ones by deliberately choosing the difficult.

Chamois shooting made me better acquainted with mountains. I was started on it by one of the greatest chamois hunters France has ever had, the Marquis de Saint-Séverin, author of the classic book on the subject whose picturesque lively text he has illustrated with crayon drawings like miniatures. He used to take me off to Lake Lovitel in the *massif* of L'Oisans. I still experience a shiver of pride when I recall those expeditions of my youth: the climb in the freshness of morning; the choosing of a stance in the shelter of some rock, sometimes on the very fringe of a *névé* or glacier, the meticulous examination of the horizon during the subsequent long wait that leads your gaze from slopes of turf dotted with alders, junipers and clumps of bilberries of such a hot flaming red as though they had been burned by the sun, right up to the domes and immaculate pinnacles shining in the clear bright air and contrasting their whiteness with the deep blue of the sky, that blue so pure, massive and at the same time light, compact and liquid, which is neither the blue of the Orient, nor the blue of Italy, but the blue of the skies of Savoy and Dauphiné purified by the air of the virgin peaks; then at last the arrival at the gallop of a whole herd driven by the shouts of the beaters charging like marauders down below in the narrow valley, the athletic spectacle of the chamois climbing the wall of a rock, the bulge of their muscles, the power of their hocks, the sureness of those cloven hooves

43   D

with their long toes which allow them to race along like a platoon of young thoroughbreds at Auteuil or Chantilly. How many times haven't I delayed to watch them at the risk of bungling my shot, unable to decide to kill them, finding them too beautiful! They would reach me and I would be able to make out every tiny detail of those little heads with backward curving horns, pointed flickering ears, gentle velvety eyes, and then suddenly having caught some suspicious scent, they would turn at right angles while at full speed, a madly foolhardy manœuvre that might easily have left them with broken bones on the stones.

It is among the rocks, sometimes on the edge of a *névé*, that you shoot chamois, yet I was to hear and heed the call of the snows. One day I felt need of the silence and solitude of the glaciers. It was at Grande-Casse in Tarentaise that I made my first traverse necessitating an ice-axe and the cutting of steps. Once you have heard the voice of the sirens, there is no more denying it, and so each year from then on I would indulge my passion, in company with a friend equally in love with high peaks lost in snow. This took me in turn to the Engadine, where we climbed the Morteratsch but had no time for the Bernina and Piz Roseg; to the Bernese Alps, where we made the Oberaar traverse from the la Concordia hut at Grimsel with a stop at Finsteraarhorn; to Saas-Fée from which we set out for the desolate hermitage of Matemarck at the foot of Monte Moro and from there crossed the Neu-Weissthor pass at a height of 13,000 feet and made our way down into Zermatt; to the Valais Alps and the Triefthorn and Rothorn, and finally to Monte Rosa which we climbed in a snow storm. Our guide wanted to turn back, but we were obstinate and determined. We went on and up through that uniform desert as far as the wall of rock covering the summit which was thinly coated with ice. Here is the Marguerite hut where we were able to rest. On the way down, however, we almost lost our way. The snow had covered our tracks and how were we to make out where we were in that immense expanse? Our imprudence could have cost us dear, yet with what delight did we reach Gressonney! All the same, we had seen nothing except when a gust of wind had swept the snow aside and we had caught a glimpse of a neighbouring peak, menacing, chill and ghostly.

Winter can provide these prodigious spectacles of mountain peaks under snow at more accessible altitudes, and that is why the mountains are most beautiful in winter. Sunshine makes them incomparably splendid, all violent and at the same time gentle. Then, indeed, the mountains call with "a siren's voice."

Among the snows, evening and isolation impart a sort of ecstasy. The virgin air that you breathe there is an austere kiss on the lips. The stars are more friendly up there, and there is a solemn importance about the silence which the deep voice of the wind accompanies like a distant orchestra.

In the mountains you see better how mysterious night comes from the earth and not from the sky; from below up to the heights. The valleys are the first to be conquered, they and the inner walls; both slow and quick the shadows climb like a crafty army. For a time victory stays with the peaks; and even the gaudiness of these snows becomes more brilliant at sunset, blazing in splendour as though day was not about to end. Then the light falters, and suddenly night is everywhere.

This is the hour for the stars. In the mountains they are not far away, as they are in the plain or on the sea. In the limited spaces between the contours of the earth they appear more friendly, one might almost say, more human. They decorate the solitude, give to the eyes that behold them caresses as pure as they are mysterious. Whilst elsewhere they are so numerous that your eyes lose themselves among them, in the mountains the very idea of the other worlds beyond their pattern of light evokes our desire for the infinite and our lust to know and to understand. Being closer in a narrow sky, a sky that is framed, they seem to banish confusion and incertitude from our thoughts and in their place put the simple fervour of our emotion. They are content to insist that God is there. All starry nights in the mountains are religious.

Meanwhile, night has given place to morning. The first rays of the dawn are beginning to colour the highest peaks. The virgin snow takes on a tinge of pink, that of almond blossom or peach blossom in the spring, and the shaded contours of the domes and cupolas have that even silken softness of slender curved things that is woman's beauty. In the light the country-side becomes animated like flesh in which life runs.

Indeed, the snow gives to both morning and evening a human profundity, the mysterious attraction of a love which will have neither beginning nor decline. . . .

5. *The Call of the Snows*

The snows do call, like the sirens, whose white softness they have and the voluptuous pearly lustre that a wet body acquires beneath the caresses of the sun. Their call is an invitation, and how can it be refused? They offer the pleasures of winter, violent, almost barbaric, to which the cold and the pure, healthy air of the peaks lend exaltation: ski-ing, skating, tobogganing, bobsleighing, sledging. . . .

Some traveller whose name I no longer remember used to say that one ought to visit the lands of the sun at the height of their summer, and the countries of the north during winter. It is then, he explained, that they are at their most beautiful, for they are frankly themselves; to know them, one must see them in that mood of frankness: the Orient in all its light, Norway and Sweden under ice and snow.

That is absolutely correct. The mountains are most beautiful during the season that we no longer dare call "bad." It has taken me a long time to realize this, but now I am sure of it. Switzerland was the first country to organize winter sports. Some fifty years ago a little group of Norwegians came to the Engadine with their skis and taught some enterprising tourists and guides how to use those long wooden skates. The innovation gained ground. From Saint Moritz and Pontresina it spread into Oberland, then into Jura, then to the heights above the Lake of Geneva, to Caux, Villars, Chambéry. From there it came to Savoy by way of Chamonix. It established itself in Saint Gervais, Mégève, La Clusaz, etc., . . . and then on to Mont Revard, to La Féclaz and Hauteluce, and so to Morzine and other places in the valleys of Savoy. It won the Dauphiné where every form of contest with the mountains has its most daring protagonists. It set itself up in the Pyrenees. Today it is sovereign in every mountain resort, yet the ski has not dethroned the skate, more scholarly, more refined, more elegant, that requires less physical strength and greater suppleness. Nor have its solitary pleasures ousted the communal joys of the toboggan built for two, nor of the long, speedy bobsleigh that rushes down ice-clad slopes at a dizzy speed. They are sought after more and more; they have their enthusiastic worshippers who make the best possible propaganda for them. I do not believe there is a more intoxicating form of exercise. This is, perhaps, because of the contrast between the icy freshness of the air and the warm circulation of the blood which gives to the whole body a delicious sense of well-being, a feeling of power and felicity, and also because of the setting, the snow so prodigiously white which the sunlight colours according to the time of day: pink at dawn, dull at high noon, violet and purple in the evening.

6. *The Mountains are a Prayer*

There are alpinists who still continue to explore the mountains, those whom I may call the acrobatic alpinists. They attack their mountains by faces seemingly inaccessible and thanks to their wonderful equipment and superhuman energy they succeed. These are people who have kept their taste for danger and peril. But there are also fervent admirers of the mountains who cherish an immaterial affection for them.

"The feeling for nature, this precious gift of privileged souls, ought to have a large share in our education . . . give me this growing child, clinging like ivy to his mother's apron strings, deprived of individuality and initiative, . . . give him to me that I may guide him through our alps. In overcoming the difficulties nature places in his path let him learn to conquer the difficulties he will meet with in life, to enjoy the rising sun seen from the crest of a mountain ridge, and the sunset that kindles the vast glaciers into flame, the moonlight sporting in a deserted valley, let him pluck the flowers which grow on the fringe of the eternal snows; let him exult at the spectacle of the heavens above the abyss of the mountains! Let him do this and that child will come back a man and his moral conscience will have lost nothing thereby."

Who said that? A future saint, one Contardo Ferrini, professor in the University of Pavia, who had a soul that burned with charity and mystical fervour. The mountains strengthened his taste for the divine: "How good it is," he wrote once, "when you are on a deserted mountain top to feel something akin to the solemn approach to God and to be able to watch His eternally youthful smile in the serenity of wild nature." His death was hastened by an ascent of Monte Rosa made under bad conditions.

Ferrini demanded the weak, lethargic unenterprising child that has lived too long at its mother's skirts for his Alps, that they might prepare it for the struggles of life; but he might also have asked for those too impetuous young people, the prey of violent desires, who are unable to content themselves with an ordinary life. For them the Alps would be a good training school; they would learn to endure bad weather, to stop when confronted by the impossible, to rise superior to fatigue, to set their feet firmly before taking another upward step. They would acquire that physical sense of balance which contributes largely to man's moral equilibrium. "Man," says the *Discours sur les passions de l'amour*, attributed to Pascal, "has need of movement and action; that is to say that he sometimes requires to be shaken by passions whose origin he can feel deep and quick within himself." Passion is the manifestation of that happy need of action and conquest which nags at man and without which he would become engulfed in the flatness and monotony of life. Michael Angelo, who carved them in stone, called them "the passions of fire": no doubt their ravages can be infinite, yet we owe to them the successful realization of some of the world's greatest enterprises. However, these bursts of passion require to be regulated and that is what the mountains will do. They will see that these desires remain in the heart, will even exalt them, they and the lusts that are the colour of our days, and through which our energies are unleashed, and at the same time the obstacles, difficulties and dangers that they pile up will constrain the most ardent to prepare themselves for the struggle, to make their plan of battle, to learn how to husband and make the best use of themselves so as to conquer. They oblige each one to find his own method. They draw you up and up, yet require that you never let the ground out of sight unless you have a firm and solid stance.

Guido Rey, in his *Mont Cervin*, quotes Rudolf Töppfer the first, or one of the first, to advocate mountain life as a moral health cure for youth. The words are very similar to those of Contardo Ferrini, though written earlier: "More than one man who had forgotten God in the plains, remembered Him again in the mountains." Ruskin looked to the spectacle of Mont Blanc to renew his power of exaltation: "The gates of the mountain," he said, "open to me a new life that will have no end, unless it be at the gate of that mount from which there is no return." And Guido Rey himself turned naturally to this verse of Dante's for encouragement on the march: "This mountain is such that always down below, at the beginning, it seems difficult. But the higher man ascends, the less laborious he finds it to be."

All mountaineers know that the pleasure of the view is but a small part of the great delight of the climb. There is no doubt that the earth changes shape when seen from above. But that can be felt, even without being seen. Some years ago a blind man had himself hauled up to the top of the Cervin, and when his guides informed him that he had reached the summit, he gave a triumphant shout. It was one of the great sensations of his immured life. For an instant he had regained his liberty. "I wish," wrote the author of *Cervin*, "that I had been able to see his poor lifeless eyes wondering at his inner vision of that splendid horizon." And he enumerated the other joys that are to be had as well as that of the view, or which can take its place: "That blessed fatigue that is one of the most intense pleasures the mountains can give us, the tenuous healthy air of altitudes of 13,000 feet, light air that has an exquisite taste, air that quenches all thirst in your breast like the purest water and that gives you strength like generous wine, the eternal silence of lofty places." All that yes, and other forces too that are in ourselves overstimulated and impossible to express. Dante understood this. In *Paradise*, he says, "There are things which he who comes down from the heights is unable to repeat. . . ."

Guido Rey, when he came down from the heights, himself addressed an eloquent appeal to the young people of Italy: "I would that all young Italians who are able-bodied and cultured should climb the Cervin at least once, so that the hidden energies of their souls might be revealed to them and that, in the noble pride of effort expended, they should feel purer, more capable of lofty purposes, more enthusiastic about their beautiful country. . . ." Of his passion for mountains which he is so eager to propagate, he speaks in his *Récits et impressions d'alpinisme* which, more intimate than his *Mont Cervin*, gives the homely simple side of his life in the mountains. He tells us how this passion was implanted in his childish heart, not by chance

circumstance, but methodically and purposefully by a noble
man. Guido Rey was the nephew of Quintino Sella, whose name
is known to all who frequent the *massifs* of Mont Blanc and Monte
Rosa, for it is the name given to several of those refuges in which
the climber is only too glad to find shelter among the rocks and
ice at 13,000 feet. There is one at the foot of the Mont Blanc
face, another on a shoulder of the Lyskamm. Quintino Sella,
famous geologist, founded the Italian Alpine Club. He belonged
in part to France, for he studied at the *École des Mines* in Paris
and obtained his practical engineering experience in the mines
of Savoy. There was nothing he loved so much as his trips in
the Alps in search of the crystals whose laws he studied; yet his
king knew that he was as talented an economist and financier
as he was a scientist, and had no compunction in summoning
him away from his crystals to be one of his ministers. Now,
Quintino Sella had a whole swarm of sons and nephews whom
he loved to gather together during the holidays at his house in
Biella, at the foot of the Alps. He would take them up into the
mountains, where he trained them in endurance at the same
time as he imparted his passion to them. One day he took his
little troop up Mont Bo and there he showed their fascinated
eyes all the peaks of Monte Rosa and told them its history. "And
there, at that moment, perhaps," writes Guido Rey, "the
powerful suggestion of that strong man and the natural intoxication of that great spectacle caused the souls of us young people
to reach out for the first time towards the eternal beauty of the
mountains and awoke within us the desire to see it close, to try
ourselves to climb that mountain which, like some colossal
phantom, we could see all pink in the blue sky of the cold serene
dawn. Oh! how intoxicating to our young receptive souls was
that unexpected revelation of a true deep love which was to
endure all our lives!"

Emile Javelle, less favoured because his greatest distraction
could never be more than a walk to the Buttes-Chaumont and
because he never saw the Alps, relates in his *Souvenirs d'un Alpinist* how his first longing for mountains came from a dried
flower in the herbarium of a botanist who was his uncle. Beneath this flower was a note: *Androsace, rock face of Mont Blanc*.
These few words, *Androsace, rock face of Mont Blanc*, a crumpled
plant without contour or scent, were enough to conjure up in

the mind of that child a whole new world of mystery. His uncle, Quintino Sella, would tell him about the flowers, and when they had got beyond the line where the last still persisted in growing, he would tell about the stones and the great geological movements which had thrust these huge masses up towards the sky, and it was his commentaries, perhaps by their very conciseness, which kindled the imaginations of these young people. For these vast white expanses, for all their appearance of being dead and insensible, have their share in the life of the centuries, and when you observe them closely, you can see them gradually come to life, take on colour and thrill like living beings. They change from one moment to the next, the play of shadow and light about them is like that of thoughts and emotions across a face. In the morning they aspire after daylight, and in the evening when the whole plain is veiled in darkness, for a long time they persist in their efforts to retain the sunlight. The silence is their language, that silence which is more impressive than any words, and that is like the converse of mountains in the peace eternal.

Just as Laura for the first time appeared to Petrach on the threshold of the church of Sainte-Claire in Avignon when it was morning, so the mountains appeared to Guido Rey in the softness and beauty of the dawn, and he was likewise captivated for the rest of his days.

Once, as he was passing through Bionaz on his way up to the col de Valpelline, Guido Rey saw a young chamois which had been caught during the winter at the foot of an avalanche. The moment it was dragged out of its stable the noble beast lifted its muzzle towards the heights and began leaping and jumping in a desperate effort to escape. "I was sorry for that beautiful creature of the mountains, born for the liberty of the high peaks, but now condemned to slavery in a gloomy hovel." The following year he again passed through that same village and stopped to ask about the prisoner. But the prisoner had succeeded in escaping: while a camera was being focused on him he had tugged and tugged and broken his halter.

Whenever he could escape from his business life Guido Rey, like the chamois of Valpelline, regained his liberty. Such liberty allows one, even though only momentarily, to forget the monotony of existence far from mankind whose vanities and nastiness, to say nothing of its stupidity, one is better able to measure from on high. *The mountains were his poetry.*

For us, too, the mountains should be poetry. Once, a chamois hunter said to me something that I have never since been able to forget. "The mountains," he said, "are God's antechamber."

Yes, in them you hear God's voice coming through the party-wall of the created world. . . .

THE CALL OF THE POLAR REGIONS

Frank Illingworth

MY first visit to the Arctic was made purely for monetary profit. War was pending, a war which I felt certain would envelop the Arctic. Thus, while my rivals in the world of journalism crossed the English Channel for a last look at Europe's capitals I turned northwards to the tundras and forests of Arctic Scandinavia, Russia's Murmansk, and to the riven pack-ice of Spitzbergen-Greenland waters. I secured my scoop. For when war flared across Arctic Scandinavia into the north-west of Arctic Russia and right across the Polar Ocean to the ice cap of Greenland and the grinding pack-ice of Spitzbergen, I was the only journalist with a comprehensive knowledge of these areas. And I secured infinitely more than a scoop. I gained from my journeys across the brilliant tundras and from the strange people who inhabit them, a new outlook on life, an awareness that spiritual greatness and peace of mind exist less in the precincts of bishops and cathedrals than in the incredibly beautiful wildness of the Great White Arctic where the mystic and the matter-of-fact have of each other a deep understanding; here in the North I saw beauty for the first time, not the transparent beauty of the Lake District, not the mauve distance of the Coolins or the leafy loveliness of a Kentish lane, but a fundamental beauty that silences the tongue and makes the finest of us feel misshapen by comparison. Sitting in the prow of a sealer as she twisted and turned between the ice-floes of the Polar Ocean I recalled the words of my old Swiss Guide, Rudolf Kaufmann, son of the famous Peter Kaufmann; "Sometimes I come into the mountains to be near my God." If indeed there is a God (which remark I present as a question rather than a statement), then surely He must reside on the top of the world among the flashing curtains of the *aurora borealis* and the unreal loom of the polar heavens?

Soon after I had returned home from this my first journey into the Arctic I felt a strange loneliness descend upon me. Without realizing it, I was feeling the Call of the North. "Once a man

53

has wintered 'beyond the North' he always returns," so they told me in the Arctic. "Living up here becomes a state of mind," a trapper said. "I'll not say goodbye because I know you'll come back," he laughed. I, too, laughed. For had I not ventured into the Arctic purely to secure a newspaper scoop? Indeed I had! But the months following my return to Britain saw a longing to be back in the North arise within me. I found myself planning to spend the spring of 1939 with the nomads who roam the tundras of Arctic Scandinavia and Russia. And no sooner was I back in Britain from this my second trip into the North than I was working out how I might return to the Arctic during the winter of 1939–40. The war prevented the realization of my plan to winter in the North. But it did not banish from my mind thoughts of the polar regions, and immediately peace returned I packed my rucksack and turned Northwards again. Six times have I journeyed North. And denied the opportunity of living in the Arctic permanently, I must, to the end of my days, annually satisfy the call that is the curse and the blessing of all men who have journeyed "beyond the North."

If the Far East exerts a call upon those who have smelt its odours and listened to the patter of its bare feet, then the Call of the Polar Regions is infinitely more pronounced. The beauty to be found in the Arctic, the people who live within its vastness (empire builders, adventurers, mystics, dreamers, hunters and herdsmen) and the spiritual and physical satisfaction it grants those who know its moods, all this and more is offered to the traveller who will take up his courage or give wanderlust full reign and venture into the Arctic regions. And having penetrated beyond the North, he will return again and again.

Six months after my last visit to Spitzbergen in 1948 there arrived on my doorstep in London a young mining engineer whom I had met in Longyearbyen, one Haakon Stuedal. He had come to Britain, he said, to attend a "board" for a mining job in Burma. In place of polar cold he wanted the heat of the tropics. And if he failed to get the job in Burma? "Well, what's it matter? I can always get a job as a mining engineer at Disco Bay, in Greenland. It would be a change to go to Greenland and nicer than going to Burma." Haakon had succumbed to the strange power of the Arctic. He did not know it, but he had fallen under its spell, for soon I heard that he had gone, not to the Far East, but back to the North. Had Haakon secured the appointment in Burma it would have been interesting to see whether the future call of the East would have been stronger than that of the North! Had the tropics "grown on him" his predicament would have been a terrible one, for here would have been a man fighting to satisfy cravings of two merciless mistresses. Yet, seductive as may be the Far East, I fancy the call of the Far Arctic would have won in the end.

One meets in the North situations in piquancy beyond imagination, and characters who might have stepped from the pages of a Jack London novel.

On the edge of the Ice Barrier I listened to a Finn, drunk from a spirit which is normally used exclusively for swabbing the skin in operating theatres, blaspheme his companions in support of a bearded Norwegian whose creed was that Christ would soon be re-born in the Arctic, and then persuade the prophet to share his bottle of hospital spirit!

In Arctic Finland I suffered the unpleasantness of having a nomad peer into my eyes so that he might read my mind, and who, having read, turned away with the corners of his mouth drooping in the manner of a reindeer in an ill-humour.

In Arctic Norway I sat in the tent of an aged nomad who asked me why men must war when all one needs is a good wife and a few reindeer. When I asked if he had heard of Hitler and Stalin he turned on me a knowing look and, pondering for a moment, replied: "Are they as great men as our poet, Johan Turi?"

And then there was Olsen, whom I met in Arctic Sweden following a journey on to the tundras beyond Karasuando, where the road ends in bog. Olsen, a Swede of immense proportions and the constitution of the ore which once he mined in the Iron Mountains of Arctic Sweden, had a capacity for liquor beyond measure. When drunk he roared like a bull, and invariably broke up the furniture, which idiosyncracy was less an expression of aggressiveness than a simple delight in his capability to tear a chair apart with his hands: having broken everything breakable he would sit amid the wreckage with a sublime expression. Drunk or sober his favourite trick was to grasp one by the belt and with a mighty heave lift one above his shoulders, thump his chest with his free hand and bellow in the tones of an enraged walrus. A little more than ten years after I first met Olsen, in the spring of 1939 I heard from the well of the Norwegian collier taking me to Spitzbergen a Tarzan-like roar that struck in my mind a familiar chord. Where had I heard that bellowing voice before? Bound for the Norwegian coalmining settlement on Ice Fjord, we had on the *Askeladden* some forty newly signed-on miners, and as I looked down on to the well-deck I saw one of them grab a companion by the belt and heave him aloft, which performance was accompanied by a further Tarzan-like bellow. It was my old friend Olsen. I clattered down the ladder and tapped him on the shoulder, whereupon he turned and, recognizing me, dropped his companion to the iron deck with complete disregard for his bones. "Ver ve meet?" he asked. My answer was the signal for Olsen to grab me by the belt and heave me aloft, in which undignified position I was introduced to the rest of the men as "Dis ees my frien' Illingvort, Ja!" Since our last meeting Olsen had crossed Siberia, worked in Greenland, and spent a season on a whaler. Four months previously he had been sailing among the ice floes of the Far South in search of fortune from whale-flensing. Now he was sailing the ice floes of the Far North, bound for the "coal mountains" barely ten degrees from the North Pole, there to earn £80 a month as a miner.

One finds in the more northerly latitudes many a man, young and old, with Olsen's outlook. On my first visit to Spitzbergen I met a Norwegian who had travelled from the whaling settlements in the Antarctic island of South Georgia to the coal mining settlements of the Arctic. When I enquired why after fifteen years in the Far South he should suddenly leave for the Far North, he removed his red skull-cap and banged an iron cup on the counter of the store of which he was in charge: "Vell, vhy not? I vonted a change. Vouldn't you after fifteen blody year in der Antarctic? Now I vont to spend fifteen blody year in der Arctic, eh?"

At least part of the attraction the Arctic holds is the knowledge that it offers the opportunity for a man to test himself. There is in some men an inner and unaccountable urge to prove themselves. For it they cannot account. But its power is great, and it can find expression only in pitting their mental and physical stamina against great odds. The man anchored to a City desk travels to Switzerland with mountaineering boots, Alpine rope and ice axe. The vast areas of the Arctic offer a considerably wider scope for this test to which a man can submit himself. The conditions under which one lives when travelling by dog-team bares a man's soul to his neighbour, permits him to search his own heart, to assess his capabilities, and if he has it in him to emerge with a greater respect for himself surely this is a great thing to accomplish? And to accomplish it is part and parcel of the call of the polar regions.

In the same category is the desire for adventure. When in 1949 I wrote an article saying that the Hudson's Bay Company required trappers I was inundated with letters from men of all classes and ages enquiring for further particulars. The article painted the trapper as a bearded giant blinking into fantastic blizzards. Those who enquired saw in the blizzards, in the hardship and the dangers an opportunity to escape from mundane things. Perhaps my reader will call this "the romance of the North." Possibly it is. But who among us can say that he or she has not at one or another time, possibly in the still of night, dwelt romantically upon the hardships faced by the man who lives in the Far North and seen himself in the position of the trapper or explorer, fighting blizzards and surviving to face hardship once again? And who among us cannot understand the thrill the explorer experiences in the discovery of new territories? Exploration offers a spiritual uplift many times more valuable than the effort put into its attainment, for tired limbs, fear, the bitterness of polar cold—these things are soon forgotten, whereas the stimulant of discovery lives past the span of the explorer's life and into the future. His discoveries are his memorial even if his name is not written upon the world-map.

Likewise there is a spiritual reward in following the steps of the early pioneers and explorers. This applies to the trails blazed through jungle and across desert, but it is more marked in the passage of snow wastes and moving sea-ice, because here the danger is more pronounced, because if in the heart of a jungle one is liable to come upon a commercial traveller from Birmingham the chances of meeting anything but a polar bear on the moving sea-ice of the Far North is remote in the extreme. Here one is alone; beyond aid; and the richer for knowing that in the whole vast Barrens of Canada there are only 16,000 people, that the inhabitants of northern Greenland, an area exceeding that of France, do not exceed five hundred, and that in all Spitzbergen there are not above six thousand people, of whom 5,980 seldom move more than a mile from the perimeter of the mining settlements, the remaining twenty being Norwegian trappers and hunters whose lives are spent among the coastal ice floes.

Infrequently one comes upon evidence of previous expeditions. Since the last war an American party found one of the cairns in which Peary placed records of his final attempt to reach the North Pole and another built by George Nares, the great English explorer. On the Greenland coast are to be found items of equipment used by such as the dead Mikkelsen and Iverser or Rasmussen and Freuchen. Along the coast of Spitzbergen lie the bones of whales and of the men who hunted them in the sixteenth century; here, too, one might find some of the petrol drums carried through the ice floes by Amundsen, or an item of equipment recalling Andrée's foolhardy effort to balloon to the North Pole in 1887. The thrill of such a discovery is yet another reward for the discomforts and, possibly, dangers, that one must accept in travelling northern latitudes.

I should stress that danger and discomfort are not a prerequisite to travel in the polar regions.

To reach the Arctic requires little initiative and entails little discomfort. The most distant of Hudson's Bay Company trapping outposts are within easy reach of Montreal in summer, when the Company's supply ships make their annual round of the northern outposts; so, too, is Thule, the Eskimo settlement in the extreme north-west of Greenland and as far north as one can find permanent habitations. Nothing more than a first-class ticket is necessary to attain points one hundred miles north of the Polar Circle; one can travel to Kiruna and Narvik by electric express complete with sleeper and restaurant car. To reach Spitzbergen I travelled by Sandringham flying boat from Oslo to Harstad in Arctic Norway, and thence to Longyear in a collier with a comfortable cabin. Lorries and motor buses roar through the forests of Alaska to the Bering Straits. The polar regions are spanned with road and rail and air services, and studded with towns complete with cinemas, beauty parlours and public bars. But step a dozen paces from the security of electric lighting and central heating and one is in the silent, beautiful Arctic where almost anything can happen. The day before my arrival at Longyear in 1948 the cook at the radio station, a bearded Norwegian with the expression of the Redeemer and the trigger-finger of a Bedouin, shot a polar bear from the kitchen window. And while I drank coffee in the snug comfort of Gallivare, in Arctic Sweden, the conversation was of the wolf packs in the mountains a little to the north-west. It very soon becomes apparent that man's grip on the Arctic is slight, which adds to its interest and magnetism.

Perhaps the most marked impact that the North makes upon the traveller is its contrasts.

The colours of the polar coast are those of a fairy's wings on a gigantic scale, and in some lights those of the rainbow—clearly defined, so that the greens are divorced from the blues and the latter from whatever colour their neighbours might be. Theirs is an ethereal beauty so intense that, like a high-pitched note, it hurts the senses.

The sea grows suddenly smooth as one approaches the ice, until it resembles an almost black mirror on which sail a mighty armada of growlers, their upper third sparkling white, their sunken foundations gleaming with the metallic greens and blues of a tropical butterfly. Here sails a pastel bomber apparently on the point of taking off, there an absurd saucepan the size of an omnibus, a glistening castle, a blue swan, a grotesque statue and a duck with a tip-tilted beak. The duck's wings are free of snow, and on their smooth surface is reflected the black apex of a nearby promontory.

An immense field of coastal ice falls into the sea with the roar of artillery, setting up a tidal wave that causes the grotesque swan and the foolish saucepan to dance and nod and bow, and thus acknowledge the birth of a bigger sister, and where the water swirls over the smaller ice it sends shafts of pale green among the white superstructures.

Refractive light born in the floes streaks the sea between the ice with an ethereal white, and the sun adds to it and to the floes veins of colour which the loom[1] lifts into the sky.

The loom adds immeasurably to the fantasy. Ranges of

[1] *Loom:* the Arctic mirage.

mighty mountains, their white minarets, domes and battlements, mounted on green foundations "loom up" their every fold and crease outlined against the black mountains of the coast; and then change of light brings them to their real size with the suddenness of Alice in her Wonderland.

The beauty of the polar coast sends shafts of emotion down one's spine. And by way of contrast from a coastal settlement comes a lung-seering stench arising from lack of sanitation.

As extreme is the change from summer to winter. If at midsummer the sun shines throughout the day and night, in midwinter it is but a memory, a chink of pink light, a blush from somewhere south of the Circle. Here beyond the North blizzards whip the world, fingers freeze so hard that knocked sharply they will snap like matchsticks and the moisture of a man's eyeball solidifies.

The beauty of the polar night is as intense as that of the polar day. For the aurora flashes back and forth in curtains of technicolor, the dog-like barking of a fox can be heard from a distance of a mile or more in the stillness, and the moon gives to glacier and sea-ice the sheen of burnished steel.

Yet the long polar night can be terrible, and during its eternity the main topic of conversation is the return of the sun, a longing well illustrated by the story of the Arctic Bird. With the end of winter, settlers in the New Siberians (the islands off the northern coast of Siberia) emerge from their caves and gaze across the gleaming face of the sea in the direction from which will fly the harbinger of spring. A white bird, it arrives suddenly, flying due north, very high so that the pink sun, straining to peer over the rim of the South, can shine on its white breast. The twilight of late winter still lies upon the North. But there in the heavens the brightness of spring shines on the tender breast of a bird, and a few days later the sun sends a flood of red across the ice so that the bergs resemble mountains of copper set in a silent, frozen sea. Whence comes the Arctic Bird, and with what species should it be classed? Who can say? For it has never been seen at quarters close enough for identification. But for all that the Arctic Bird is very real in the minds of the men who survive winter darkness and cold so intense that to draw in a sharp breath can shock the heart to silence.

Inevitably the loneliness has a marked effect on those who

spend a lifetime among the northern ice fields. The story is told of two Norwegian trappers who, after many years of living on their own, decided to share a cabin on the condition that neither spoke. After eight months of silence one of the men commented on the bareness of the larder, and immediately his silent companion packed his gear on to a sledge, hitched-up his huskies, and returned to his own cabin forty miles down the coast; he would not live with such a garrulous chap.

I met in Spitzbergen a trapper who entertained me with the best in raw liquor and fur bedding, but spoke not one word.

Men have been known to go mad during the long polar winter. At the least the loneliness may prey on a man's mind so that he talks to the pin-up girl tacked to the brown paper with which his cabin walls are lined. The Arctic can indeed be terrible; frightening. Legend tells of men unable to withstand the beautiful woman whose kiss meant death. The Arctic holds something of her quality, and like that of the death-kiss, it is beyond refusal.

News of the arrival of a woman in the North travels along the traplines with the speed of wind. A woman! In the Arctic men will trace-up and drive fifty miles for a few words with a newly arrived nurse or school mistress. But the woman who goes North is not only of an independent nature but, there being at least four males to every female in the Arctic, she takes a marked pleasure in leading by the nose every man from mountie to missionary. One must be very worthy to win a wife in the Arctic, and the majority of men turn to liquor for solace.

Drinking in the polar regions lacks finesse. It is indulged with one purpose—to get drunk. Thus, on my first night in Spitzbergen I was entertained with a bottle of brandy, followed by a large bottle of Grand Marnier consumed, not in the manner of a connoisseur, but by the quaff. This might have been considered sufficient for four men for one evening. But at midnight there was produced a second bottle of brandy, and then a pint jar on which was pasted a label bearing the words "96 PER CENT." This proved to be hospital spirit, and the next thing I remember I was struggling out of my bunk at noon to find my shot-gun on the rocks outside the window and in my bunk four dead auks. In the miners' barracks and the bachelors' mess the scene was probably the same. A man need not drink if he does not want to, and many in the barracks and mess are teetotal. But liquor and poker form the two main relaxations. The miner here suffers from a peculiar lethargicness known locally as "Spitzbergen fever." Its victims lie in their bunks in a torpor, and when they recover it is often to return to the bottle and the poker pots of perhaps two or three hundred pounds.

Undoubtedly the reader will enquire why a man should leave Social Security and the forty-hour week for the discomfort, hard work and, sometimes, danger and fear of the North.

The answer is readily apparent. In return for hard work the North offers wealth, given reasonable luck wealth no less than that earned during the Klondyke Days. Among the men who "strike North" today are many in whose minds lurk thoughts of wealth in gold, silver, antimony, and uranium. They can travel across the tundras by aircraft, at their elbows all the aids of modern science: but in their blood is the spirit of the early pioneers who left a trail of dead right across Canada to the Pacific Coast, and then northwards into Alaska, the Yukon and the North-East Territories.

The Canadian North and Alaska are being developed industrially at a phenomenal pace, and so it is throughout the Soviet Union to the most northerly shores of Siberia. Twenty-five years ago the population of Igarka in the Russian North comprised forty fishermen; today Igarka is a city exceeding 40,000 workers. Yellowknife, in Arctic Canada, did not exceed a dozen souls thirty years ago: today its output of gold is higher than any other settlement in the Dominion's "North."

Whereas a century ago the cry was "Go West, young man! Go West!" today it is "Go North, young man! Go North!" And there is no lack of reply, for the spirit of adventure is as rich as ever it was. Many of the men and women sent into the Arctic during the war have returned to make its development their life's work. They found not a terrible wilderness but a land of opportunity, and falling under the spell of the North, they returned to savour the feeling of vitalness apparent in its industrial centres. The greenhorn soon finds himself swept away by the enthusiasm to build, drill, dig—to work, for this in which he lives is a New World with an immense appeal.

The modern pioneers are pressing ever farther into the Great

North, beyond a dozen parallels to within less than the length of Britain from the Pole itself; and their reward is measured in more than the fabulous salary paid to technicians in the Arctic. It includes the mental stimulus in the knowledge that they are working in perhaps unknown territory, building therein the foundations of new Provinces; it includes the benefit which the wiser of men can gain from enforced comradeship, and the knowledge that their one weapon against failure is a quality deep within their characters.

And on the tundras, where the trapper works? Here the alternative to work is hunger, and death. But it is not the alternative that sends the trapper on to the bleak tundra. He is a trapper because there is within him an urge to pioneer, and perhaps to submit himself to the most strenuous trial a man can face, a trial both physical and mental, the former in the battle against the element, the latter in that against uncertainty and loneliness.

The vastness of the polar regions, the intense and appalling loneliness, produces in one an acceptance that only the polar bear and the seal could survive here. Yet one constantly comes upon evidence that others, no doubt impelled by the North to ever greater travels, have preceded one along the polar coasts.

I recall the occasion when, standing on the shores of Ice Fjord, I imagined to myself that even had others passed this way before me, none was likely to have stood where I was standing. Overawed by the loneliness, the beauty, the incredible silence broken by the boom of bergs carving from the glaciers across the water, I was fulfilling the subconscious desire we all have to be an explorer. It was a great experience, this knowledge that there was none to call upon in case of emergency, that the world here was untrodden, as clean and unsullied as when the Creator first made it. And then I came upon the last thing one would expect to see in the grand solitudes of Ice Fjord—an American pulp magazine! Its fluttering pages brought me to my senses with a jolt. The cover was torn and the first word of the title was missing. But the letters ASSION and the outline of a lady who lost her head at the time of the cover's mutilation left me in no doubt about the theme of the creased, cockled pages. I turned away in disgust that the world of the polar bear should be contaminated by that of a lady whose only name was PASSION. Subsequently I learned that a Norwegian trapper had passed this way four months previously.

The trapper undoubtedly possesses in large measure the desire to travel where none or at least few have travelled before—to satisfy the inner craving that is the basic reason for a man "striking North."

There is another reason for the trapper adopting a profession that only the most robust and independent soul could contemplate. In his youth he sees the supply ships return from Longyear and Kingsbay, from Clavering Island and the mainland of Greenland, and he succumbs to the romance of the trap-line. Alternatively an unresponsive woman drives him to exile. Such was the reason for the arrival in Arctic Greenland many years ago of a little Dane, Antoscue. A once-successful circus clown he forsook the ring and the bladder for traps and furs, and judging by the fact that he has never had a team of huskies without at least one bitch called *Karen* he has not forgotten the reason for his self-exile.

But whatever the reason for a man turning to the trapline for a living, once he arrives in the Arctic he is doomed to stay there for as long as health permits. First, the North very soon lays claim to his soul. Second the trapper too often spends a year's profits in a month's riotous living, and, incapable of earning a living at any other profession, he has no alternative but to return to the Arctic. Such was the experience of the famous Norwegian trapper Henry Rudi, a diminutive but incredibly tough Norwegian who has spent a lifetime hunting polar bears along the edge of the sea-ice between Spitzbergen and Greenland. Rudi made £2,000 in one season from bear pelts, and arriving at Tromsoe (Arctic Norway) bought himself five suits, five silk shirts, five of everything including five silver-headed walking-sticks—hired a local hotel, and flung it open to anyone who would accept his hospitality. Within a month Rudi was back on the trap-line. The trapper does not learn from experience. When the annual ship is about due to arrive he may turn the last of his potatoes into raw liquor for immediate consumption, and even if he manages to retain sobriety until his return home the temptations and luxury comfort of civilization soon undermine any will he may have to resist the most expensive compensations for eight months spent in icy exile.

Included in the "Call of the North" is the desire to know the strange, slant-eyed nomad herdsmen and hunters of forest, *fjell* and tundra—the Lapps and the Eskimoes. At first one is inclined to regard them as one would an exhibit at a zoo, or as carriers of water, hewers of wood, and killers of game for the white man's table. But very soon one comes to respect the Eskimo who has not fallen too far under the spell of canned goods, circular saws and chewing gum. He gives to the North a piquancy not to be found in any other part of the world. Only in the Arctic could one hope to meet a gentleman proud of the fact that he is the illegitimate son of an Eskimo woman and the first man to reach the North Pole (Peary), and another whose name, Anaqaq, translated, means, "The one who empties his bowels quickly." Only in the Arctic can one meet a race that has stepped from the Stone Age into that of the Atom without hurt to its basic charm. The Eskimo of the more southerly settlements, particularly in Canada, is often a sorry specimen who has adopted many of the white man's failings, from bad teeth to insincerity. But the Eskimoes of the less accessible areas of the American North and Greenland are unspoiled, their minds as beautiful as the lands in which they herd and hunt.

The Polar Eskimoes never lie, for they believe that the liar's untruths will appear in his expression for all men to see. The bedtime stories told in the mud-and-stone huts of Thule feature not witches and ogres but the last man to tell a lie. Murder and theft are unknown in this riven world of ice where a man's first duty is to aid his neighbour no matter what the circumstances. Life here is frequently grim, grim to the extent of death. Yet one hears more laughter among the Polar Eskimoes than perhaps any other people. They consider Man to be fundamentally good. It follows then that there are no fundamentally naughty children. Thus there is no need ever to correct a child, for he will surely grow into a good man or woman.

I found a similar outlook among the Lapps of Arctic Scandinavia, at least with those whose nomadic lives keep them to the less accessible forests and *fjells*, and particularly among the Skolt Lapps of Finnish Lapland.

When I first met the Skolts, travelling southwards down the Arctic Highway from their little wooden settlement, Suenjal, in the extreme north of Arctic Finland, I dubbed them "savages." But I soon found myself in many ways their inferior. When the Skolt Lapp rubs noses with the stranger he "looks into his eyes and through them into his soul." I found it embarrassing to be "read" by a savage, who after reading my soul turned away with a distasteful quirk about the corner of his lips.

My meeting with the Skolts was unexpected. I had not heard of this remote tribe of fur-clad Lapps when I set off up the Arctic Highway from the railhead at Rovaniemi, on the Arctic Circle. I knew that Petsamo, the (then) Finnish port at the northern limit of The Highway, enjoyed electric light, running water, cinema, hotels, beauty parlours and the other benefits of civilization. I was not interested in these benefits. I wanted only to travel—northward. The Arctic Highway pointed due north to the Polar Ocean and the Barentz Sea, named after the Dutchman who died in the search for the fabled route around the corner of the world to Cathay, and because it pointed due north I had no alternative but to climb into a car and bump along its rutted surface, through forests, and *fjells* until, reaching its northern miles, I heard that comparatively nearby through the spruce trees there lived a strange fur-clad people whose origin was unknown beyond a hint that they may have migrated across the roof of the world from Tibet in the very dawn of time and whose legends were yet to be recorded. The "call" to visit these people was beyond refusal, and thus I met Gariloff and his family, complete with furs worth at least £300.

In the company of the Skolts I felt strangely tranquil of mind. For these people seldom quarrel. They never lie. Theft is unknown. There is no hatred. No illegitimacy. Evil powers are pitied for they must be so unhappy at their evilness. In the great silent forests live the spirits of men and animals, some evil but mostly good, for there is more good than evil. Sometimes, particularly on still winter nights when the cold crackles among the spruce and pine and polar willow, the lights of their subterranean homes gleam through the snow. Always you can hear the thoughts of the woodland's spirits whispering among the branches, or playing tag with the wind-driven snow that whorls and rustles around the feet of the trees. The songs sung by the invisible inhabitants of the forests is one of praise, for they speak of the trees and the rocks and the sun and the aurora, all of which are so beautiful. The fantasy of one's surroundings is such that one is inclined to stop and listen to the whisperings. In blizzard weather tree and boulder seem to move, for a dozen white wraiths whorl among them, causing one to cast sidelong uncertain glances at boulders which have not moved since the Ice Age and to watch for movement among trees which one knows are securely anchored. Perhaps this is but the effect of extreme cold on the brain. Or are the forests full of magic, and enchanted with the spirits of kindly peoples and animals, as the Skolts say? I think they must be.

Care must be taken not to hurt the animals of forest and tundra, and the fish which form the major part of the Skolts' diet, for they are the abode of human spirits. Beneath the flickering flames of the Northern Lights I was told about the beauty of life after death. To the Skolts there is no sorrow in or fear of death, rather a gay gladness. I recall one old man who insisted on his burial celebration being held while he was yet alive and hearty, because he wished to secure the full benefit from his passing!

The Lapps' knowledge of poison gas and bombers is specific, and they are well aware of the value of money. Meet them on the *fjell* reindeer trails, and you stop and invite each other to coffee, and having brewed coffee among the heather and boulders conversation will descend to the level of the price of reindeer and that of the coffee, and the possibilities of securing better equipment. You are equals, and your company is welcome. But the Skolt shows his dislike of the casual visitor by pursing his lips in the manner of a disagreeable reindeer. He has an understanding of, indeed an affinity with, the reindeer. It is not present in his words but in his eyes, and in that he can read the animal's mind and is therefore able to converse with it. The reindeer is a gentle, serene animal, and the Lapps of Sweden and Norway no less than Finland reflect its gentleness and serenity. The Skolts greeted me with the courtesy one would expect, but it was the reserved courtesy that the reindeer shows the traveller. I thought the Skolt not only a savage, but off-hand. But in time I learned that within him are qualities that lift him above the white man in matters of intrinsic honesty, kindliness and beauty of mind.

It might perhaps be thought strange that the Arctic should produce so delicate a flower. But this is not so. It requires only a short visit into the wilder areas of the North to appreciate that to survive there men must pull together. When Man knows conditions of hardships and danger he develops, in the course of time, a mental insulation against the conditions under which he lives. Among the Eskimoes this insulation is provided by an ability to laugh at the slightest provocation, and among the Lapps by a mellow philosophy and a delightful sense of humour.

Typical of the latter's humour was the legend told to me in the cloth-tent of a Lapp, pitched some two hundred miles north of the Polar Circle in Finland. It concerned an old woman by the name of Mariska, who refused to accept Christianity. Her neighbours cried out after her "Ya-ha! The only heathen in Suenjal! Why aren't you a Christian like the rest of us?" But Mariska preferred to continue in the worship of the Sun and the Trees. Day after day her two sons, Merca and Voca, tried to convert her to Christianity. "Why" they asked, "do you still blow kisses to the Sun?" And Mariska would answer, "I would rather worship a God that I can see than one I can't see." And when her sons asked why she kissed the Trees she replied: "Because I prefer to salute a God I can feel than your Christ." "But the trees fall and die," her sons argued. "What if they do?" Mariska retorted, "I prefer to worship a fallen God than one that's invisible." Burning under the taunts of their neighbours Voca and Meca decided to win their mother around by subterfuge. Carefully they hatched a plan, and then approached the old lady. "Mother," they said, "if you'll be a Christian we'll give you the pelt of the finest white reindeer in the forest." Immediately Mariska's eyes narrowed with avarice. This was sensible talk! "I agree," she said. "Go, get the priest—and the reindeer pelt." And as the two boys left their old mother in high glee at the success of their plan, Mariska blew a kiss to the Sun—just a little kiss, for had the Sun not been instrumental in making her adopt Christianity?

One shaft of humour such as this is ample reward for many hardships. As biting as the wind that sweeps across the snows, it yet reflects a deep understanding of human nature and an acceptance of human weakness, and it is the foundation of an outlook calculated to render worthwhile the most arduous journey into the extremes of the North.

The surprise element is marked in Arctic travel. One can never be sure what lies around the next corner. The constant jolting of the bus that took me northwards from Kiruna to the road-head at Karasuando was beginning to pall when a *pulka* (a light sledge usually drawn by a reindeer) containing the body of a dead Lapp was hitched to the back of the vehicle. The bus did not slacken speed for being transferred into a hearse, and at each corner the *pulka* swung out across the white surface of the road, threatening to pitch its occupant among the grey boulders. On his way to a burial ground, our companion in the *pulka* transformed what is usually a tiresome journey into one of infinite piquancy.

There can be no certainty about anything in the Arctic beyond the change of the seasons. When the nurse at Longyearbyen married the local priest her first patient as a married woman proved to be her husband. "We drove off from the Radio Station in great form," she told me. "The dogs pulled well, and the weather was lovely. But by the time we'd reached the cabin where we were to spend our honeymoon my husband's ears were frostbitten."

Shortly before this episode Longyear picked up a radio message from the Soviet settlement deep in Ice Fjord calling for a doctor. It appeared that the wife of the Russian Commissar there, one Fudor Fetchin, was expecting a difficult time with her first confinement, and the Norwegian doctor at Longyear immediately traced-up the huskies and set off by sledge on a dangerous sixty-miles journey across mountains subject to intense blizzards.

Blizzards follow sunshine with startling suddenness. Summer months see the forests and *muskeg* of the sub-Arctic steaming with heat and humming with mosquitoes, but in the North Arctic and in the vicinity of permanent ice fields even summer weather is fickle in the extreme, thereby adding to the interests of travel. A change of wind can bring the temperature tumbling down. I recall a day when, barely eight hundred miles from the North Pole I stripped to my boots and lay down on a slab of black rock to sunbathe. The rock was warm to my skin, the sun soothing; the bark of seals floated up from the off-shore ice floes, and above me the snout of a hanging glacier glistened in the clear atmosphere of the Arctic. Nearby grew patches of yellow polar poppies, blue poppies, and masses of cotton-grass; across the *fjord* rocks and tundra were streaked with brilliance. This was indeed a moment which could never escape a traveller's memory, even if his feet were saturated from crossing melt-water. And then suddenly the wind changed. From around the nearby bluff came a wave of cold that caused me to leap up and scurry into my windproofs.

A change of wind can turn a perfectly safe situation into one of extreme hazard. Winter is the time for long-distance travel in the Arctic, at least inland, for then the ground is iron-hard and clad in snow. But in the extreme north sea-ice may offer suitable conditions for travel by dog-team both in summer and winter. Subject to intense blizzards between October and April, in winter the sea-ice will probably be too thick to break up, but in summer a change of wind can cause the most tightly packed floes to move out to sea, necessitating on the part of the traveller a strenuous race against time, and one which he is by no means certain to win. There have been many instances of Eskimo hunters supporting themselves by hunting the seals with which they share drifting sea-ice until a change of wind blows the floes against the coast again. It is nothing uncommon for the Polar Eskimoes to spend the winter months hunting polar bear and seal among the floes drifting slowly southwards through Smith Sound (between Greenland and Canada's Ellesmere Island), returning to Thule in the spring after a sledge journey of perhaps five or six hundred miles. It is also not uncommon for the traveller never again to see land when the wind carried the floes out to sea—which adds a certain spice to serious travel in the Far Arctic!

Summer can be idyllic in the Arctic, a time of laziness and good feeding, and of laughter, for the world is brilliant and alive with life.

Some five hundred species of spider have been discovered on the island of Jan Mayen alone. There are no bees to pollinate the flowers of the extreme north, but fifteen species of fly have been recorded among the rocks of Jan Mayen, and as many as three hundred springtails are found to the square inch. In some parts of the Arctic insects flutter and buzz in black clouds. Bluebottles buzz in their thousands around the rubbish dumps at King's Bay, Spitzbergen, where I counted thousands between the double windows. When first I visited Lake Myvatn, in the north of Iceland, just south of the Polar Circle, I commented on the haze hanging over one of the islands. "What is it?" I asked, "Steam from a hot spring?" The boatman replied, "No, just insects—gnats." The cloud was so dense that from a distance it resembled summer haze. In parts of the American North mosquitoes hum in such myriads that to close one's eyelids quickly is to trap half a dozen pairs of legs.

Poetically, butterflies are the harbingers of spring in the temperate lands which I leave annually for the North. In point of fact I have seen butterflies many miles farther north than one meets poets. Some one hundred varieties have been recorded north of the Arctic Circle, one of which I saw caught in flight by a bunting perched on a rock outcrop with its feet in everlasting ice.

Travel in winter, especially on short cuts across the ice caps, or on sea-ice, can offer the most intense hardship. There is, as previously explained, a certain pleasure in this hardship and in the feeling that one is emulating the greatest of polar explorers. But at the same time the mind grows numb with cold, and inevitably one toys with the fears that arise from the loneliness and the ferociousness of a world which appears to be as " dead" as that of the moon. To meet another traveller in a world of life or greenery, where snow and contorted ice stretch to the horizon is an immense pleasure. There is no question of two travellers nodding and continuing on their way. They stop. They brew coffee or smoke a pipe, and chat about the conditions of travel each has met, about mutual acquaintances and the possibilities of good hunting in this or that direction, not only for the practical purpose of exchanging news but also for the pleasure of hearing a human voice

Desolate and forbidding as are the northerly regions of the Arctic, in summer these support an immense variety of life. A post-war Danish expedition to Peary Land (in the extreme north of Greenland) recorded two hundred varieties of flowers, lichens and flowering grasses. Cotton grass, lupins, forget-me-nots, polar poppies, stitchwort and saxifrage render the Arctic brilliant with wealds of colour between May and August or September. In the more northerly regions the forget-me-nots may be dwarfed by cold, but they form an enamel-like carpet that merges into the blue-greens of the heavens and the ice. In Spitzbergen I found the polar willows not above eight inches from roots to crown, but the rocks were streaked with red, yellow, white, orange and olive lichens.

On the coastal miles of the Arctic millions of seabirds scream, and swirl in clouds that throw grey shadows across the snow and ice . . . geese, duck, sabine gulls, ivory gulls, delicate-winged terns, glaucous gulls, immense and lumbering in their noisy grey-and-white dignity, sea-kings whose piercing cries fill the air, and whose unplucked bodies the Eskimos thrust into a seal skin until the flesh is red-rotten and tastes like ripe cheese and you pick the feathers out of your mouth as you eat.

Most startling is the tameness of the wild life. Hunting gyr falcons in Arctic Swedish Lapland, many of the birds I found waited until I was less than a dozen yards from their eyries before launching themselves over the rocky valleys, to show the whiteness stamped on their breasts by the Arctic. One could knock ptarmigan down with a stick, and a weasel fought me for one bird, clinging to its head even while I severed it with a jack-knife. In Greenland, white hares come running to see what all the banging is about, and thereby present themselves an easy target to the worst marksman. Coquettish, lovely, foolish, they provide the polar traveller with hours of amusement, for they will prance at his feet. The polar bear is less aggressive than it is inquisitive; the musk-oxen that roam the moraines of Peary Land and Ellesmere Island may sometimes permit one to approach to within a dozen yards before charging. In Iceland I heard how blue foxes sat around the Norwegian hunter, Henry Rudi, and watched him build his cabin beneath the towering heights of Mt. Beerenberg, King of Jan Mayen: "And after a day or so of watching, in full sight mind you, the foxes ambled over and stole his hammer and nails."

An increasing number of travellers are "going North" to study or hunt the Arctic's wild life. Improved conditions of travel are opening up many parts of the polar regions which a dozen years ago were beyond the reach of all but the best-found expeditions. For example, it is now possible to fly from Chicago to the extreme north of Alaska, there to hunt polar bear, or should one say " shoot polar bear," for the tourist company that arranges this trip guarantees its clients "complete safety from risk and from discomfort." But it is beyond possibility that air-craft will one day make the polar regions available to the extent where they become a tourist paradise. For the Far North is on the edge of the world. Tourists may perhaps touch at its capitals, at even some of its outlying settlements. But conditions of life in the Far Arctic render millions of its miles sacrosanct to the fundamental traveller—to him who feels the Call of the Polar Regions, and who can never hope to explain in full why he must return to their wildest, most terrible recesses.

THE CALL OF THE SEA

Adrian Seligman

FROM earliest times the sea has been feared and often hated. It remains so to this day; unloved and, on the whole, unlovable. With senseless indiscrimination it reflects the lusts or longings of all who gaze upon it—just as it reflects the sky; ready, at the first puff of wind, to tumble them all together and obliterate them with a shrug.

So we do not love the sea. At least no seaman who has served in smaller craft than liners could truly say he loved it. Understanding he may have of some of its more obvious moods, and a deep respect for its powers of destruction— even a certain grim affection, such as one feels for any close companion no matter how disgraceful his behaviour on occasions. But not love.

I remember an old captain in the Baltic timber trade standing on his poop and gazing—at last almost with pity—upon the face of the sea. Tears of exhaustion and desolation were running down his cheeks, and he was muttering over and over to himself—"You senseless brute. You senseless brute. Oh, you poor damned senseless brute of a thing" . . .

We had left the Finnish port of Kotka with a cargo of *splitväd* (short planks for sale as firewood) at the beginning of October, and had taken a whole month to beat down against perpetual south-westerlies to the Sound. From there, our course being northerly past Copenhagen and up to Skaggerak, we were blessed with a fair wind at last. And, wonder of wonders, when the coast of Norway came in sight, the breeze fetched round into the east and sent us scurrying across the North Sea in fine style, almost to the mouth of the Thames. There it fell light, then round it came again into the south-west and began to freshen.

For us lads, of course, the week of gales which followed was not so bad. We had a fine dry forecastle, well protected from the sea by the deck cargo of firewood (which we plundered enthusiastically to keep our "bogey" roaring). We emerged for an occasional hour on lookout or at the wheel; but, since the ship was hove-to with the helm lashed—all the sails except three having been blown out or furled on the first night of the gale—this was scarcely an arduous duty.

It was quite an experience, though. I remember one big sea in particular that leaped on to the deck cargo and, scooping up a pile of planks, flung them into the air to be scattered like autumn leaves by the wind. I also remember how we roared with laughter at the sight, and clapped and yelled encouragement.

"It'll cost the shippers thousands," we told each other ecstatically (and incorrectly).

But for poor old Captain K. there was no pleasure in the spectacle. He was sixty-eight, and this was his last voyage; more than just his last, in fact, for he had retired some years before and had only been persuaded to make this single trip (against the wishes of his wife and family) to fill a sudden gap. An additional inducement, moreover, had been the very fact that since it is not possible to insure deck cargoes from the Baltic in winter, the consignees had offered a handsome bonus for every *standard* he managed to bring into the Regent Canal Dock. So, carrying the whole responsibility for the safety of vessel, cargo and our graceless lives upon his bowed old shoulders, K. stood for six days and nights on end, there on the poop, with nothing but a helpless ship upon a sea gone mad to look at, no music to comfort him sweeter than the howl of a November hurricane and, after a time, no hope.

He seemed to shrink visibly, hour by hour, as though his very insides were being sucked out by the force of the wind and by the loathsome green tongues of water, furred and livid with spray, that lashed incessantly about the ship and him. Stubborn and eviscerated he endured, till there was nothing left of him within the flapping husk of an old tweed overcoat except two eyes, red-rimmed beneath a squat fur cap, first burning with anger, then stony, then dimmed with an enormous pity—not for himself, he was past that—but for a sea condemned to an eternity of vileness.

And what finally broke him was the sight—in a clearing between squalls on the seventh morning of the blow—the sight of the Naze of Norway again, ten miles to leeward and exactly where we had seen it a week before. He sat down then on the cabin skylight and cried.

F

But the sea, you may say, is not always in so violent a mood. For weeks on end it may be blue and smiling, caressing the shore with enchanting sighs.

Beware of that enchantment. Beware of the sea in its brightest, bluest humours, and of the unswerving malevolence which those very aspects only just conceal. Above all beware of what you say, or even think. . . .

We reached London eventually on the last day of November. I was paid off there and never saw the ship or Captain K. again. My best friend, a Finn (who wanted to come with me on a ski-ing holiday for which we had been saving up throughout a whole round trip to Australia in another ship), also left her. But for him it was not so easy: there were immigration laws, and K. was obdurate.

In the end Holgar forced the old man to remain silent about the intended desertion by threatening that, if the police caught him, he would claim to have jumped ship through fear—fear of sailing any longer under a master who must inevitably lose her one day, since he drank at least a bottle of whisky in every twenty-four hours. (He did, as a matter of fact, but what happened to it then no one knew; probably the wind got it along with his tormented innards. At all events no one had ever seen him the worse for alcohol.)

We were base. There was no excuse for us. We had forgotten, by then, all about old K.'s agony in the North Sea and the compassion we had felt for him. We were pitiless, with the stupendous pitilessness of youth. And though, of course, we would never actually have split on the old man, we made no bones about threatening to. We were set on that ski-ing holiday.

About a year later—in the saloon of a tramp in Alexandria harbour—I ran into another friend who had been shipmates with us that trip.

"What sort of a passage home did you make?" I asked him.

"Pretty smart, as far as it went."

"How d'you mean?"

"Put her ashore on the coast of Jutland."

"Good God!" I was thunderstruck. The sea slapped gently against the strakes of my felucca alongside. One could almost imagine it, like a grossly gorged Oliver Hardy, tapping its fingertips in monstrous self-satisfaction. "Poor old K." I said at length.

"Yes," agreed my friend, but grudgingly, then: "Took us a bloody hour to get the old runt into the tug that came off to us —just sat on the poop there blubbering, he did. Had to pick 'im up and sling 'im overboard in a bowline at the finish . . . silly old fool," he added.

I was horrified. To think that we, for our own ignoble ends, had half predicted this. Not that we would ever have expected such a thing to happen, or even believed it possible; but we had thought of it.

K. is dead now. But I learned a lesson that day which I have never forgotten. And no wonder that sailors are superstitious, when the sea has this unpleasant habit of eavesdropping upon their lightest words, absorbing them into its passionless depths and keeping them there, sometimes for years, against the day when it can suddenly hurl them back with crippling force.

Yet the sea still calls to men, and it has many voices. Its oldest cry, heard by Columbus, the early Norsemen and, before them, by the Polynesians of the Western Pacific; the summons to discovery—that ancient call, like the voices of the little people, is seldom heard today except by children and the simplest folk. Too much is known about the sea and all its islands for the essential element of surprise to attend our voyages still. The black jag of Teneriffe like a shark's fin upon the horizon, one hundred and four miles distant; a fabulous city of mosques and palaces upside down above a desert coastline; the loom of ice—these are but momentary surprises: we know what is there and what is not there, we are not discoverers. Nor, until the next great earth convulsions, like those which drowned Atlantis, can there ever again be unknown oceans out of which a peak, an island or a point of land may spring as though by magic.

But it calls; and as strongly as of old. To some it offers escape and a road to various freedoms, to others a living, and to all companionship. The evil nature of the common enemy and the perpetual war we must wage against it merely to cross from one side to the other of the thing without being eaten alive, makes sailors cling together in their ships like men besieged. Like beleaguered men, too, they surround themselves there with small comforts (some of them ridiculous) which they would never dream of asking for ashore.

And they are loyal to each other. For loyalty, like intimacy, is inescapable at sea—imposed by an authority against whom there can be no appeal. It is there while you work about the decks in trade wind weather, or in the beargarden atmosphere of the forecastle when a pig has been killed and the old man has sent a bottle forward to help it down; at night in the brooding calm of the doldrums, on the upper topsail yard in a gale of wind, or at the lee fore brace when the ship is running heavily and big seas are boarding. It is still there, too, during the un-hallowed occasions of waterfront life. In sin or solitude or high endeavour seamen will support their kind.

They are not alone in this, of course. Loyalty, as well as a passion for unauthorized luxuries, is found among politicians, prostitutes, the bandits of Corsica or any others who live by direct conflict with the forces of nature or man's desire to im-prove his lot, and whose fortunes are transitory. Yet nowhere, do people choose to live on terms of such exacting propinquity as do seamen. It is the prime condition of all sailors' lives.

They are not different, of course, from other folk—more com-panionable, perhaps, but the same men. Their attitude to life, though, is sometimes different. For instance they have no sense of property. How could they have? Who can possess the sea? Even the great winds, aspiring sometimes to rule it, can do no more than ruffle its surface for a while. Yet the landsman en-joys his privacy, and above all he likes to own—his house, his garden and his country. So the brave and patient earth must suffer the scars of succeeding ages; the forts, the ramparts, boundaries and walls. But not the sea. It will never be con-quered, bought and sold or occupied, nor suffer slow disfigure-ment by man—be labelled, parcelled, painted green or pink. The sea, after all, in its implacable contempt for man and all things living could hardly care less about such vanities—more arbitrary than women's fashions and often as impermanent.

No more could sailors. Their country is the sea; but they have no wish to own it. Nor do any problems of race or nation-ality exist in ships unless enforced. Provided a man knows his work and is reasonably good-tempered, the mere accident of

his birth upon some piece of land convenient to his mother is un-
important—a petty matter, a matter for landsmen. The
Albatross, that classic friend of mariners, may join a ship at
Algoa Bay, and leave her off the Horn; but who will pronounce
him African or Fuegan? He was surely born somewhere; but
from the moment of leaving the nest he has been at sea—afloat
or on the wing. So constantly, indeed, that he cannot even
walk. His feet are soft; even a wooden deck will tear them. His
legs are so weak that when he tries to stand he falls over. He is
a seaman. He never goes ashore. And, like the sailor, should he
ever do so he will only get into trouble.

So the sea speaks to the men who have known her, afloat or
ashore. A gust of warm wind; the flicker of gulls behind a
plough; the smell of steam—these carry its voice. One hears it
across the plain of Lombardy with mist lying like spume between
advancing waves of grape vines, white houses for sails and masts
of sudden cypresses. The patterned tumult of the factory shed;
even a motor cycle's horn in fog can recall the abrupt indigna-
tion, incongruous and sad, of penguins in a winter's calm.

It was a misty night in February—and still, there was no
wind. The ebb had just come away, and the current running
strongly down the London River set the lights from Rother-
hithe astir upon the water.

I was sitting on the verandah of the Prospect of Whitby at
Shadwell. Across the Lower Pool the cranes were nodding and
pecking above a yellow glare, like slow flamingoes scavenging
in hell: in Surrey Docks to be exact, with their far-sounding
names—Quebec and Greenland, Russia, Canada and (a touch
of sentiment here like the posy in the stockbroker's buttonhole)
Lavender and Lady Docks.

Around the brinks of these the prim, selective derricks for-
aged, lifting up into the light each drab and costly morsel—a
bale of hides, some timber, sacks of nuts—swinging it gravely
round for our inspection with the selfconscious rectitude of
maiden ladies plucking brands, then letting it fall with loud and
disapproving rattles.

All at once, from far upstream, came the beat of a steamer's
screw; and presently she appeared—a hoary tramp—nosing
round the bend from Wapping. Every head turned to watch

her as red, green and white her steaming lights flung banners on
the water; and soon above the plunging of her screw one heard,
upon that silent night, the music—manifold and simple—of her
passing: the hiss of steam; the quick clatter of a windlass rounding in moorings; the lift and whine of a main feed pump; and,
by and by, the rising purl of bow waves as she came abreast
of Cherry Gardens pier, and gathered way down the wider
reaches.

She was magnificent. She was a regiment with colours flying
and band playing for our enchantment. One wanted to cheer.
The cranes across the water paused in their angling and seemed
to watch her as she passed. Beside me a man grunted—a man
whom I had never seen before and couldn't see properly now.
"Outward bound, eh?" he said.

Uninspired? Maybe. Yet I suppose the passing of that ship
meant much the same to him as it meant to me. It was like the
passing of a friend into some bright hereafter. It stirred up
memories, personal and shared, out of the river mud, and left
them tumbling in its wake . . . the slender airs of Schubert re-
monstrating mildly with the stars in high south latitude . . .
Alf, the steward, who went courting a "young lady" in the
West Indies and got lost in the jungle without any trousers . . .
a burst of sunshine after a week of gales between Japan and
Vancouver, and thirty cages of canaries blazing into song all
over the ship . . . mist upon the coast of Ecuador . . . a dour
Finn quoting Shelley in a storm off Iceland. All these and many
more came dancing to the surface as the old tramp passed.
They were memories, not of hardship, stress, and ocean solitude,
but of crowded life; the life of a seafarer, diverse and conventional, requiring no justification because of the singleness of its
purpose and the unmistakable quality of its achievements in a
world where success can be so difficult to prove.

"Outward bound, eh? . . ."

"Wish you was in 'er?"

"Yes."

Is the call to sea, then, a call to escape and no more? In a
sense it is. But not an escape from duty to a life of indolence:
the sailor's responsibilities are numberless and he is never without them, at sea or in harbour. For most, though, an escape is

involved . . . from false gods to true ones; from the conflicting codes of commerce to the clearcut demands of an ancient profession; from the vaults of churches to an arching sky upon its pillars of cloud, where there is nothing between one's triumphs and the stars; no lesser audience than the universe.

Nor other tribunal. Sailors are by nature tolerant. They feel themselves too small before the brute immensity of the sea, too deeply in need of fellowship, to judge each other.

Men have striven in all sorts of ways for international brotherhood, and will no doubt continue to strive for it until the first invading force from Mars unites them unconditionally and at once. But seamen, already united against a power at least as formidable as an army corps of Martians, find no difficulty in living peaceably together.

Diversity of language is rarely a bar, for sea terms are self-explanatory, and "sea sense" universal. So yachtsmen, bluejackets and merchant seamen; the Italian sponge diver, the Spanish sardine fisherman and the West Indian negro fresh from his crazily ballasted flying-fish boat or casting his blossom of a net into the shallows; the London bargee, the Baltic schooner-man and the Dutch family in its *boyer*—all, when they meet, can get on well enough for sympathy and the common needs.

The great colonizations—of Africa, Australia and the Americas have been moderately successful in uniting men of different origins. So have the Church, the Cinema and Communism. Yet in all these brotherhoods there is either a marked preponderance of one race over the others or an element of profit to the mother power. Jealousies within and disparagement from without have always resulted.

But the sea seeks no profit, nor sovereignty, nor indeed any favours of man whatever. The sea as a uniting force is above suspicion. It is also all-powerful. You may re-interpret your faith to suit a national emergency or the aspirations, worthy or unworthy, of your rulers. You can change your country. But you cannot deny the ocean or temper its demands; nor appeal for special dispensations to the stars, studying their mute reflections in the sea and giving not a damn for anybody.

So you stick together. If you divide, the sea—listening always, knowing your thoughts, watching day and night for the smallest chinks of pride or sentiment in your ranks—the sea will have you. There's not the slightest doubt about it. . . .

During the war I worked for a time with some Greek caiques on special service in the Eastern Mediterranean; and one morning early, just as a boat of ours was about to sail, a junior staff officer rang up to say that an enemy submarine had been reported some hundreds of miles away—what were we going to do about it?

He was a young man who had always been openly contemptuous of our "dirty little false beard" flotilla; and the submarine, it appeared, was bound in the opposite direction from the one intended for our caique. So we, entirely within our rights (and yet a thousand times wrong, of course) said: "You're the Staff. You tell us."

We must have known he wouldn't—or even care to call out his superior at half past six in the morning.

In actual fact I doubt whether anyone would have stopped that sailing on so slight a chance of danger, or even that it would have been right to do so. But that is hardly the point. The point is that we had allowed ourselves to become divided, and the sea to know it.

"Nudge" Mason, the skipper of the boat, who was an Australian and therefore happily unfettered by the chains of naval etiquette, told everyone within earshot and many who were not, in the nicest possible way, to go and do things to themselves; he was sailing.

The sea smiled. And for many blue and sunlit days thereafter, with a gentle breeze ruffling the smiling, the damnably smiling face of the sea, we waited for news of Nudge. Neither he, nor his boat, nor any of his crew were ever heard of again.

Floating wreckage was later reported by an aircraft about thirty miles from the course he ought to have steered. It might have been the remains of his boat. There might, indeed, by some horrid coincidence, have been a second U-boat about, of whose presence we had heard nothing. Only the sea knows— and knew . . . the sea who loves no one and is for ever unloved; who respects neither persons, nor aims, nor the hopes and fears of men: the good-humoured gallantry of Nudge and his crew, the ferocity of a U-boat captain firing on survivors, or the weariness of simple, peace-loving old Captain K., who had given it fifty years of his life—fifty years, I don't doubt, of faithful and uncomplaining service.

All were one to that implacable monstrosity. With a shrug and a chuckle it obliterated the first, bore the second on to further slaughters and brought ruin, in the end, upon the third.

But once you have acknowledged the sea's mastery—been chastened, disciplined, and learned to fear it in the fullest sense; then the ocean, which covers five-sixths of the earth's surface, may become for you a place of peace. The calm routine, the daily occupations; making sails or painting ship or waiting for the sun at noon to tell you your position—these are peaceful pursuits. As peaceful as the shaping of a long Great Circle course.

A Great Circle, paradoxically, is the nearest approach to a straight line which may be drawn upon the globe. It is also, as one might suppose, the largest circle. The plane of it cuts the world in two: its arc is the shortest way across the sea it spans.

Landsmen are forced to move upon more devious routes, revolve in tighter circles, chasing their tails. But steamermen go straight. As straight as they can; yet still, obedient to the curve of Nature's earth, drawing, not straight lines on their ocean charts, but the arcs of circles . . . circles which, when complete, would enclose the earth—through which, as it were, the long-enduring world might at last be made to jump. And it is navigators who are licensed by the nature of their craft to draw such circles. Who better, since so few of them have ever cracked a whip?

They are humble at heart, like ships themselves. And a sailing ship at sea is one of God's most modest, patient, yet most steadfast creatures. So those who live with her, who watch her running bravely, lying becalmed for weeks or yielding with grace to the slope of the wind—such men begin to learn from her in time.

They learn above all to appreciate simple pleasures. I can so well recall an almost sensual delight in one's first real wash after weeks in oilskins from Australia to the Horn. On the first warm Saturday after passing the Falkland Islands and entering the "horse latitudes," all hands would heat their buckets of fresh water on the galley stove, then strip and scrub themselves all over before putting on clean shirts, clean underclothes, dry trousers, socks and slippers. After that some might begin to pare their broken nails; some would even scent themselves with eau de cologne. And, as often as not, a final gale would come rollicking after us that very night, sending everyone back into oilskins. It didn't matter. The first all round wash of the passage had been a luxury beyond all luxuries.

It used, I remember, to have a strangely intoxicating effect: sleeping was difficult after it. One became seized instead by a passion for squaring up and bringing out on deck one's queer belongings—the clothes, the books, the stuffed lizard (gone a bit on one side), the string of shells, half finished models, letters from Liz, and the patent marline-spike which never really worked. All would be spread in the sunshine, gloated over, sorted, sighed at, classified I don't know how, then stowed away again to become at once the dear and senseless jumble it had always been—of passing whims, ideas, ambitions, memories, which sometimes give to us the feeling that we're really not such duds: "just look what we could have been or had or done if we had wanted to—if we had never sold that farm to go to sea."

Nevertheless one sleeps sounder at sea. And a good deal more. Ashore there is always something one should or might be doing instead: at sea, off watch, nothing. The landsman may say: "My God! To think one spends a third of one's life asleep, when life is so short!" but not the seaman. Life is not short to him. There are times, even, when he can feel himself to be part almost of infinity—one with the clouds which form, fly by and then dissolve interminably. "Watch how you go, there, Charlie; you'll be a long time dead, you know—look at old Henry VIII . . . " is an amusing but curiously finite point of view to the sailor. Death, to him, is less forbidding for all its permanence.

Not that the idea of drowning or suffering pain is less repulsive to him than to others; but about life *after* death, he feels, I am sure, no great concern. He expects so little—the projection of his life on earth into infinity, that is all. For, surrounded as he always is by a prospect of infinite size—containing an infinity of worlds proceeding composedly upon their infinite occasions—he sees no reason why his fate should be different from theirs. They seem to have been going round and round for quite a while, and so has he. Why, therefore, should either of them ever do otherwise?

So he works and sleeps in peace. Peace and security. His food is there, his friends, a sheltered bed: he feels quite safe at sea. He knows that so long as he takes no liberties, he has little to fear from all its furies.

The hardships and dangers of his life have been exaggerated. To any healthy boy a year in sail, at an age when he enjoys most violent exercise, is something of a picnic. He is safe there for a time—from plague and pestilence, from pride, from the sins of yesterday and the temptations of tomorrow; safe even from himself. And, above all, he is safe—to use the picturesque language of the mercantile charter party—from "restraint of princes, rulers, peoples . . ."

Even in time of war this was frequently so. One was often safer at sea. . . .

It was an hour before dawn when our caique snuggled in alongside the cliffs of a cove at the southern end of Naxos. The Aegean was fairly quiet at that time; for Italy had just surrendered, and only a few German raiding parties were left to range from island to island bullying the peasants and stealing their food.

Our business was to find out the size of one of these which was known to be working in the southern Cyclades. I slipped ashore. The caique shoved off and crept away to hide among the rocks of a nearby islet, while I began to scramble up the cliffs and out of the cove.

In the darkness I could see no track, and loose stones kept flying from beneath my feet to bound away among the boulders of the foreshore. A dog began to bark. I stopped and crouched down among some bushes, waiting for daylight.

When it came at last I found a small farmstead near the mouth of a stream not far away. The crofter, though startled by my sudden appearance, was friendly. He even provided a donkey to carry me over the mountains to Filoti in the centre of the island. And his son, a cheery, fair-haired lad, offered to go with me.

Our journey across the hills took several hours, and was enlivened by frequent meetings with groups of peasants who, when they heard I was British, rushed forward to grip my hand, or hug and even kiss me in their enthusiasm.

I was more worried than embarrassed by this performance, for terrible things were done every day by the Germans to peasants who had "harboured revolutionary elements." It made me feel more absurdly out of place than ever upon those barren hillsides.

There is often something almost majestic about a sailor on a donkey; especially a big fat sailor, helpless, good-humoured and generously ready to make sport for the onlookers. But I was neither big nor fat, and only likely to make trouble. If it came, too, there was little doubt that I would be able—helped by these very people—to escape in time; while they, bound to their hills, their homes, their families and friends—what could they do?

Eventually we reached Filoti and the house of the headman, where I learned with relief that no Germans had yet reached the island; so for the time being everyone was safe.

They were very kind, those people: the headman himself, a fine type of mountain peasant with a magnificent moustache; his mother, dressed all in black with a black shawl over her head, saying nothing, but watching me with anxious hooded eyes; and several others, men and women, who came crowding in to listen, silent and curious, to what went on. Some of them smiled at times; but mostly they looked bewildered, like injured beasts who still retain some hope. And indeed the life they were living then was little better than the lives of the few animals that were left to them. I knew this only too well; and our visits to such islands were always heartrending. We landed, looked on their misery, and left; there was nothing we could do. Penniless, tethered to their stony hillsides, earthbound yet insecure—and starving, they remained.

While we talked, the daughter of the house, a child of fifteen or so, came in dressed in quaintly townish clothes with high-heeled shoes. She bustled about looking pleased with herself, and in due course set a plate of eggs and oatcakes and a dish of black olives before me. I was not hungry, but I ate the food: they insisted so passionately that I should. It seemed to mean so much to them—to the little girl in her gallant and inappropriate finery; to the headman giving his moustache a jaunty twirl, and to the others nodding and half smiling behind him.

But meanwhile I was intent on getting information.

"What do you know about these German raiding parties? Have you heard anything from the other islands?"

"A little."

"How many men are in them!"

The headman shrugged his shoulders and made a sweeping gesture with both arms, as though waving a host of soldiery towards him across the hills.

"How many ships?"

But he was clearly unwilling to talk. I didn't blame him. In fact I had decided to give up for the present, when the door opened and a young fellow burst in, gabbling excitedly. I couldn't make out what he said; but I heard the old mother draw in her breath. The rest of the people dispersed quickly. The headman turned back to me. "From there you will see," he said, pointing through the window to a low hill not far away. "They have just arrived."

The sky was overcast and spitting with rain, so the headman, the boy and I were able to climb at a good pace without discomfort. But none of us spoke as we plodded up the screes.

When we reached the top we lay down among some rocks, and I brought out my field glasses. Below us the slopes curved gently down through stunted pines and scrub to olive groves. Beyond these to the sea was cultivated land except where, three or four miles off, lay Naxia harbour edged with houses. I examined it for less than a minute; the landing craft beside the quay and two patrol vessels anchored off told me all I had to know. Not more than a company of soldiers could have come in those three craft, and from the bustle of boats between the ships and the shore it was clear that they were landing in a hurry. We dodged away and made off down the hill again to Filoti.

As we approached the village we heard motor transport coming up the road from Naxia. The two Greeks stopped, looking nervous; so, to be on the safe side, I took off my uniform cap and put it behind my back. In my khaki shirt, without shoulder straps, and grey flannel trousers, I then looked very much like one of them.

We had just reached the road when a German staff car containing two officers and followed by a truck full of soldiers came roaring into the village. As they tore past us we could see quite plainly the caged and brutal looks upon the faces of the Huns, sitting dull and upright in their seats. The headman raised his cap and bowed. I thought it prudent to bow also; but I felt unaccountably free at that moment and safe from those inhuman louts, so erect in their hurrying pens, hands on knees and staring without enthusiasm at the greyish napes of each other's necks.

One of the officers in the car glanced at us contemptuously and lifted an arm in the Nazi salute. We replied with a loud "hurrah!"

It was time now, for all our sakes, that I went—as fast as I could, which wouldn't be very fast I knew, donkeys being sensible beasts who never hurry unless they have to.

The boy and I started off; but we hadn't been long upon the road when, glancing back, I saw a distant figure in a grey uniform coming after us. I looked at the boy walking beside me. He was singing, as Greeks always do in the mountains; and when I pointed to the figure which had just rounded a shoulder of hill about a mile behind us, he only shrugged and went on singing.

The track was steep, and very rough. On one side of it a precipice fell sheer into a rocky valley; on the other the cliffs reached up into the clouds. The donkey picked its way with maddening deliberation; and now, some distance behind the man in uniform, came a second figure in civilian clothes.

More for form's sake than otherwise I dragged the cumbersome old Webley .45 out of my pack; but this only added embarrassment to my anxiety: if there is one thing more ridiculous than a sailor climbing a mountain sitting on a donkey, it is a sailor climbing a mountain sitting on a donkey waving a revolver (which he has never fired in his life).

My distress was short-lived, however. The fellow in uniform turned out to be the local police constable and far from wanting to arrest me, he wanted to come with me. I agreed to take him, then pointed with a look of enquiry at the second figure, still a good way off. "Sergeant—Chief of Police," he explained with a touch of pride.

Night was coming on when we reached the cove where the

caique lay hidden. The sergeant caught up with us while we were waiting for the dinghy to pick us up. I was rather relieved to learn at once that he did not want to join us as well, because we were already crowded aboard the caique. Instead he brought out a notebook and said, in passable English (probably the only words he knew; cherished from some boyhood visit to a mainland cinema): "Name and address please."

His grave expression and polite but determined manner were perfect. Even the way he licked his pencil was just right. I wrote down for him: Mae West, The White House, Washington. Then the constable and I said goodbye and clambered down to the foreshore. Ten minutes later our caique stole out of the cove, rounded a headland and stood south into a darkening sea.

The sergeant and the boy watched us go, together but a little apart as befitted their stations. They grew smaller against the hills looming massive with the dusk and distance. Over the shoulders of the nearer ones climbed the higher inland peaks, as though in horrid eagerness to pounce upon those two small figures by the shore.

The boy waved once. The sergeant saluted. He looked absurd in his brown civilian suit without a hat, and very brave, till at last the night joined forces with the hills and swallowed them.

I have never been back to Naxos, and I often wonder what became of them there. One small incident gives me hope, for the sergeant anyway. When the Germans found out the names of any of us, they used sometimes to make capital out of the fact in their local broadcasts. Always the same silly formula, imaginary and unimaginative—"Reactionary elements under allied orders yesterday attempted a landing on Naxos. They were repulsed due to the vigilance of the island's police force. The only casualty was one constable missing, believed captured." ... Then, in dark and hollow tones, in English ... "Don't worry, Mr. West; we're ready for you. We'll get you, Mr. West. Don't worry."

And, of course, we didn't. At sea in our boats we were safe. As safe as houses? Much safer, of course, in these days.

REMOTE PLACES

Freya Stark

IT is usually assumed that the traveller who prefers lonely places, the desert traveller, so to say, is one who wishes to escape from his world and his fellows. The popular conception gives to his wanderings a touch of misanthropy. To him the gentle things of every day make no appeal: the intercourse of humanity—that fragile house of cards built with such delicate and assiduous labour through millenniums of time, threatened by every cataclysm, and which yet stands because of the mere fact that every card leans up against the others—this finite and infinite structure of civilization is supposed to be the object of his aversion, the atmosphere from which he turns away.

I should like to offer a far less negative interpretation of the longing which leads men out into the wastes. The Lord Byrons of this world,

> "Sated with home, of wife, of children tired,
> The restless spirit is driven abroad to roam;"

are rather bogus spirits more often than not. I have a suspicion that Lord Byron himself might easily have settled into a domesticated middle age if his fates had not cut the thread so soon. The discontented are the least capable of all people to live with themselves for very long; and the same goad which has driven them out into the wilderness, will prick them home again.

The true wanderer, whose travels are happiness, goes out not to shun, but to seek. Like the painter standing at his easel, he moves constantly to get his perspectives right, and feels, though half a country may be spread out to a far horizon in his view, that he is too close to his picture and must get away now and then to look at it with an eye of distance. This necessity keeps him for ever on his feet. He touches and retouches the tones of his world as he sees them; and it is to make the proportions more accurate that he travels away from them, to come back with a more seeing and a rested eye.

It is of course absurd to think that one gets away from the world by moving into lonely places. All that happens is that one reaches a simplified world, with few personal attachments of one's own. In its less crowded atmosphere, it is easier to see the proper shape of things, since other shapes impinge much less upon them. The human figure itself takes on immense majesty when you meet it solitary in a landscape that scarcely speaks of humanity at all—where no fields, no walls, no hedges, no milestones, telegraph poles and unnaturally straight lines of road, make the single human being seem less important by adding continuity to the image of humanity as a whole. Ruins go well with deserts for this reason—the human continuity is visibly broken by them, and the rare human figures you may meet among them stand doubly isolated in space and time. Even without ruins or deserts, the mountains or the sea can create the same impression, of dignity and gallantry, round the fisherman's boat aslant in the trough of the waves, or the shepherd with his flock, alone on pastoral edges where the high rocks come down. The smallness and the weakness of the human creature is there made unmistakably apparent, and yet at the same time you feel in yourself the elation of victory, the knowledge that the solitary puny being is the master of his immense horizon: and if you yourself are sharing the life of solitude and hardship, you feel that you too have a part in the victory which you see.

This is a true feeling, presenting humanity as it is, amid the antiquity, the size and grandeur of earth. It is worth a long hard journey to attain it, for it is scarcely to be found in towns or easy places, where men triumph so habitually one over the other that their more cosmic victories are difficult to distinguish. For every victory of man over man has in itself a taste of defeat, a flavour of death; there is no essential difference between the various human groups, creatures whose bones and brains and members are the same; and every damage we do there is a form of mutilation, as if the fingers of the left hand were to be cut off by the right; there is no pleasure in it, nor any deep sense of achievement or of peace.

In the policies of nations, in the life of towns, of industry and business, even—too often—in family life, this secret murder and mutilation of our selves is going on all the time: every injury that is done to others hits us with an unknown wound; we are being hurt constantly, not in our individual quality, but in our state as parts and members of the human family on earth. And the process is so general and so continuous, and the sight of it so frequent in the more thickly inhabited parts of the world, that the real victories of mankind in their spiritual progress, through mineral and vegetable worlds and animal transformations are obscured, and only the very detached and the very clear-sighted can follow them, under our suicidal acts of every day.

Therefore we like the country, and even more so the comparatively desert places, because there we can take pleasure in watching with far less interruption the progress and the triumphs of mankind. The countryman is not, I imagine, nobler than his fellows, nor is the sympathy that we, travellers in Arabia, feel for the rough bedawin a result of any marked superiority of theirs over other men. Their violence, their crimes against their own kind and therefore against themselves, are, if anything, greater than the average that our civilization allows: and yet we are happy because we can see behind these crimes a background of real and vast achievement, the primitive vanquished background of earth. The courtesy of the desert Arab who stands in his poor tent to receive the stranger, is not greater necessarily than that of the diplomat at the head of his staircase: yet a difference is made by the darkness of the surrounding hills, by the stony hardness of their paths, by the scarcity of food and water. Even the smallest crumb of grace or virtue is a triumph when the whole darkness of earth and time lies around it; and we are constantly comforted even for the worst crimes in those lands of treachery and murder by the sight of a victory immeasurably greater than these defeats, wrested by the whole of humanity out of the "fell grip of circumstance."

This is, I believe, the obscure reason which has lured not only explorers, but hermits, saints and philosophers into their solitudes. They are not anxious to leave the paths of their fellows, but they do seek out the less frequented stretches, where—free from obstructions—they can comfort themselves with the certainty that the path does go uphill and not down. It is, of course, not impossible to make sure of the same fact in other surroundings. More discrimination and more imagination are required, and also a mind less sensitive, less alert to the impact of what surrounds it, so that it may keep the essential truth in sight through all the contradictions of times and men. Socrates loved the market place and his sense of proportion was not impaired; but perhaps he is not a fair example, for the light of Attica is a very clear light and preferable to most deserts even now. The artist, too, if he is sufficiently in earnest, can follow his vision in a crowd, and is made happy perpetually by the victory of the human spirit, in which he has the delight of taking an active part; and of the scientist, pursuing knowledge for its own sake, the same may be said. But to most even of these, and to many of lesser calibre, it is a help and a rest to get away for a while to where the pattern of mankind is traced in less complicated lines, so that background and direction show clearly beyond the tangle of our self-inflicted sorrows.

I have often noticed that the eyes of sailors and hillmen are free and quiet. Countrymen, too, when they walk among their fields, and women who surround themselves with love in their homes and think rather little of what lies beyond; old men contented with the end of their journey; and painters, carpenters, and all makers, when happy in their jobs: these and many others, men and women who have found their true vocations, share the same atmosphere of certainty and peace. I have noticed too that the business of these people is never such that it makes them consciously share in the wounding of their fellows whether through rivalries, or vanities, greed or envy; not only are they free of such impulses in themselves, but the happiness of their condition is such that they are largely exempted from watching this strife in others, either through the solitude of their lives or through the absorbing interest of what they care for. For it is to be hoped, and I think believed, that the worried look visible on so many city faces is more due to the constant witnessing than to the constant infliction of pain—though both must take their share in a competitive life. Those who are so happily free from this affliction have no need to travel; they can sit quietly and continue to be philosophers at home.

To the rest of us, the roads lie open and lead to a true and happy panorama of our world. We will avoid mere sight-seeing and rush of trains, or cars, or liners, where the suicidal tendencies of mankind are just as visible as in a street of bankers; and will confine ourselves to two sorts of landscape, each of which can give us what we need by different means. We may go to some quiet land, not over-populated, where there is enough natural prosperity for contentment, enough leisure for beauty, enough poverty for kindness, and enough labour for health—some mountain land like the Dolomites, where the harvests are sufficient to feed their villages, and the families go in summer to cut their hay and live in their wooden chalets high up amid their pastures in the sun. Here one need not search to pick out one man in many hundred with the look of contentment in his eyes; one meets it, clear as the current of the mountain streams, in the glance of almost every passer by; and that is the human comfort of the hills.

Or one may go to the wilderness where there is no consolation of human peace, but where the magnitude of nature is so apparent, the reality of her obstacles so visible, that the smallness of our achievements matters no longer. The fierce and tiny tribes can tear and lacerate each other; we see that this is a mere incident in the colossal triumph achieved by man in his mere existence, with whatever small measure of order, courtesy and goodness he has managed to collect. And we are comforted because we know in our hearts that the city and the desert background are the same, and the noise of our machines is not much louder than the tribal battle-cry, and is just as temporary against our tremendous background in space and time.

THE LURE OF SOLITUDE

Colonel P. T. Etherton

THE desert has always seemed inimical to people of the West attracted to the cooler living ways of forests and rivers. The hot wind that blows out of Africa and Asia has in history and story imperilled their well-being and sometimes their lives. Yet the Second World War has done much to end this orientation of thought, this belief built up largely on the sands. Those who fought with the Eighth Army tell stories in plenty of the redeeming quality of the desert, and many of them would give the deserts of Africa preference over other environments as a campaigning ground.

Indeed, to anyone who has actually lived in the desert and braved its desiccated reputation there must come an awareness and appreciation of the special beauties and benefits of the hot yellow pancake portions of the earth found in the equatorial zone. The Sahara, Kalahari, and the Gobi, the three great deserts of the world, possess to anyone who has no fear of the sun, a haunting and soul-searching appeal not to be forgotten and not easily put into words. A visit to these unearthly regions has in it something of the flavour of pilgrimage rather than travel; the road is often a golden one stretching out beyond the tinkling bells of caravans to those lost and glamorous places with chiming names, Samarkand, Timbuctoo, Baghdad, and when night falls the heavens become biblical with stars.

There is no contrast so satisfying as the descent of cool night after the hot and thirsty day, no sunsets more fabulous than those on the desert, no pleasure greater than pitching camp in the evening and sitting down quietly under the peace of the sky. A wide open environment has its spell and desert life has a strong philosophy of its own.

The dominant influence is loneliness, but of such a kind as to leave the traveller sustained and fortified by a vastness comparable in some measure to the reach of the sea. Yet on the paths of ocean man leaves no imprint behind him, while on the sands he can look back and see something for twenty miles behind him, no other footsteps but his own.

To those who believe and find that a long horizon brings liberation to the mind through the eyes and that an uninterrupted arc of sky, day or night, sustains the spirit, traversing the desert places can be an experience indexing the inner self and not to be forgotten. Stripped of all the world's prized possessions and ambitions, without a sense of time or even of ordinary succession, life takes on a condensation of its own, with a sense of an essential purpose and a still more necessary direction. Those who live and travel in the desert shed their petty selves and link with larger things, for destiny and divinity seem to meet each other—it is not for nothing that the three great religions of the world came to life in the desert areas.

It is not only the desert that has its peculiar attractions and its call to those who are tempted by the lure of loneliness. There are many who have been drawn by the magnet of the snows, who have set out across the mountains and the passes to the Roof of the World, to seek solitude and live a carefree life. In them the true spirit of the traveller in lonely and remote places runs high, with a disposition for courting and defeating dangers rather than shunning their companionship.

We are told that the great travellers who crossed China in the seventeenth and eighteenth centuries were thrilled with the wide open spaces that would appal less resolute characters. In reading Marco Polo and Huc and Gabet, amongst others, the bare list of the names of places gone through in the long and wonderful journey provokes curiosity and speculation, not only as to the physical geography of those *terrae incognitae*, but as to the inhabitants and the tidewaters of civilization now breaking around the frontiers and shores of the haunts of strange tribes and nomads.

What are the essential qualifications for the traveller into the unknown? He must have a certain training and experience beforehand; he must from his youth up be fond of travel; he must have a sound constitution and active frame, with frank and decisive manners, and possess that look that dwells in the eyes of men who have seen things in and out of dreams and fear naught. If he seeks the Roof of the World he will need all the energy and enthusiasm he can muster, for once beyond the frontiers of civilization he will find only tracks that twist and turn and wind by profound ravines and narrow valleys enclosed by stupendous mountains. All day long he runs the gauntlet of snowslides and avalanches. There are great glaciers to be traversed, some of them as long as from London to Brighton, which lead to passes never before used by white men. The ascent is coated with ice and the whole surface like a sheet of glass. The way leads down and up among the Pamirs, the Roof of the World. One might imagine that this is a tableland, that movement is unrestricted, with plains stretching away to the horizon. The reverse is the case; the "roof" is no tableland, but rather a mighty mass of lofty, high-pitched ridges and gables, with narrow valleys, hollows, or leads between them. Such soil as there is has been formed by the detritus of avalanche-swept shale and gravel, and it is amongst these interminable and formidable leads that the inhabitants gain a scanty subsistence by herding a few flocks. This region holds plenty of snow and for the rest bare rocks. It looks a land of waste and desolation, as it certainly is in winter.

There are extremes of temperature to guard against, as well as the frequent blizzards. The temperature can be provided for; the danger lies in the searching and wounding wind, and then it is that one seeks the shelter of the felt tents or *yurts* of the insanitary nomads and finds them most delectable.

Yet with all its drawbacks it has a fascination of its own and the hardy Kirghiz, who have made it their home since time began, would not exchange it for all the corn in Egypt.

They are a sociable and hospitable people, but they decline to live in houses. Instead they have the khirga, or felt tent, a circular construction on a lattice framework, from twelve to twenty-five feet in diameter. The lattice-work walls are about four feet high and from them wooden rods are stretched to a hoop forming the crown of the tent. The framework is covered with felt made from goat and camel's hair and an opening left at the top to let out the smoke. The tent is bedroom, sitting room, dining room, and kitchen, all in one. The Kirghiz tell you that it has no equal; you can set it up or take it down in twenty minutes. Could I do that with my house, a Kirghiz chief asked! No place on earth could compare with their windy and icy habitat; from time immemorial they have lived there, generation after generation, and why cannot life go on like that ... always ... in calm beatitude. Although they occasionally descend into the valleys and mingle with the people of the plains, the warmer and more comfortable life there fails completely to attract them; the warming rays of the summer sun, the fruit from the teeming orchards, the luscious grass, the tall and waving poplars. To most of us these would be a welcome change from the cold and ice and winds of the uplands, but on the Kirghiz they exert not the slightest influence. Their flocks provide most of the things they require and they look upon the outer world as a thing apart and give no hint of finding their lonely life wearisome. They never wish to leave the uplands and, in any case, are not likely to miss what they have never known. "We have immense pastures up here; when one area is getting thinned out there are others; we are lords of the uplands and the heights," they concluded. Such is their philosophy of life.

In this solitude the wants and ambitions of these simple, carefree folk are few. The yak provides several of them, a queer creature that revels in the cold and seems to fade away in the slightest heat. Its nearest ally is the bison of North America and in colour it is generally black. Found at a greater altitude than any other animal, except perhaps the burhel or mountain sheep, it thrives on the coarse grass growing there. The yak is an accommodating creature and, apart from being used for riding and the transport of goods, provides milk and cream, from which a cheese is made, whilst the flesh is not unlike beef to eat. Yak dung is the principal fuel; it gives out great heat and is a precious asset, being collected and then dried in the sun for storage and use during the winter months, for the cold weather lasts from September until the following June. Altogether the yak is a godsend to the people who live up there.

The yak is a slow-goer and cannot be hustled; he keeps up a steady pace of about two and a half miles an hour, and any attempt to make him go beyond that speed is met with grunts and kicks. On one of my visits to the Roof of the World—I have been there five times—I organized a yak Derby in which there were nine starters, the winner coming home at the rollicking pace of five miles an hour.

Other sports they have but they are mostly on horseback, for these people are born riders and their lives and pastimes are lived and played within an amphitheatre of mountains.

These mountains whose colossal height and solidity seem to break the current of time itself; it is there that man resisting the revolutions of lower regions retains through innumerable years his habits and his rights. While a multitude of changes has re-moulded the people of the West, while languages and laws, dynasties and creeds have passed over it like shadows over the landscape, the tribes who went to the mountains thousands of years ago are there now, and show in face and figure, language and dress, what their fathers were, in striking contrast to those living below them. They show, moreover, how adverse is the spirit of the mountains to mutability and that there the heart of freedom is found for ever.

Whilst serving as Consul-General and Political Resident in Turkistan I had unique opportunities for coming into contact with peoples and places almost beyond the ken of man, where loneliness could soon turn to terror and the fireside and friendly faces seem a million miles away.

One such journey was to Ordam Padshah, a shrine in south-west China, one of the world's sacred places, to which devout Moslems flock like trippers on a summer pilgrimage to Brighton and Blackpool. In the past nine hundred years only five white men had penetrated to Ordam Padshah.

Luckily I was on the best of terms with the Chinese author-ities and so it came about that the delicate matter of my pro-posed journey to the shrine was successfully arranged, the Mos-lem leaders, despite predictions to the contrary, raising no ob-jections.

A couple of weeks later I was en route through a land of con-trasts, for Chinese Turkistan is all that, especially in its general physical formation. Over part of the way to Ordam Padshah you pass through orchards and cornfields, interspersed with sandy stretches not yet connected up with the main oases. The track is a rough road which it is possible, though not comfort-able, for country carts to bump over. In places the road be-comes a narrow lane flanked by lofty poplar and willow trees, usually in double lines, with a canal of running water between them. Here and there these canals cross the road by a bed with solid earthen banks forming miniature water jumps for a horse. Sometimes the canal is spanned by a bridge of rough-hewn planks, or trees and logs thrown transversely and covered with branches and earth. Farmhouses and dwellings, singly and in groups, dot the landscape, low-pitched structures of mud and beams, generally without windows and devoid of architectural plan.

One essential idea of house construction has been retained throughout China and Central Asia, and the profession of architect is unknown. The same plan upon which every house is built is followed with a constancy that gives it the aspect of a moral principle revealed from Heaven, and handed down through generations for the architectural guidance of the people.

Most of the houses have a courtyard and verandah embowered in trees where in the warm weather the women sit and gossip whilst they weave the rough but durable white cloth of Turkistan.

The landscape is typical of these parts; stretches of oasis and desert alternating, for all this area is really a desert traversed by rivers which give the requisite incentive to vegetation and the creation of cultivated ground.

This was the setting through which I passed with the Chief Beg, or official in charge of the district, and a mixed following of Moslem soldiers and servants.

For the traveller in Turkistan the Beg is an important individual; a district as large as Yorkshire in England, or Rhode Island in the U.S.A., is in his charge and over it he exercises a despotic influence, which may be kind and benevolent, or harsh and grasping, according to the temperament of the man. He is the pivot around which the life of the villager revolves and nothing can be done without his sanction or approval. For a traveller like myself he is a sort of courier, the man from Cook's, and with him in one's entourage all goes merrily as the marriage bell. Moving about the country in my official capacity I was accustomed to Begs in general; they are mostly peaceful, hardworking fellows whose principal vice is a tendency towards bribery and corruption, but as this fault is common to all officials throughout Turkistan, I suppose the Beg cannot be blamed for making hay, or rather money, whilst the sun shines.

The Chief Beg who accompanied me on my expedition was a man of middle height, sturdily built, and, dressed in European clothes, he could have passed for a southern Italian. He wore a padded robe of brown cloth, with an edging of fur, and a small round cap like a beret, likewise edged with fur. White linen trousers tucked into black riding boots completed his attire and, taken altogether, gave him a dignified appearance.

The following morning I was seen off by the Governor and his officers and wished God-speed on my journey Nothing now but the dagger or the bullet of a fanatic stood between me and my goal.

We were mounted on sturdy ponies and for the first few miles after leaving Yangi Hissar passed scattered farmhouses, beyond which lay the edge of the desert proper. At one or two settlements I was met by the local Beg, who had prepared a *dasturkhan* laid out in front of his house—fruit, nuts, boiled and roast mutton, meat dumplings, doughnuts, and cakes of every kind.

The Turkoman is a hospitable soul, and if you know his language and can talk of the things nearest his heart, there is nothing he will not do for you. The dasturkhan is an institution, served at every village and halting place, increasing in proportion to the size of the place until in the larger ones it becomes breakfast, lunch and dinner rolled into one.

We camped that night in a house put at my disposal by the local Beg, on the outskirts of the cultivated region, which was gradually merging into the arid and sandy stretches. The next morning saw an early start as I wanted to get as far as possible that night.

It was late in the afternoon when we came abruptly to the point where the gardens and the cultivation end and the desert and real solitude begin. It is like passing the gateway of a walled garden beyond which is only a wilderness of violence and oblivion, yet within there are the flowers and the fruit, the murmuring streams, and the mosques and cloisters where seems to have fallen that peace which passeth all understanding Once the desert is entered not a trace can be discovered in the famished and desolate waste of what you have left behind.

At this parting of the ways we had our midday meal. We were getting to the limit of cultivation and could see ahead of us the sandy country. By five o'clock we had done some twenty miles when we plunged into an infinite sea of sand, the dunes extending as far as the eye could reach. The track, such as it was, threaded these dunes, making progress exhausting, for at well nigh every step we sank into it up to the knees and often as far as the waist.

It was a mystic region I was traversing and one that has originated all sorts of ghost stories—creepy tales of fairies and gnomes peculiar to the superstitious Asiatic. Certainly one cannot marvel at the legends, for the stretches of sand have a dismal and depressing effect upon the traveller. There is no sign of life, human, animal or vegetable, no sound of bird or beast, nothing to relieve the sepulchral silence. No wonder the people believe this eerie desert to be the abode of demons and evil spirits.

It is the sort of place where fear can be felt, as Guy de Maupassant puts it, a sensation as if one's soul were disintegrating; a convulsing of the mind and heart, a nameless horror of which the remembrance will evoke a shudder. These sand dunes are apt to conjure up fantastic terrors, and anyone who believes in ghosts and thinks he sees a spectre in the night, experiences fear in all its horror when he finds himself amongst desert sand dunes. I must admit that they had a depressing effect upon my nerves and sometimes I was almost ready to jump away from my own shadow. I had been up and down and round the world, but the creepy, supernatural nature of these dunes would shake most people's nerves; in my own case, when it came to straightforward open fighting and tackling a danger that was tangible, I was not afraid of anything.

What really affects one is the total absence at times of life and sound. The land is silent as the grave by day; it is only broken by the drumming sand dunes, filled with weird, mysterious, and dreadful sounds, a feature in the life of this unique desert. The whistle and rush of a sandstorm, which occurs at infrequent intervals, may also break the uncanny silence.

The aspect of these dunes is monotonously the same—successive rows ranked one behind the other, and seen from above they would resemble ripples along the seashore. Continually pouring in from the east, steadily and pitilessly they overwhelm the land lying in their path. Settlements are engulfed by a gradual process of encroachment; at first the walls of the houses keep out the advance guard of the sand, but gradually it climbs over them. Then the courtyards are invaded by successive storms which rage with great violence in this region—the drifts slowly mount to the roofs and complete the work of destruction, leaving no trace of human occupation and removing man and his works from the map.

These buildings of a long-past age are composed of sun-dried bricks, and a kind of matting, made locally, is used in the foundations. The climate of Turkistan is wonderfully dry, and sheets of this matting are often found beneath the walls of buried towns, often in a marvellous state of preservation although the ruins date back for at least fifteen hundred years.

Night had fallen when we were well within this grim section of our route; all day we had toiled on, and when we decided to halt my party was almost overcome with heat and fatigue and parched with thirst as the burning desert itself. Our day's stage had been one of about twenty miles and I felt we had well earned a rest.

"Let us stay until the shadows fall," said the Beg, who although in solemn mood seemed pleased with the success which had attended our efforts so far. The sun sank lower and lower behind the sandhills until it disappeared altogether; long shadows fell across our halting place, a breeze sprang up and moaned among the dunes. Then it died down to give place to something far more creepy. From somewhere near at hand, but exactly in what direction I could not make out, came a mysterious drumming as though someone were gently beating a drum. To get an idea of this blood-curdling sound you must try to visualize the strange tract of country I was in. You know what the smooth level sands of a sea beach are like, running on and on interminably. Now picture in your mind the ocean itself turned to sand in the middle of a hurricane. Imagine a tempest without sound and with billows of yellow sand that never move. To the height of a hundred feet and more they rise, these irregular waves of all shapes and sizes, and with the rays of the sun beating straight down upon the sea of sand, lying there without sound or motion. A journey across these hills of sand is one continual ascent and descent without a moment's respite or a vestige of shade.

We sat there listening to this phenomenon, which though

familiar to travellers in those God-forsaken parts, has never been explained. The beating of the drum was distinct, now fairly loud, now soft, now dying away, now resuming its weird tattoo.

In the Sahara, travellers have often been startled by this singular sound, which is reputed to be caused by sand scudding before the wind and brushing against tufts of dry grass, the echo being intensified and multiplied to considerable volume by the valley formation of the desert region. Apparently the phenomenon always occurs near small plants burnt up by the sun and as hard as parchment. According to this theory the drum is merely a sort of sound mirage, nothing more.

That night round the camp fire we talked of the things of this world and the world beyond, of the stars, the sun, and the earth, for in the moonlight, conversation tends to become universal. In any case, Moslems never talk personalities to the same extent as Westerners. Some of them had a keen knowledge of the sky and could find their way about at night with ease. "Allah has many eyes in the darkness," one of them said to me; "and he watches over each one of us when we are defenceless." In my own case I inwardly hoped this would turn out to be true.

When in Ordam Padshah the residents of the place formed the major part of my evening audiences. I asked if they found life monotonous at times and it drew their views on the subject in general. They were happy to be within such sacred confines and spoke of the outer world as a thing that did not concern them, nor did they find their lonely existence in any way wearisome. "We have no wish to leave here," they said, and there they left the matter. This was the centre of their world, a world that to most people would be eerie, strange, and oppressive; but to these people Ordam Padshah was everything and they regarded the land around it as one of ideals and dreams.

"What do you think about it?" I asked my henchman the Beg. His reply was non-committal. "'Tis a holy place and blessed are they who live here!" At the same time I felt that the flesh-pots of the gardens and orchards and the lovely ladies of Turkistan would prove more attractive to him than our present surroundings. As if to put himself right with the rest of the company he added, "The way hither may be dark and difficult, but we have our reward on arrival." He glanced round as if waiting for someone else to speak, but all eyes were turned on him, and then he began the story of a tragedy in the desert.

"Some time ago—many moons have passed since then—I came to the holy place; there were four of us in the party. One night we camped within a ring of sand dunes; they were as high as the sacred sheaf. After the night prayers we talked of many things, of this world and the next. Suddenly a night breeze sprang up, moaning and sighing among the dunes like unto the voices of a thousand souls in torment. It was the same drumming sound that we heard together a few nights ago," he said looking at me. "One of our party got up; his heart seemed to stand still and dire forebodings seemed to rush upon him. Then, before we could stop him he went off into the darkness as if to discover what this dreadful interruption might mean. When, after some time he did not return we went a little way as far as the darkness would allow; we called out, but only the echoes came back . . . there was no sign of our companion.

"Then, when we were hoping he would come back, the moon became overcast, the night seemed to get hotter; it had been warm in the daytime; now it was oppressive." He paused and we kept silence; after musing a little over the tragic event he went on. "He had vanished, no one knew whither," at the same time looking round on us, on whom the full meaning had already dawned.

"Through the night we waited, in fear and trembling, wondering what had happened. At dawn we went out again; a cold hand seemed to close round our hearts; it was like some evil dream."

"Did you find no trace?" I asked, with an indefinable sense of horror.

"No," said the Beg, "our companion had gone into the Land of Shadows; we never saw him again."

The heart of Asia still holds first place in the realm of solitude and mystery, especially that unexplored range of the Kuen Lun Mountains along the northern border of Tibet, where the Chinese hold shadowy dominion over the highest inhabited portion of the globe, a maze that is a sealed book to the rest of the world.

There I found a Buddhist sect who have as near neighbours more than a score of peaks exceeding a height of twenty-four thousand feet, and glaciers covering hundreds of square miles. This curious band numbering not more than six or seven hundred are doing penance for the rest of the world, for the sins of you and me and all mankind. They regard solitude and isolation as prime factors in their belief; they are happy in their incredibly austere surroundings, totally unmindful of wars and upheavals and the rise and fall of nations. They are following what they consider to be the original precepts of their ancient religion, as expounded by the Buddha six hundred years before the birth of Christ.

I will pass over my journey thither and come direct to arrival at the monastery and my reception by the abbot who offered the ceremonial tea as a gesture of welcome.

At the monastery only the abbot and I partook of the tea, the entourage stood looking on, acting up to the character of respect and adoration of their chief which was stamped upon them. There was nothing servile; perhaps after all even the head of a monastery did not seem so very important to people whose ancestors had probably been part of this ancient institution hundreds of years before the twentieth century. These people were devoted to their work; they were clinging to the theory of splendid isolation, working out their destiny and that of the world in general, in their own way.

If ever there was the simple life, it was here; the wants of these people were few and easily supplied; at long intervals a small convoy with food, mainly rice and tea, would arrive from the plateaux of Tibet, or the plains of Turkistan; as for drinks there was the purest spring water. Wine did not appear on the bill of fare. They had never tasted it, so had no dreams of some soft-flavoured nectar; whoever might visit the monastery and dream of such a drink would not find it realized here. Looking at their life dispassionately I thought how wonderful it must be not to have such feelings. In the heat of summer, and it can be extremely hot in these altitudes, I, personally could imagine nothing better than a drink from the juice of the grape, the full flavour of the natural grape turned into wine. This cool drink, of the colour of pale gold; you feel glad that the day is hot, and that you are alive and well to taste this real nectar of the gods.

However, what the eye doesn't see the heart doesn't grieve over.

As for money they had no use for it; even if they had there were no shops within four hundred miles as the crow flies, and when they reached them they would find them like kennels, open to front and sides, the shopkeeper sitting among his wares with an air of complete indifference. In fact, he hardly deigns to notice the customer. Money may, indeed, be the most important thing in the world, and all sound and successful personal and national morality should have this fact for its basis. Money controls morality and every teacher who denies or suppresses it is an enemy to life. The monks have never had any money, and are, therefore, quite indifferent to it.

These earnest and romantic men give a new outlook on life; they work with quiet energy and do it in an unobtrusive way, but the work is hard and genuine, and they would despise the go-slow man in this country, who wants the maximum amount of pay for the minimum of work, who rarely hurries himself, but is not above getting something for nothing when the opportunity offers.

These followers of the Buddha are free-souled creatures, sensitive, industrious, wrestling with great natural and physical difficulties, but intent on the aim for which the sect was constituted—the redemption of all mankind.

Whilst sitting there talking to the abbot I had time to look round and take stock of the central hall. It was about fifty feet long and twenty-five to thirty feet broad, with massive granite walls and a floor of granite slabs, each one about six feet by four, and fitting exactly. Indeed, they were so well cut and bevelled that one could hardly detect the dividing lines between them. The builders and joiners who had laid the slabs knew their job.

The conversation between us went on for several minutes; the abbot had a singular charm of manner, listened to what I had to say as though my conversation was the only thing in the world that mattered, and showed no evasiveness or hostility. All the same, I had a certain feeling of uneasiness and was wondering what was going to happen next. The monks with him stood behind, and in a crescent shape round us; they took no part in the conversation, but were eyeing me intently all the time.

They had the gravity and self-poise of the Buddhist monk;

they looked fit and as if they could tackle a mountain climb for the simple reason that it was high and difficult. I had never seen this particular type of man before and would like to have gone deeply into their history. For hundreds of years these people and their forbears had lived in the mountains in a freedom all their own. They were a community entirely unto themselves; their faces had not the subtlety of expression seen in those of a race whose interests and occupations were larger and more complex. So far as everyday life was concerned it was plain that they were people of simple straight ways; the same as their ancestors before them; they were living right outside the world —and didn't seem to feel the loss.

Yet it is astonishing what knowledge they possess, and they claim to have gained it through a life of solitude and study. You might class them, and others like them with whom you come in contact in travels over China and especially Mongolia, as ignorant and knowing little of the world above and around them. Nothing could be farther from the truth. I once met an old Buddhist priest who knew all about the solar system; in fact, he knew more about it than I did. The universe was important to him, as the world in which he lived. It was a planet, he said, and quite a small one at that, it revolves around the sun and does this in company with other planets; he spoke of asteroids and orbits, of stars, of meteors, their aims and origin. He treated me to a learned disquisition on the celestial family generally in the vast void of space.

I thought of this old priest when talking to the abbot and how he had spoken of the giant meteor which fell some years ago in Siberia, blasted hundreds of square miles and laid low trees by the thousand. Dr. Eckener who passed over the area in the Zeppelin, told me the effect of this meteor was felt several hundred miles away, for men on the Trans-Siberian railway far to the south heard a roaring sound like the thunder of massed artillery; they even felt the air wave that spread out from the point where the meteor struck the earth. I tell this story about the old Buddhist cleric, since it shows that these people have knowledge, although it may be latent, and that it does not do to stamp them as ignorant without first putting them to the test.

Beyond the walls of their monastery and the peaks and canyons that hemmed them in, they would be in a totally artificial world, founded on long-established ideas of convention and money; it would be so utterly foreign to them that they would have no sympathetic understanding of it. They take life with restful ease, and when not working know and appreciate the full value of leisure, and for this blessing they thank the Buddha.

Their code of morals is simplicity itself, it is based on the attainment of the one and only aim in their lives and is original all through. Probably they know that the ordinary man, as revealed by outsiders and books and manuscripts they have at their command, has no time for ethics and principles for he can neither understand nor apply them; what he can understand and make sense of are arbitrary rules of conduct. Some of these may be destructive and opposed to human wish and thought, but, at any rate, they are clearly-defined regulations which tell the ordinary individual where he gets off and what he may and may not do, without finding himself up against the law. Here the monks have no need to worry about that; their lives follow a certain definite line and the doubtful blessing of progress has not fallen upon them.

They are wise with the wisdom of simplicity, men of the mountains and the open air, contented people, and imbued with the love of solitude. Here all were on a common level, the arts and wonders of the world outside were an unknown quantity, and as such entirely unheeded. Perhaps they have missed something, but, at the same time, they have grasped a great deal. They owed allegiance to no one except their head; he dictated the policy, what should happen in the course of everyday life, and his rule was unhesitatingly accepted. He was regarded as a reincarnation of the Buddha; his followers therefore became a concrete body bound together by the cement of loyalty and devotion.

As I have already shown, the lure of loneliness and the call of the wide open spaces is not confined to the mountains. The Sahara has peculiar attractions, with its spirit of quiet and solitude, and its oases at rare intervals, some with a palm tree sheltering the camel-hair tents of the desert nomads, others with thousands of date palms with good water and land where the people cultivate barley and millet.

I already knew the Sahara; in this sinister and mystic land live the Tuaregs, the People of the Veil, very little known to the outer world. They are the overlords, the Knights of the Desert, whose home is under the blue sky, for they will not stay under a permanent roof regarding it as ill-luck and an outrage on Nature. "You talk of solitude and of our being lonely," they said; "Not at all; for us the desert has an irresistible attraction. We are here in the high court of Nature; in the midst of her nobility. Is it not so? The wide desert is our home. In the day-time we have the sun and at the night the moon and the stars are everlasting lamps."

The Tuaregs are happy in their environment; they shun the world in general, regarding the desert as their own and disliking the sight of other men. No one knows exactly whence they came; they are so difficult of approach and hold themselves so much aloof that they are called by other tribes "The Abandoned of God." Physically they are a magnificent race of people and live by raiding—a battle-loving, plunder-hungry tribe whose custom it has been for ages to go pillaging and killing in the lands adjacent to the Sahara. These things constitute their prime occupation, their business, and their sport.

The Tuaregs are the most mobile raiders on earth; gigantic, silent people, as silent as the desert that surrounds them, they are mounted on camels trained to rise quietly, to move off, and to cover as much as two hundred miles in a couple of days. These raiders are Moslems, but totally unlike any other follower of the Prophet. Religion is not a passion with them and I doubt if a Tuareg has ever made the pilgrimage to Mecca. They are no tillers of the soil; there is little to till; in fact, they disdain all work and devote themselves to the pastime of war.

The outstanding feature about these people is the veil, worn in all other Moslem countries by the women, but here in the Sahara adopted solely by the men. How the custom arose none can say—not even the Tuaregs themselves. Perhaps in ages long past it began with a desire for protection from the rays of the sun and the whirling sand of the desert. At all events, the Tuareg would consider himself steeped in shame were he to un-cover. He does not even remove it when he goes to sleep. These children of the wide open spaces take to the veil when they are about fourteen, and thence onwards it is an inseparable part of their lives.

For food they rely mostly on dates from the oases. These

oases are often of enormous size, as many as fifty thousand palm
and date trees, and an adequate supply of water. Some are only
a few yards round, but all are known to the Tuaregs whose lives
are strenuous and romantic. The Tuareg girl will sleep for days
and nights on end on the tomb of an ancestor for this will give
her a view of her lover who is away on a distant raid, perhaps
hundreds of miles down in the all-conquering desert.

I talked to these veiled riders of the desert. I asked what they
thought of the wonders of civilization as expounded to them, of
the amenities of life as I knew it. They were scornful and suspicious of modern science and civilization. They asked for
nothing better than their own habitat and the illimitable freedom that was theirs. They pointed to the blazing sun, "Could I
alter that?" They next showed me a camel. "Could I change
that into a horse?"

I, who have travelled widely in the five continents, and seen
some mighty truths shattered by modern invention, could
answer nothing. "A man can juggle with little things, but
not with the universe," the Tuaregs declared.

I changed the subject to the topic of veils. "How did the
custom arise?" I asked. They stared at me in astonishment.
Why did I wear those curious trousers? I said I hadn't the
faintest idea.

The Tuaregs remounted their camels, saying that Allah in his
wisdom had not made all men alike, else who would there be
left to raid?

A French writer, the Baroness Renée Roques d'Esplas, speaks
of the extraordinary attraction of the desert and the charm of
being alone in its vast solitude; of the flowers to be found there
and the birds that come to the oases from cold northern climes.
Here in the Sahara, the world's largest desert, larger than the
United States, is a land of curious contradictions, for apart from
sands hot enough to burn shoe leather, there are oases where you
can pick apricots and peaches as you might in California. To
these oases come the camel caravans, plodding over the white
sands, meeting the domestic donkey that can really call itself the
oldest inhabitant. Coming here long in advance of the camel-
man and the Moslem faith it ambled over this desert country
even before the three wise men rode into Bethlehem.

The camel caravans which have traversed the desert for untold generations take their leisurely course along traditional routes determined by the presence of oases where one can never really be lonely. Unexpectedness and contrast are the highlights here. I came across brilliant flowers, and a rose that was finer than a Maréchal Niel. It was a sign of beautiful life within a wilderness of sand; I refrained from picking any of them for I wanted them to remain serene and undisturbed so that they could delight others who might pass that way.

Whilst I was admiring the rose in its strange environment there came the soft notes of singing, and then a number of birds resembling goldfinches perched on some nearby bushes. Their song was a joyous one and brought out the sharp contrast wherein lies much of the charm of the desert. Only when the sun went down would they cease, to give way to the beauty of the night sky.

Looking back on all I have seen and experienced, a highlight is the individuality of man which he has preserved throughout a constant and close touch with Nature. Most likely the dweller in the deserts and the mountains is too occupied and never gives a thought to the marvels around him, to the mountains that are the wonder of the world. Yet he has an intense love for his environment and to him it is the land of his dreams.

Loneliness and solitude are not so much a doing without as an emotional discipline, a contrasted inner strengthening, a self-integration. At its best it is a straight line in life, opposed to oscillation and change; yet Nature herself believes in curves and variations and not even a Roman road went on straight for ever.

For these reasons the man who is wedded to loneliness and solitude for a lifetime, like a Trappist monk and the inmates of certain Buddhist monasteries, is no longer quite human and not always quite sane. The desert road is a good one, straight and strong, but the fleshpots of Egypt still call; indeed, must call, to give the desert its full savour. The wide open spaces can be empty of avarice and alluring sometimes as the hinterland of Paradise, but the television of the market place and the happy throng still remain like a secret parcel marked "Private: to await arrival." Solitude after all is not an arrival but a departure from the press, the speed, and the perplexities of modernity.

Despite the lure of heights, the charm of deserts and the breadth of distances, I should not be a happy seeker of solitude if I could not sometimes get back to the civilized smell of early breakfast and the comfortable crumpling sound of the morning paper. If Wellington was right when he said that the best general is he who knows at what point he must retreat, so the best traveller is the one who knows when to come home again. To get anywhere you have to start from somewhere; you can settle down to wandering, but even a cat finds you cannot settle down to loneliness.

MY PHILOSOPHY OF TRAVEL

Ella Maillart

I AM lucky. I have been able to satisfy my urge to travel by going five times to Asia after spending many a summer on board small sailing ships. When I started travelling I was eighteen; I was then instinctively obeying a strong urge. But today, at last, having reached the middle point of my life, I can analyse that urge and see where it has led me.

It goes without saying that I wanted to learn a few foreign languages and therefore I had to go abroad. Also as soon as I reached Paris, London or Berlin, I enjoyed becoming another person—starting an unforseeable chapter of my life, putting on new clothes, meeting new people, reading other newspapers, developing new interests.

Sometimes being abroad meant a much less enjoyable pastime: patiently, tiresomely, looking for a job. At that moment such a finding was of paramount importance to my purse; but today I see that the lasting value of these jobs was to make me travel up and down the social shelves that build the rather water-tight compartments of our so-called democratic age. Thus I gained a direct knowledge of the life of the poor in big towns: I have felt the narrowing mechanism of its conditioning and feared it.

But from the beginning I wanted to live my own life, and patiently I shored up that desire against wind and tide. The usual channels of university studies or secretarial work did not appeal to me; and today I see clearly that time and again I cherished most difficult dreams because only through a few hard-won victories could I prop up sufficient confidence in myself. Of course I needed much self-confidence, if I did not want to be depressed by the gap existing between my weakness and my ambition.

Have you ever asked yourself the question "Why do we travel?", and here let us eliminate all departures motivated by a need to gather—or impart—information. Scientists, craftsmen, businessmen, politicians and missionaries being left to themselves, we remain with the adepts of that "pernicious habit" mentioned by Masefield in his introduction to Marco Polo: "Wandering in itself is just a form of self-indulgence; if it does not add to the stock of human knowledge it is a pernicious habit." How long I had to wait to annihilate my guilt-complex due to a sentence I was too shy to correct!

But first of all who do I mean by the "we" I use in that question "Why do we travel?"? The science of today, according to genetic laws and the theory of chromosomes, insists on the fact that humanity is made up of an infinity of different individuals. Therefore it might be true that each of us travels for motives exclusively his own. But now, for convenience sake, I shall only mention a few of the impulses that force people to leave their home.

Certain travellers give the impression that they keep moving because only then do they feel fully alive: going from place to place gives them the feeling that they are mastering their particular circumstances. Others, more complex in their reactions, are keen to see if natives other than us, live better than we do without heat in pipes, ice in boxes, sunshine in bulbs, music on black discs, images gliding over a pale surface—all of which makes our life sapless, indirect, lived at second or third remove. Those who appreciate the ways of simple tribes where every activity is direct and immediately understandable, can remain among them as Alain Gerbault did in Polynesia, or Peter Freuchen among the Eskimoes. The others can come back. I think it is Paul Morand who wrote: "One cannot go too far in order to feel the desire to return home."

Travel can also be the spirit of adventure somewhat tamed for those who are no Frobishers ready to find new straits, but who desire to do something they are a bit afraid of—you can feel as brave as Columbus starting for the Unknown the first time you decide to enter a Chinese lane full of boys laughing at you, when you risk climbing down into a Tibetan pub for a meal smelling of rotten meat, or simply when addressing a witty taxi-driver in Paris.

But I often think that one of the main points about travelling is to develop in us a feeling of that solidarity, of that unity without which no better world is possible. That feeling builds so to speak, the second movement of the pulse of travel. The Chinese

Master Chuang Tzu said: "If we see things from the view-point of their differences, even liver and gall are as far from each other as Ch'u from Yüeh. If we see things from the viewpoint of their sameness all things are one." For me, during the first movement of travel, it was normal to see chopsticks, turbans, wooden saddles, fermented mare's milk and they were dutifully recorded in my books. Today I much prefer to note what emphasizes the inter-linkedness or the common background, of all thoughts. And I like to underline that when the heart speaks, its language is the same under all latitudes.

When I see something, it is certain that for an instant I am one with what I see. Also I am sure that instinctively we want to expand, to be the all, to possess it—why this desire to cut the rose or marry the lover, otherwise?—but shall we ever succeed in seeing "the ten million beings" of the universe simultaneously in order to be the all in that way? I think it is in answer to that human urge that the Buddha said: "Not by any travelling is the world's end reached. Verily I declare to you that within this fathom-long body with its preception and mind lies the world, its arising and its ceasing and the way that leads to its cessation." Today I am certain that to live is to travel towards the "world's end," returning to the unity we have lost. Or at least, if we feel too weak to do it, we do keep searching for signs of that unity.

To develop that solidarity I have mentioned, one must not travel like that charming English family I met just returning from a round-the-world tour. I wanted to know how the South Sea Islander lives today, but I was only given details about the different tennis-clubs visited in those islands!

No. We must develop more interest and a deeper understanding of the people we meet here or abroad. Like us they are passengers on board that mysterious ship called "Life." The sooner we learn to be jointly responsible on that ship—instead of simply blaming the staff—the easier the sailing will be. Special efforts must be made with those passengers who are inimical, isolated, convinced they are wronged. Forgetting differences but emphasizing traits common to each being, our comprehension has to be piercing and total: thus becoming absolute love, the only level at which we can find an inspired solution to the inner and outer chaos which has uprooted us.

Every time I took long leave from home I felt as if I were to conquer the world; or rather, take possession of what is my birthright, my inheritance. We want to feel that this earth is all ours, like our parent's house when we were children. No sooner had I left school to cruise the Mediterranean than the following question absorbed me—which kept me company during my later travels: "How much does one 'kill' the journey by accomplishing it, by realizing it?" or, "How much does the real journey, the taking possession of a new land, fulfil the promises of the dreamed journey?" Though he has never been there, does not Arthur Waley know China better than I who patiently sampled many bugs and pubs, jokes and quagmires, without mentioning the evasive governors, of that great country? And consider Rimbaud writing the *Bateau Ivre*, probably the most compact sea-poem there is, before having ever approached the sea? Are not such abstract journeyings more real than a concrete meeting with the earth?

I wonder why more books have not been written on the subject. I know one which is fascinating: *Equipée, Voyage au Pays du Réel*, by Victor Ségalen the archæologist, writing about his expedition to the upper Yang Tse River. He describes masterfully the many days of painful progress during which only two moments were rewarding and sufficiently intense to plunge him in the fullness of the present. For myself I have come to the conclusion that the benefit brought by the realized journey is not to be counted in the amount of such perfect moments, but in what it does to our character. Not only does travel enrich us with a new system of reckoning; but by endeavouring to know other parts of the world, we enliven latent aspects of ourselves which would have remained unknown had we stayed at home. Our broadened consciousness will help us to judge ourselves better.

Having visited this planet, we shall react differently towards our drab neighbour, our raw climate; and I had to live in a desert before I could know the full value of grass in a green ditch. Based on personal experience, I suggest the following definition: the true traveller is the one urged to move about for physical, æsthetic, intellectual as well as spiritual reasons.

It is true one also travels to run away from routine, that dreadful routine that kills all imagination, all capacity for enthusiasm. One travels in order to learn once more how to marvel at life in a child's way. Blessed be the poet, the artist, who keeps alive his sense of wonder!

Yes, one also travels to escape from it all.

But that is the great illusion, it cannot be done: it was always myself I found at the end of the journey and I wish it had not taken me so many years till I had the courage to face that self properly.

When I crossed Asia with my friend Peter Fleming, we spoke with no one but each other during many months, and we covered exactly the same ground. Nevertheless my journey differed completely from his. One's mind colours the journey as if one wore individually tinted spectacles. It is our mind we project outside and ultimately decipher when we think we meet the "objective" world.

But first of all let us go into that escapist idea. I want to translate the French writer Saint Exupéry: "A certain cheap literature has told us about the need to escape. Of course one runs away in search of wide horizons, but a wide horizon cannot be found—it has to be rooted, substantiated in us. Escaping never leads anywhere."

These words could sum up my life.

The wideness of the horizon has to be in us, can be nowhere but in us, otherwise we speak of geographic distances. Only those who can grasp, comprehend the wideness, can possess it—after they have found the means to express it. I see now that a concept or even a feeling has no sense unless, out of our substance, we spin around it a web of references, of relationships, of values, of sense-reactions. Until a child can conceive hotness, the hotness of the stove will remain for him in a world of automatic stimuli. For the camel crossing the desert there is no wideness, only steps taken, blisters, burning sands and the desire to rest. Or take an inveterate reader: intellectually he can conceive what is meant by the idea of love, but unless he dares to engage himself across the Gobi desert of love, he will never know the reality of love, its barren stretches, its gushing oases. The timelessness of a concept has to be woven into the running warp of dying time—that vertical power to be wedded to the horizontal earth.

To enjoy reality one must meet it in action. Passivity or contemplation alone cannot lead to a full life.

Already during my youth I searched how to enjoy water and wind, sun and snow in their entirety, in their *reality*. (Sun-bathing *quasi* religiously for months yielded nothing, of course!) Then I tried to be wedded to these elements, to "root" them in me while living among seamen, mountaineers, nomads.

I am fond of cats and sometimes feel related to them. You know how a kitten behaves in a new home; how it pokes its nose into every corner, climbs up all sorts of peaks and faces many a precipice till it knows its domain by heart? So for me, a Genevan girl, it had been normal to push the nose of my sailing boat into every creek of our big lake; or to point my skis down every possible gully of our mountains.

Why stop after that? Was not the Mediterranean waiting to be conquered? And the vastness of windswept Tibet? It be-came a necessity as soon as I was convinced that a town life would asphyxiate me. But how could I make the good holiday life last all the year round instead of two months only? Grown-ups, of course, were too silly for words and there was no need to follow their example. They think it is intelligent to travel at sixty when one has retired from business and is stiff with rheum-atism. No. I was going to think for myself—or at least live my own life. One does not need much brain in order to do great journeys in the open. One must know how to want one thing at a time; and then, only a huge appetite is required, a desire to swallow and assimilate people and places—with a pinch of con-centration now and then. No special training is needed: endur-ance comes by itself when you stick to what you want to do. Past habits must not act as blinkers. Having erased what we owe to the town-rut, we can try to acquire what peasants and sailors enjoy as their birthright: the worthy carriage of head of those who have unlimited sky around them for the best part of the year.

I will tell you what I did. I missed my last examination be-cause I had been too busy founding the first ladies' hockey club of Switzerland. Then the urge to sail became paramount. My best friend recovered from a grave illness and was ordered six months' rest in the south of France. She was still in the nursing-home when I bought for her a seaworthy three-ton sloop. Two months later, in January, we were living on board at Marseilles, joyful and ready to sail for Corsica—in spite of most alarmed letters from our families.

A six-months' cruise took place during which we met many adventurous sailors. It became normal to nurse great plans. Exams were forgotten. A year passed. I found a job on an English yacht, the *Volunteer*, in order to learn navigation. Two years later we sailed for Greece, being only four girls on board our yawl, *Bonita*. On a bigger ship, a converted pilot-boat, we went tunny fishing in the Atlantic, training for the South Seas. But my friend married, my hopes were crushed; and the first part of my life, sailing, came to an end.

Once more I tried to think. I was not a kitten and could not remain in the country where I had grown up. My moorings in the centre of Europe were not suiting me, or else I did not know how to breathe in that musty air. A world war had maddened the Continent, nonsense ruled everywhere—why remain part of it? Why not search the world for more harmonious surroundings. Why suppose I had to fit into a struggle for life which was not leading to a life worth the name? I was useless anyhow: I had learned nothing except to fit out yachts. In the big house called the world, I might find a corner suiting me better than my depressing room near the failing League of Nations.

Because I had not followed my father's advice, I had been obliged to earn a living as I mentioned before—teaching French and English abroad, typing in Paris, acting in ski-ing films, also going on the stage. After that, in a small way, with my rucksack on my back, I started eastwards, I went to Berlin, writing articles, then to Moscow, the Caucasus, Turkistan . . . trying to join those proud nomads seen once in the documentary film made by the Citroen expedition. I began to see clearly that I was looking for a tribe or a place that would be less nonsensical than our crazy Europe where men torture and exterminate each other every twenty years.

I wanted to reach a valley not yet upset by our ideas. There I wanted to "substantiate" the wideness of Asia, to relate it to my life, thus establishing a living relationship between the stability of traditional Asiatics and my European restlessness. Could not that escapism lead to freedom, the freedom of man's entity? Reach beyond one's self by going through one's completed self—instead of doing it by reaching outside one's self, what some people seem to do when plunging into a life of frantic activity, or in the queer world of drugs. By trying to understand the cause of both the Asiatic and the European attitude towards life, transcend them both and reach a standpoint liberating me from my limitations. Lasting peace cannot be reached as long as we are tempted by conflicting possibilities. Oneness is bound to be the ultimate truth: only then can questioning cease.

During that long journey made with Peter Fleming I learned a lot—by being cut away from the world for many months. While through the power of his thought, he remained linked with his world, I, perhaps through the lack of power of my mind, became detached from the world. And, by the way, this is the main reason which makes me prefer to travel alone: a companion is in himself a detached "piece" of Europe and he is bound to behave according to his breeding; thus his reactions will contribute to keep alive in me a European frame of mind. I dislike it because I want to forget my Western outlook; I try to become blank inside so as to let the journey sink deep in me. In that way I can grasp better what I see; I can feel the whole impact made on me by the newness I meet at every step. When I have a companion by my side, together we build a foreign cell, a "resistance" which can only with difficulty blend into new surroundings. The amusing fact is that my behaviour ends by defeating itself: my inner blank having made me plastic, I soon find everything normal around me. And thus I miss that impact which I wanted to feel more vividly while travelling by myself! I console myself thinking that the pernicious habit mentioned by Masefield is none other than that shock of newness, a fascinating experience which might easily become a kind of drug.

But to return to the emptiness of Northern Tibet. There we were, having travelled to the end of space, as well as to what seemed the end of time. Nothing ever happened. We had no accidents, no bandits attacked us, we never suffered badly from hunger, no prison closed on us, no aeroplane was sent to our rescue. There I even came to think: though we came so far, there is hardly anything worth writing home about.

Nevertheless these were thrilling months, but on a different plane of being. Detachment was slowly becoming part of me. It was normal to belong nowhere, or everywhere; to feel one is an eternal traveller . . . I discovered I was richly contented, away from my people and my friends—without a roof, without a wood fire, without bread even. In winter at twelve thousand feet of altitude with two cups of barley flour a day; at ease in a reality which was a void.

Isolated explorers in the Arctic, or in the desert, sometimes discover that fullness which is latent in all of us; it is not true that we have to be herded together by the millions in order to be human. In my own case, Europe was forgotten and I knew she could do without me; immensity, solitude, were becoming part of me, were being related to me. They were unveiling a few of their meanings. For instance, the faintest track of an antelope acquired a new significance. It became filled with my own longing for the water-hole towards which we had been marching for ten hours. Man is a knot of relationships; he is only fully developed when he has become directly related to a number of people, feelings, countries, ideas. And I was becoming related to primitive life. Since it was due to my choice, no grumbling was possible, I remained open-eyed and became aware of real values. Mariners and mountaineers had already much helped towards disentangling the brambles of superficialities that hobbled me. I aim at grasping the essential quality of things beyond appearances, at remaining truthful to my highest aim as well as to my friends, while constantly lessening the disagreement between my thoughts and my acts. I must stop being a living lie.

Never I hope, will the lack of a table, a sheet, a lump of sugar, a slice of bread or a friend make me feel miserable—they are not essential. But at the same time, having been without them, how I do appreciate them when I have them. That is the beauty of it: the more you become non-attached, the more you enjoy life; the more you live fully the present moment. But to cease to desire, you must feel that fullness is in you—not outside you. You will say that you cannot leave for Tibet as I did, but it was only my silliness that made me go so far.

Then, how are you to find your fullness? Each one among us who is a seeker, will have a different Tibet—his own void—to cross. No one but himself can find that treasure at the end of detachment. His searching will determine his finding. It might be the wisest man who finds it in his kirk or in his cabbage-patch.

Today it is fashionable to quote the Zurich psychologist Jung:

"The age of discovery began when men would no longer believe that the Hyperboreans inhabited the land of eternal sunshine, but wanted to find out and see with their own eyes what
existed beyond the boundaries of the Northern world. Our age
is bent on discovering what exists in the psyche outside ordinary
consciousness." So, was I typical of our age when I wanted to
learn how to grasp reality?

What goes under the name of spiritual problems of the
modern man became a fact for me when I saw that having had
all I wanted, I was nevertheless miserable. Material security,
welfare, humaneness—they were not sufficient ideals to me.
Now at last I know with absolute certainty that we travel to
find ourselves. By placing ourselves in all possible circumstances
which like projectors, will illumine our different facets, we
come to grasp all of a sudden, which one of our facets is fully,
uniquely, ourselves. Through it, go beyond it, having then
exhausted our particularism.

Or, in another way, if I represent one of the innumerable
possibilities of the cosmic ideation "looking at Itself through
myself," I want to place that particular "point of view"—that
open window which is me—in its right frame: my genuine way
of life. Then, instead of tearing me apart, my gropings will
interlock themselves peacefully since I shall know myself.
A window is not important in itself, but only because of the
light passing through it and the unique angle of vision it provides . . . showing the marvellous wedding of the changeless
Light supporting the ever-changing scenery.

Having so far mentioned what I did, I hope you will now
allow me to take a bird's eye view at my different lives, in order
to philosophize after the event.

While still in my teens, I gave myself to the seas—having to
burn my family "boats" behind me—and I had much pity for
the life of the landlubbers. The sea meant the "good life," the
most sensible way to live. Then also, without noticing it, we
learned to make up our minds, bearing the sometimes dangerous
consequences of our decisions. Handling our own little ship,
sailing sometimes through squalls with beautifully curved sails,
meant a clean life away from the mean jealousies and mis-
understanding of crowded places. To move always among

wind and water provided a more *real* life than anything else I could think of at that time. And my person was harmoniously active since my physical, emotional and mental selves lived simultaneously. Also I must mention the joy of being alone and self-contained between water and infinite sky, utterly free—having kicked the Continent away when jumping on board; and the joy of intense peace of mind in good weather. This, of course, in our antithetic world, implies its contrary: fear, fight for shelter, blinding fog and dragging anchors. Yes, my heart was in love with the sea and never could a man make it feel more wonderfully great than did a departure for a new cruise.

That life at sea could not be maintained and after ten years it petered out.

When living ashore, the hills of Central Europe helped me to be patient. They mattered more than the rest of the land. Hard mountaineers and self-reliant guides were more manly than town people. In their proud heads their eyes were clear under a clear sky. The intoxication of ski-racing, the radiance of the snowfields made me forget the drabness, the misery of our industrial age. Up there it was easier to tend towards fullness, towards purity.

But unless I married a seaman or a guide, how could I relate myself to sea or alp? I was not one of them. I had to find another solution.

Nearly penniless, I went to the country of the Soviets—once more acting against the will of my people. . . . If there was more justice, more dignity in the Russian way of life, I was ready to settle down there. After two stays of six months each, living exclusively among Russians, I felt sad, disappointed, at a loss—having exhausted the cheap satisfaction of doing something which was considered difficult.

But then, after having visited on foot the most remote valley of the Caucasus, I started a new phase of my life. I felt as if forbidden places were challenging me: Samarkand, Chinese Turkistan, Tibet and the Himalayas had to be reached. I started to will it. A life of daily thrill peppered with the sharp taste of risk, the pleasure of using one's wit, the joy of realizing what one had thought out, became mine.

Nevertheless, deep down in me I knew it was a stop-gap activity. I still needed an acceptable answer to the question:

why live? I wonder if Masefield would think that such an answer adds "to the stock of human knowledge"? Thank God, it was because I was too silly to add to that stock that I could slowly discover what I was looking for.

Seeker is really another name for traveller—whether one seeks sunshine, fun, inspiration or wisdom. I would travel till I did not need to seek any longer. Ultimately, all pretexts being eliminated, I travelled to become wiser. So I came to pretend that my living among Asiastics would give me a vantage-point showing me where we, the Westerners, went wrong.

Central Asian nomads are less tormented than we are. They are at ease in a world at their measure, where the causes of well-being and hunger are easy to understand; where man is not a lonely individual struggling against the whole world; but where man is supported by the clan, an organic whole, the unit of these regions; where man is part of something bigger than himself, is not an end in himself . . . a restful way of living. We Westerners suffer, unable to belong to a living concept bigger than ourselves; we have not yet formulated what will replace the nation-idea.

Four times I started for Tartary. I would not settle down in Europe. But each time it was my own discontentment which I found at the other end of the journey, which was colouring everything I saw. Each time local disturbances prevented my researches; and somehow forced by circumstances, I landed in South India in 1940. There I discovered what I needed and could not name before I had approached it.

For a few years I lived the stability of a traditional group: built upon a metaphysical concept of the universe, it provides for the spiritual, mental and physical side of man and each side is given the degree of importance it needs. Linked to the eternal laws of heart and nature, inner and outer man stands up as a whole; in the West, most of us are lost in the crumbled frames of family, culture and gnosis.

East and West, though, have reached a dead end where both feel terribly uneasy. But, Siamese brothers hinged either at the Urals or at the Carpathians, Europe and Asia are complementary: the "*homo faber*" cannot do much without the "*homo divinans*" and vice-versa.

In South India at last, I had time to sum up, to weigh my

travels in my heart—and not in the balance of time and space. At the hour of my death what would the meaning of these travels be? They were important to me in so far as they had changed me, brought me nearer to my real centre. Slowly they had led me to what matters most. Only the inward journey is real. I found myself. Which is the same as to say that I found the way to become freed from my preposterous ego. Now I know that there is a way to the unchangeable Centre—that Core which is the same in all of us. And because of It, I can try with sincerity to love my neighbour as much as myself. Feeling no longer divided but concentrated, I can march with patience towards that oneness which we all feel, is the ultimate as well as the first word of life.

THE ARTIST AS A TRAVELLER

Cora J. Gordon

THE artist is a privileged traveller, for his is the only quest that is almost bound to be successful. In other respects, too, artists on their travels enjoy more privileges than other mortals. For one thing the simple people of this world seem to have an innate sympathy for them, at worst a sort of tolerance.

This means that once at large in the country, wandering about with sketching kit or sitting at his easel, an artist is regarded by the peasantry or the man in the street as a fellow worker. Immediately there is a bond of sympathy. Countless are the times I have made some suitable answer to the remark "chacun son metier" grunted over my shoulder after a critical survey of the painting.

Also, as to £ s. d. On the Continent painters have long been looked upon as simple impecunious "rapins," with a certain aura of irresponsible charm.—After all, that is often true. . . . Soon after our marriage, though longing for a few months away from hot stifling Paris, we couldn't muster enough money for the average painter's "holiday." All the recommended spots were far beyond our resources so in desperation we laid out a map of France, clasped our hands round a hatpin, shut our eyes and jabbed the pin down on—Camarez, not very far from the point of Finisterre. Never having heard of Camarez we reasoned that, although near the sea, it must be cheap. After a long train journey, followed by a soaking trip on a ferry boat, we found ourselves in a *diligence*, a covered wagonette filled with friendly old women balancing market baskets on their knees. When asked about cheap hotels they said, "Five francs a day is the usual price." (4s. 2d.) Our faces fell.—"Beyond our means." "Well, you could try Madame Barbu; she has a fisherman's inn." We visited Madame Barbu, creeping through a low doorway into a dark room where fishermen were drinking penny brandies at the "*zinc*." "My poor children, couldn't possibly take you; I've only got one big bedroom crammed with fishermen," said the white-coifed old Madame Barbu. Some-

how the French habit of calling young grown-ups "my children" warms the heart. Jan explained that we were painters
hoping to live cheaply. She softened, said she would cook a nice
lunch and insisted on lending us clothes belonging to her niece
and nephew while ours were dried. We purred while consuming
all the things one couldn't afford in England, such as lobster,
washed down with white wine. I wore the niece's *sabots* and a
full skirt of serviceably thick material, while Jan in the nephew's
clothes looked thoroughly nautical with arms akimbo. She
questioned us a little more—"Oh, well,"—hesitating—"I have
just furnished a tiny room—too small for both to dress in at once,
—three francs a day all found, wine thrown in, of course. . . ."
And that was the beginning of our travel adventures.

We realized that just because we were living on the cheap
among the people it was really possible to learn about their
life. Though foreigners, we were artists first and foremost and
so in a sense belonged to our surroundings. If not the most comfortable way of travelling, this must be one of the most infor-
mative. We also learned that for those who travelled as we did
it is often necessary that taste and digestion should have their
share of the spirit of adventure. This was brought home to us
by Madame Barbu's little granddaughter who took "*les jeunes
peintres*" under her wing and spoilt us. But one day, noticing
that she was turning the pump on to a heap of mysterious some-
things in a bucket, we asked, rather nervously, what they were.
"Snails," she said triumphantly, "for you." Much embarrassed
we explained that though oysters, prawns, and even winkles
were eaten in England, we hadn't been brought up to appreciate the excellent food value of snails. "Ohhh," she cried—
"and I've been *all* the morning in the churchyard collecting
these for *you*." Since then we accustomed ourselves to braving
some hair-raising "dainties."

After all, everything to which one is unaccustomed may seem
barbarous and the sooner one is enabled to shed one's prejudices the better. Certainly for that travel is the best tutor.
When we told an old Frenchwoman that red-currant jelly was
eaten with mutton in England she said, "What barbarians!"

A painter's sole enemy is inclement weather. Friends he finds
even among the customs officers who, after being shown the in-

evitable pound of tea, glance at a certain proportion of palettes, paints and serviceable old garments and shrug their shoulders indulgently.

The answer to this might be that painters seldom travel with much that is dutiable. I think, however, that customs officials, the French *douaniers* in particular, use some considerable psychology. Artists may as a whole wear an ingenuous kind of air. On one occasion, after studying for a year in Munich, we were seen off by thirty-five student friends who sang to us as the train moved out. We had no idea that thirty-five presents, including some boxes of cigarettes had been surreptitiously stowed on the rack behind our luggage. At the frontier we were visited by the *douane* and our bags were chalked without being removed, and the officials even expressed surprise and pleasure when we displayed a packet of French cigarettes, saying quite honestly that we always smoked *Caporal Doux*. Later on, when we discovered the thirty-five gifts our horror can be imagined. Most certainly guilt would have been visible on our faces had we knowingly smuggled such things. A sophisticated looking woman we once met in a train told us a different story. "I never get through the customs without a struggle," she said. "The officials take one glance at my face and I am done for. I have been through rigorous experiences—yet I have never tried to smuggle—luckily for me."

The excitement caused either by seeing or by doing new things seems to have a magical effect on one's emotions and mentality. Like freshly dug soil the whole quality of one's being becomes temporarily 100 per cent better. In Art Schools the *cliché* "to grow stale" is often applied to the condition reached by an over-conscientious and plodding student. This "stale" condition can soon vanish under the stimulus of a thorough change. Things seen or experienced for the first time may stir one more deeply than far greater beauties to which one has long been accustomed.

Our adventure with the thirty-five students reminds me of an incident which occurred while we were studying in Munich among the thirty-five well-wishers. The *Pension Fürmann* was then famous as the abode of the liveliest and most impoverished students, sub-editors, teachers and cranks of the city. Fürmann, a fatherly man with a kind eye and a formidable chin, had in his youth emigrated to America. On returning he inherited a small farm situated in the bohemian and formerly outlying part of the the town. He added to the building and for three marks (2s. 6d.) a day you got a room and excellent board with high jinks and dancing on Saturday evenings. Once a month we paid two marks each towards the fee of a little peasant dance orchestra and also enjoyed a barrel of beer in the kitchen.

On first arriving in Munich we had asked for the address at a stationer's in the district. They looked at me appraisingly, pursed their lips and said; "Ach, das ist nicht für eine *Dame*." (That is not for a *lady*.) However, with our usual persistence we found Fürmann's and spent a very happy winter. Those monthly balls were treated by us as great occasions for which we designed fancy dresses and made quite elaborate decorations.

Art in Munich was looked upon as progressive, but their modernity had not moved beyond "*Secession*." This could be labelled mostly as a development in several directions from Impressionism. "We will do you a mock *Salon des Independants*," said we, and being supplied with cheap tempera mixtures and huge rolls of canvas paper, we perpetrated in two days nineteen big and ridiculous pseudo modern pictures, painted with our tongues in our cheeks—*fauves*, *cubist* and *futurist* and any other 'isms that we had seen but had not yet understood. The result was that, released from all our former Art School discipline we were possessed by such a spirit of fun and vitality that in many ways we painted far better than we *could* paint, having abandoned our usual rut—to which we returned with permanently heightened powers. The occasion was publicized; journalists came, including the editor of *Jugend*. An old English lady who little realized that we had perpetrated the pictures begged us as decent English people to make a firm stand against such atrocities. There is no doubt that mental excitement while observing or while creating may have such a tonic action that the effects can never be completely lost.

Embarrassment is occasionally the lot of all travellers and not even the artist is exempt from it. Some people feel it when struggling with a new language; others don't like being stared at. Perhaps my most embarrassing experience was during our first walking and sketching tour in the Tyrol. Gradually we had made our way to Mittenwald on the German side, a place where they made cheap violins and hung them, after being varnished, on to the clothes lines to dry. There we stayed for six weeks, painting on little panels of wood matured for violin making. Our next choice was Erwald, a village over the border in the Austrian Tyrol. Though anxious to climb the Zugspitz, we were weather-bound for many days, the soft snow on the mountains was considered dangerous for climbers. As I had some illustrations to do for the *Jongleur de Notre Dame*, I got on with them. Our landlady was greatly impressed with my rendering of monks, angels and archangels and gossiped about it all with the neighbours. The pious peasants, far away in the mountains, soon heard that a holy woman was getting sacred pictures straight out of her head. They banded together and made pilgrimages to our lodgings. The landlady ranged them in queues and every now and then she knocked at the door. At the sight of poor embarrassed me, they crossed themselves and begged my husband to show them the drawings. Never a word was addressed to me for they felt they were in the presence of a saint.

After the student days were over we went to many places, and for many years quite one half of each year was spent in travelling. Later on we spent part of the other half year in writing a book about our experiences. Why did we go to those places? Why does the artist travel?

There are certain parts of the world that inevitably attract the painter. Due to some magic quality in the soil, or whatever the reason, the ground and everything on it is so arranged as to form ready-made compositions. Such are the south of France and various parts of the British Isles. I have not mentioned these, because to visit them is hardly to court the unknown, as it was, for example, when we set off to make our way to Lapland. The artist is continually in need of new experiences to freshen his perception. Whether travelling abroad or hiking at home the experienced realistic painter is always in possession of that magic talisman, a trained eye.

Years spent in looking for subtleties or strengths of colour and tone, seeing the possibilities of massed shapes and developing a sense of general form cannot fail to give the painter an advantage over his fellows. The untrained man can see shadows as little more than grey shapes, while the painter discovers at a glance which of the many delicious colours may be embodied in the tone of a shadow. For example, to the uninitiated light and shadow on a white house mean nothing much, yet when a painter has translated it into pigment it can readily be realized as something beautiful.

Most of us know that to enjoy a long walk without fatigue one must have trained one's walking muscles through a certain amount of practice. However that deals merely with the physical side—the painter's eye is trained both physically and mentally, in neither case to avoid strain but to apprehend clearly.

For a painter I would hardly recommend the hasty survey of places that is sometimes dismissed as "globe-trotting." Our most profitable summers were generally those during which we settled down for some time. This means, of course, that you arrive in a place without any idea where you are going to stay. You then at once set about reconnoitring, walking around until you find the ideal spot. We first adopted this technique in the Balearic Isles. On our arrival in Majorca, after walking round it we came upon a little hillside village with a deserted inn perched on the crest of the hill. We wanted that inn. A French painter friend negotiated with the owner and for 8s. 4d. a month its nine unfurnished rooms became ours. We borrowed two beds, two chairs and a table. Our cooking pots and cups cost us five pesetas and we settled down for three months, living on grapes, figs, rice and the golden fish that abounded in the incredibly blue sea; and a delightful child served us and cooked for fivepence a morning.

For the first few days we wandered round—falling more and more in love with the character of the place, sometimes scribbling possible compositions in minute sketch books. Without hesitation or erasure Jan could, in a four-inch sketch book, set down panoramas of mountains, olive groves, or perhaps whole towns seen from an altitude. He ascribed this power to having been an engineer, but that hardly accounts for their beauty. Generally he had to put up with a syncopated draught down the back of his neck, due to the heavy breath of some admirer peering closely over his shoulder. In Spain we were often asked why we did not put in the trees behind us. The onlookers thought we were putting down what we knew, not what could be seen from one position only. After this, as we were training ourselves to see quickly and to aim for breadth and decision, we used our smallest oil sketch boxes with panels fitted into the lids, often painting from five to seven little sketches each day, trying to find out how to express the terrific effect of sunlight on olive groves and farms. Our failures, smeared over and almost baked in the yard served again for further research.

We were hardly more than students but of course looked upon ourselves as mature. Certainly for the immature this is a good method. Lots of fun it was. Fun and experience, and after our second summer we eliminated enough to be framed with pride for our first "two man" show in London.

To the artist the mental atmosphere of a country means a lot. Soon after the end of the first Great War the feeling in most countries of Europe was depressing and unhappy. Spain, we felt might be the one carefree country in Europe and so we decided to go there. A painter friend, Wyndham Tryon, lent us a flat in Murcia and a cottage, really a wee Saracen castle, in Jijona. Later we looked round the outskirts of Murcia and found Verdolay, an ideal village for sketching, and we were able to rent a tiny vacant house for next to nothing. For beds we laid mattresses on packing cases. La Mechora, a charming woman who ran the village provision shop, befriended us. She and her cronies sat outside the little shop after working hours, and we joined them in the blue night, perched on short-legged chairs that people insisted on treating as if they were fitted with rockers. A sound of sharp clicking could be heard along the streets as little sets of friends grouped themselves, sometimes round a guitarist and singer, sometimes just to gossip. Our Spanish improved rapidly for La Mechora was very helpful, and soon we were able to hold our own. Conversation among the Spanish peasants was rich and fruitful. An old man's mind was always stocked with proverbs full of everyday horse sense, such as: "If your wife asks you to jump off a roof, pray heaven it's a low one."

La Mechora's father was a delight, and we collected many of his proverbs. Like so many old countrymen in Spain his face had refined with age. Life was simple—natural work, light but palatable food, music, poems and proverbs in the evening, wine, but no drunkenness, for that was uneconomic and disgraceful.

In Murcia the rare drunks were quickly dealt with by law. They were forced to drink some horrible potion which turned them a bluish colour, so for a time they carried their shame with them. I persuaded the beautiful old man to pose and painted a little portrait. Having had the pleasure of painting him, I felt that possession would be worth more to them than to me, so I gave it to La Mechora. She was entranced and knowing that we had admired her huge old Sevillian basin she offered it to me. The design was built up of blue and green rhythms which, after intelligent diagnosis, could be pronounced "cat recumbent." The pottery was quite an inch thick. La Mechora had been bathed in it as a baby yet now she regarded it merely as a useful washtub for small effects. "I can get another the same size for a few ha'pence," she said. I refused it four times, for to refuse something three times is merely a sign of good manners. After that you really mean "No thanks," for the offer is sincere. However one day we found the basin sitting on our kitchen floor, and now it is in my studio admired by everyone.

After living for six months in Spanish villages we made up our minds to walk through the South. A tiny donkey lugged a cart filled with our sketching materials, guitars, and oddments. At first we thought that it would be profitable fun to paint small portraits on our way, but we soon learnt the low rateable value of Art versus photography. Our way took us to the homes of the cave dwellers of Andalusia. We had an introduction to the richest man there, a peasant who had inherited £40 a year. These caves are comfortable, cool in summer, warm in winter. Each dwelling has at least two square rooms carved out of rock, a fireplace, chimney and front door. The rich man's son was a gaunt consumptive youth. His mother asked if one of us could paint his portrait. I offered to do so, and to my surprise she hurried me outside into the lean-to pigsty. Apparently she wished for privacy in order to do a bit of bargaining. I assured her that I would do it for nothing. Her face fell. Surely in that case it could have no value. She really longed for a photo. I felt crestfallen; while the pig looked interested. However, I set to work and painted a tiny portrait by the light of the open door. The consumptive was satisfied but his mother looked pointedly at our cameras, so Jan took a photograph of the whole scene and we sent along a print later.

Spanish innkeepers are a race apart. To obtain one of their rooms is not a mere matter of enquiring whether there is one vacant and how much it costs and then striking your bargain, but a lengthy procedure that is almost ceremonial. You must arrive long before dusk, settle yourself in the general room and order penny glasses of wine, until the innkeeper deigns to enquire who you are, where you are going, where you have come from, etc. This you hope will lead to the *offer* of a room. It was often a lengthy catechism that generally ended with: "What! husband and wife! We thought you were brother and sister, for you get on so well together." Once, during that tramp with our donkey, we startled the host of a lonely mountain inn, called *La Tonta* (The Foolish Woman) by arriving at nine o'clock in the middle of a thunderstorm, wet through and all three of us tired out. Spanish inn-keepers are not to be bounced like that. This time we were turned away, for they feared us and swore that this was not an inn. It, they said, was just around the bend. So into the wet we sadly turned with the donkey. He knew a good inn by its smell and moaned with disappointment. Off we trudged wondering how this could end. But the innkeeper had a heart and she sent her little boy after us. He said, "The inn that mother *says* is round the bend is shut today. You can stay here." Our previous misery was worth the joy we felt, and there we stayed for several days. I painted little portraits of her two small daughters and presented them. "Now that *is* kind," she said—and in gratitude refused to charge us for the morning's coffee.

Often in many a Spanish market place could be seen some journeyman artists standing on their colour boxes with handsome easels fitted with acetylene lights for evening sessions. They seemed to have learnt by heart a set of pictures which could be knocked off quite cleverly in about twenty minutes. During the performance the artist's wife or partner busied herself distributing raffle tickets—three chances for a ha'penny.

One day in a muleteer's sixpenny dining place we were befriended by a shoemaker who had been asked to leave his native village. His story was that he was so superior to the only other shoemaker that he was asked to move out in order to give the the other man a chance. We hid our incredulity. "If you are as capable as from your faces I would judge you to be," he said,

"I would suggest that you do paintings in the market place and I will collect the money." An amusing proposition, thought we, but our shrewd suspicion was that he would move elsewhere with all the ha'pence—without being asked. Still, it is a pity that we were too prudent to do it. The things one has never had the courage to do have a way of haunting one in later life.

Sometimes the artist traveller meets with unexpected disappointments. The Lapps have from our point of view unusual and very interesting faces with their high cheekbones and general shortness. As usual, I vowed I would draw everybody who consented to pose. Unfortunately many years before they had been converted from Paganism to a form of Christianity, Calvinistic in severity. As their art and music had been the outcome of pagan rites, the Lestidians who converted them put a firm foot down on music and any form of imitative drawing. Like the Moslems, the Lapps were allowed to pose for nobody. But occasionally a Lapp might giggle, saying, "Well, for sure it's a sin, but I'll let myself be drawn—for it's such a pleasant little sin."

There are many other advantages enjoyed by painters. They are not necessarily searching for man-made beauty, such as magnificent buildings, nor do they crave for grandiose scenery. A painter looks for subjects that he can recreate into pictures. He wants something that touches a chord to which he reacts with an excited desire to fashion something that he intends to be beautiful . He may even get what he wants out of a backyard while repudiating Alpine glories or the Grand Canyon of Colorado. You might then say "Why go abroad?" But the new and strange has a power to thrill. Coming back to his own country a painter sees more clearly not only the characteristics but the light of his own land. Those who live and paint in England alone, to my mind, do not see that the English countryside is lighter, at any rate, than any pigment, although it may not be so luminous as southern countries. Compared with the sky white paint is darker. However, that subject could be debated at length.

Another point is that while travelling we painters often discover the things that are destined to thrill us more than anything we had heretofore seen. On looking back I remember many thrills. Perhaps my favourite subjects are white and colour-washed villages writhing their way like snakes up hills. I first saw them in France, later in Portugal. Engineers or roadmakers might possibly explain to us why these serpentine tracks were laid up one hill, down another, in so decorative a fashion. Anyway, to a painter they present a perfect set of rhythms.

The whimsical side of one's nature may respond to the sight in Albania of little haystacks looking like fat tassels hanging on trees, just high enough to elude marauding goats or mules. In the Tyrol there were farms with ramps from ground to attics where the hay was kept all winter and little shrines stood by the roadside, weatherproof with their tiny pent-house roofs.

Among other thrills were Portuguese boats with fascinating prows like huge birds—Swedish girls sitting on roofs and calling the cattle by blowing through four-foot horns—Swedish wooden churches with their steeples standing demurely by their sides— the farm *bonarden*, decorations painted on material which is kept rolled up and only brought out for festival seasons.

To see clouds beneath one, from a mountain top, can stir one; so can the twinkling lights of an approaching boat in the blue John mine of Castleton ; or a herd of reindeer on trek in Lapland. There was much to be said too for the gay many-coloured little houses built on stilts in the Lofoten Isles, which we visited in a cargo boat which carried six grumbling baby polar bears in packing cases. I remember, still with pleasure, the long strands of vegetation hanging from trees in South Carolina forests. Also the housetops of the English Black Country seen from the high railway route are hard to beat. Pittsburg dimly realized through sinister shapes of smoke can never be forgotten. The grandiose sham façades in the Hollywood studios rendered strangely tragic and picturesque with their leaning supports, poles, planks, bits of driftwood, had some of the grim beauty of bombed London.

All these had to us an element of the surprise that is some-times the "open sesame" to a real æsthetic thrill. As I am look-ing upon foreign travel as occupying only a section of one's life these surprises are healthy and not merely a superficial stimulant.

Actually, one of the biggest visual thrills I have experienced was when riding through the Balkan Mountains, both in Jugoslavia and Albania. Towards dusk we often descended towards some village, chiefly inhabited by Moslems. Standing on the tall minarets the priests intoned the evening muezzin. This was always looked upon by all the neighbouring crows as their bedtime signal. Up they rose from their daily labour of scavenging the streets, round and round the singing priest they whirled, adding their raucous accompaniment of caws. Directly he stopped, off they went to roost in the woods beyond the village. At dawn they answered what they took to be the priest's call, went through the same manoeuvres and plunged down to breakfast. Somehow, the dignified minaret, silhouetted against the copper sky, the whirling curves of the crows above the clustering roofs of the houses below, gave a complete feeling of peace and inevitability.

Something so expressive, especially of eventide, I have never experienced elsewhere.

Although art, music and poetry take a large place in the lives of the more primitive mountaineers all over Europe, portrait or landscape draughtsmanship is so rare that to them it seems like magic. After working all day mountain peasants spend their evenings singing home-made poetry. Round the fires built on their floors Balkan fathers and sons will sing to the buzzing accompaniment of the guzlar poems sometimes composed on the spot. In Serbia during the 1914 war our hospital patients often amused themselves by playing flute-like instruments, blowing and humming simultaneously—a baffling bit of technique but rather fascinating. Art is evident in their skill with colour harmonies. On Sundays, far down in the villages the old women form committee meetings outside the churches to judge the colour schemes and technique of any woven or knitted work brought by young girls from the mountains. "That," they may say, "can be copied by anybody." Or they will turn down a clumsy colour scheme saying, "Never to be copied."

Through constant trial and little error they have learned to combine the brightest contrary colours and achieve rich colour harmonies, a far more difficult and interesting task than our gentle interweaving of pastel colours. They have never heard the word "art" yet these unlettered people stand high among those who instead of crushing have developed the touch of the artist included in nearly everybody's make-up.

In 1915 when leading a party of English hospital orderlies out of Serbia in order to escape from the oncoming German army, we often had to camp by the roadside, sleeping sometimes in the open for we had been obliged to throw away our cumbersome tents. A kindly innkeeper who had no room for us, as even his floors were covered with refugees, let us rest while enquiries were being made as to whether a neighbouring cottage could put us up. On his wall we saw some large bits of paper decorated in a manner that nowadays would remind one roughly of Paul Klee. We admired them. "Oh, those," he said. "I do that to pass the time on winter evenings. Could I sell them? Well, I couldn't let them go for less than 2*d*. each. You see the paper cost me a penny a sheet." Needless to say we bought some. To him and to most simple people the desire to decorate was natural.

Yet when the Serbs saw us drawing people they would cry, "Look, they are *writing* us."

Before riding through the Albanian mountains I vowed that, no matter how tired, I would draw every Albanian we met, although after riding for some thirteen hours along bridle paths flanked mostly by precipices, one might have preferred to relax. Espying the arrival of strangers our host-to-be (usually a heavily moustached old grandfather) always emerged from his chimney-less home, bowed, and often pressing his heart, offered us hospitality, saying to Jan, "Are you a man?" (Their equivalent for "How do you do.") They gave us of their best, but there were no beds, no chairs and the foot-high table was brought in for meals only. Round it, cross-legged on the floor, we sat, each with a section of the table napkin on his knee. This napkin, like a roller towel, had no beginning and no end. It was hand-woven, gay in colour and just large enough to go round the table, lying on our knees. When the old patriarch wished to wipe his honourably long moustache the tug communicated itself to his neighbours and in a trice the whole assembly lifted the napkin and wiped.

Afterwards I always drew the chief man and his sons. With Christians there was no difficulty, yet the Moslems in the mountains were not very strict. The women went about the villages unveiled and I even once drew a Moslem priest with his rather coy consent. Drawing heads after a long day's ride was no joke, especially as the laws of good breeding in Albania demand that you must never show any signs of fatigue or hunger.

On our trek we were treated as medicine men, able to cure anything. The mountaineers have a trained power of projecting their voices so that messages can be shouted from mountain to mountain. The news was soon transported on the air that marvellous strangers with a bag of cure-alls were riding through. Like the spokes of a wheel, little parties of sufferers slowly converged daily to our next halt. The waiting around reminded us of the outpatients' department of Sir James Berry's war hospital unit in Vrnjatchka Banja, Serbia. Having assisted and interpreted there for Dr. Helen Boyle I could sometimes be of use.

In one far away eyrie the family had many ailments—doctors and hospitals were unobtainable. After our hospital experiences in Serbia during the 1914 war I could give each sufferer a little advice, mostly horse sense. We had aspirin, cascara, linseed, liquorice and chlorodyne lozenges, and an ointment for the itch (this we had been advised to take in case of mishap). Afterwards I drew them all. The handsomest and most intelligent of them was deaf and dumb; yet he appeared to lip-read or to guess my meaning and by signs and queer sounds he clarified my advice for the others. Suddenly he clasped my face and scraped it with his stubby unshaven cheeks. I was much taken aback though Jan grinned. Apparently this was a great honour, for he was inaugurating me as a blood brother, a compliment never paid to women—barring those who had forsworn womanhood, taken to trousers and men's work, thus being treated with the respect due to men.

One day we were accosted by several turbanned men, picturesque in their thick white handwoven trousers cut to the shape of the leg, and voluminous coloured silk belts circling their waists. One man had the sneering allure of a lounge lizard. He explained that he had shot his foot accidentally some months before. Could we look at it? Many rags were unrolled and at the sight of his foot I was horrified and said, "You simply *must* see a doctor." "How can I hop down the hills for six days to reach the nearest village?" said he. I did what I could, gave what advice I could and asked if I might draw his portrait; and we moved on. That evening we were put up by a charming old monk who had a gift for compiling wonderful sauces and apparently he was known throughout the mountains for his power of brewing and administering simples for the sick. That night the chief of police, a soldierly looking man, was also a passing guest. We told them about the wounded man, and I showed the drawing. "Why, that's Vuk (Wolf), the brigand," they cried slapping their thighs. He was one of the worst murderers in the the mountains. "Told you he shot himself, did he?" said the policeman. "I shot him, and with this." Dramatically he flung an old pistol on the table. Vuk's house had been burnt by order, but he could still be at large, they explained, because the government had changed.

Next day the monk's customary crowd of outpatients turned up, including the brigand who had apparently managed to hop there. Jan took a group photograph, including monk, chief of police, the armed soldier who accompanied us by order of the government, myself, a dragoman, out-patients and the brigand, who outstripped everyone in beauty.

Those daily journeys were generally gay. Each old chieftain who gave us hospitality would send all his sons to accompany us for the next day's journey in order to guard both the soldier and ourselves. They had all taken a blood-feud vow, called a *besa*, that they would kill some male relative of any scoundrel who molested us. "But really, *you* are protecting the lot of us," they said to me. As it is the worst of bad form to kill any man in the presence of a woman, it seems that my sex was a great comfort to our protectors. If we came across a solitary man, slogging along the narrow path, our escort would joyously stop him, saying I had made a vow to draw everybody, so for the first time in his life he would be a portrait model. In some places after a night's rest I had a patient queue of young men anxiously waiting to be drawn.

One of the handsomest of my models was a young murderer whose father was putting us up for the night. We were travelling with the young *juge de paix* in charge of the case, who was to try him after the supper courteously offered us by his father. The murderer, having greeted us with a limp hand shake, acted as butler. After our meal the testimony of witnesses was taken and he was committed for the next assizes.

Queer were the people we met and strange the impression some of them made on us. It is, however, the visual experiences of travel that are the most profound, not only for the artist, but for any who merit the name of travellers. Some of those that have impressed me most have had nothing to do with scenery or with the things in which man has consciously found his art, but were little unexpected things.

Once in Serbia, during the 1914 war, when we worked as V.A.D. and orderly in a hospital intended chiefly for soldiers, but to which out-patients flocked especially during the outbreak of typhus, a lovely thirteen-year-old orphan child serving the owners of a neighbouring farm, was sent to us suffering from a violent fever. Eventually she was sent home apparently cured, but within a short time there came an urgent appeal to go and collect her. I was sent with a man and two oxen slowly drawing one of those carts that look like a bunch of planks bound together. She was alone in a dirty room inhabited by a score of hens. There she lay flushed with an incredible temperature, on a wooden chest covered by a gay but tattered homespun rug. I rolled her up in our clean blanket and we put her into the bottom of the cart. Slowly we meandered home. Oxen always seem to be carefully striving for a race in slowness. She was placed with another girl and during her recovery the other one asked, "Why do you call her Cinderella when her name is really Mirka?"

With great confidence I embarked, in Serbian, on the Cinderella story but came to a stop at the word "pumpkin." I just didn't know the Serbian for pumpkin. I described the thing; but still to them the story was a mystery for they had never seen a coach, a carriage or a car. The only wheeled vehicles they had ever seen were the simple straight plank farm carts. How *could* a pumpkin turn into a cart? So my story lost its point. Nevertheless they understood that Cinderella married a prince, though why he bothered about the size of her feet they couldn't imagine. Prince Alexander, afterwards the King of Serbia, had recently visited the hospital, so they knew about princes. Even now I can picture the hen-coop room, the gay little chickens matching in colour her two golden plaits, the beautiful colours of the dirty rug and the cool blue-washed walls.

During this war I considered that the best work I could do

was to fill some teaching and lecturing vacancies. The present difficulty is to prevent the twelve-year-olds from losing their childish imaginative quality, while at the same time allowing them to learn what they feel they lack in drawing and construction directly they desire it. I tried to devote an occasional lesson to encouraging the naive and charming picture-making that children so often drop as they grow older, but the results were worse than poor. The girls were bored and wouldn't bother. Then I thought of telling them stories about children I knew in our travelling days, such as the little Lapp who, admiring my unbrella, said, "What a practical rain hut you carry around." After telling them about some child and its doings, I would say, "Here are your colours. Now do me a picture about it." Immediately they were fired with that excitement which is the mother of inspiration. The place hummed with vitality. Questions about costume were asked. One child while illustrating the Cinderella story said, "Would you be mortified if I put you in the picture?" The results were grand, and I still prize them. They were full of the child genius for design and for contrasting colours. Allied to this they showed a growing knowledge of the construction and draughtsmanship for which they were craving. So my visual memory, filtering through the minds of some thirty-seven little girls, was still of value.

The power to observe and set down a face quickly is an enviable quality, not always to be found among trained artists. How often do we notice that special gift for getting a likeness enjoyed by some amateurs, while many a professional artist may achieve beautiful drawings, full of character, yet they have not caught the likeness of their subjects.

Whether travelling abroad or wandering about in one's own country, the sketcher of heads is bound to fall in with many unusual adventures. My own experiences came through a long course of sketching with a fountain pen. Realizing that over-carefulness was getting me no further, I sallied forth with a Waterman pen and attached myself to the fringe of the Hyde Park rostrum crowds. No tentative methods were possible, once the pen touched paper a statement was made. People bent over my shoulder. At first my heart beat and my hand shook. Then I thought, "Who cares, anyway?" and found that people's faces are twice as interesting when they are interested and not posing, while when heckling they were at their best. The work was so fascinating that I would stand drawing for even four hours at a stretch, walking home afterwards feeling as if my heels were creeping up my spine. At first most of the drawings were only fit for the wastepaper basket; three minutes was the maximum time possible.

"'Ave you noticed," said a soldier to me one day, "it's the long-nosed folk who stay quiet and the short-nosed folks are fidgety and walks orf?" I ran through my sketchbook—quite true. There were many finished sketches of interested looking long-nosed folk and countless snub, piquant and turn-up noses were started but the faces were unfinished. It was interesting to see how one's technique became almost as unconscious as breathing and stodginess gave way to freedom. In the Hyde Park crowds people did not seem to mind being drawn. On the whole I found that in continental cafés no one resented the attention, while in English restaurants and tea-houses one must use the greatest discretion and circumspection.

Turning from heads to animals, I found that even with animals an artist has some advantage. For one thing, he is quiet. Animals respect and fear movement. At first, when I strode into a Cornish farmyard with sketching stool, the pigs, geese, ducks, hens, all ceased living their everyday lives and became watchful and suspicious, regarding me as a potential enemy. But when I made a practice of sitting for hours, turning out innumerable scribbles, they carried out their usual barndoor dramas. Once I saw a quarrel between two goose families. A white goose had insolently pecked one of the grey gander's family. He challenged the white gander to fight. Unfortunately the white gander won. I felt it was most unfair. He jumped on to a garden roller, head erect and screeched a song of triumph. His white family stood around the conqueror, waving their heads skywards, applauding the boss. Meanwhile the grey family lowered their heads to a horizontal position and slunk away in grieved humility. Had I moved, the whole performance would have stopped. In the Tyrol I drew goats and calves; the latter used to creep up to me, look questioningly into my eyes and then begin to chew the corners of my sketch book. I had to draw with one hand and with friendly gentleness push the calves aside with the other. In the Tyrol cows don't seem to approve of goats sharing their field. I was drawing a goat that took lovely positions. A cow came up and tried to turn out the goat. I kept pushing the cow away. She looked outraged. I'm sure she got a lump in her throat and in desperation she blew a trumpeting blast on my knee. That, of course, stopped the session.

Mules in Spain are worth painting when they are on the road. With stylish straw hats on their heads and bright coloured wool streamers on their chests, they are protected from flies and serve as first rate colourful models.

The bisons and oxen in Jugoslavia don't seem to worry about fidgety people. With minds apparently above all mundane cares, they lounge at rest in the market place, chewing the cud with know-all expressions and looking down their noses. Somehow for a draughtsman, a reclining old cow has more possibilities than the most beautiful of horses. A cat has more rhythms than a dog, and above all, a goose is worth any amount of swans. It is very difficult to gain the confidence of a frog, but a toad will soon befriend you.

The artist is, as I have said, a privileged traveller. Almost everything is grist to his mill and his art provides him with many opportunities of achieving at least in part that financial independence without which true travel is impossible.

When driving and camping through all the Eastern States of America we were possessed with the desire to visit a show boat. We even had a letter of introduction to the captain of one for which we searched in vain. At last we heard from some retired actors who were running a hot-dog pull-up, that the Show Boat had gone far out of our reach, while another was only twenty miles away. So we were soon able to present our letter to the wrong captain, who smiled amiably saying, "I guess I'll serve as well." He asked us to camp in a nearby field and have our meals on board for a few days. We offered to return the hospitality by doing a turn that had been suggested to us by an old millionaire barnstormer. On the stage Jan should play Spanish Flamenco music on his guitar, while I would do lightning portraits of the actors. These were easy as among them were "Uncle Sam," a Red Indian in war paint, and other exaggerated types. "My, that went over big," said the captain, offering us the job to stay with them for the season and perform daily, all found, for about £14 a week. Again we deplored the necessity for turning down such adventure. We had contracted to write a book about our worm's eye survey of the States and we had to move on.

Looking backwards even to the easy-going years before the First World War, I have tried to pick out the incidents that could only be possible when artists are in question. Many strange adventures spring to one's mind which could have happened to anybody, not necessarily an artist. The strange dishes we have had, strange people we have met, musical adventures with gypsies, some night's lodgings, bizarre and Spartan—as we said at the time "nice to look back upon."

One I might legitimately describe as we had made a special journey to a place in Dalmatia, known for its beauty, but not yet popular. There was a pleasant-looking inn just opposite the railway station, but the innkeeper would have none of us. His ideas were very hazy as to who was on whose side in the 1914 war in which he had lost two sons, and he looked upon us as enemies—after all, perhaps his sons had been in the Austrian army. A man who resembled Phil May's once-famous advertisement for Pears Soap entitled *"Since when I have used no other,"* stepped up saying he knew of an excellent inn, "The one I stay at. . . ." "I'll look after the luggage, and you'd better go with him," said Jan. We swung along the road at a good hiking pace and reached a frowsy little place kept by Moslems. The cook, unveiled (so she might have been a Christian), welcomed me into her greasy kitchen. I felt grease didn't matter. English people generally object to greasy cooking but Jan and I throve on dishes cooked with plenty of olive oil, such as Spanish rice dish, goulash and Turkish mix-ups with odd names. But when I saw the bedroom my face fell; it was awful. Still the cook was pleasant, so I engaged it and thanked "Since when etc." very gratefully for his help. On reaching the station again Jan queried, "Well?" I murmured, "We'll have an interesting night." That night was pretty bad, not so bad as some we had on our Serbian retreat, but those nights have nothing to do with Art.

To begin with we found the smell overpowering. "Wonder if it comes from outside?" said Jan. We climbed on to a high window seat. There was a narrow passage between two houses. It was being used as a pigsty. A dirty looking old sow lay smiling, with six grubby little piglets. We shut the window. The smell was no better. We opened the door. Just outside "Since when" was asleep and snoring on a table. "Could it be that?" Then we noticed that the floorboards had slits between them. We applied an electric torch. There below, with no ventilation, was a flock of hot sheep. That was the smell, and barring skunks, I defy anybody to find anything worse. There was nothing for it but to shrug our shoulders and go to bed. Even then our troubles were not over. Out came the crawlers, out came the rats which noisily gnawed the legs of our beds. Having experience, some technique and remedies in bottles, we shooed away our tormenters, but slept little, for a consumptive woman in the adjoining house coughed till dawn. Then the cocks crew and the geese expressed themselves with hideous cacophony. At breakfast time I crept apologetically into the kitchen. "We shall have to leave," I said to the cook. "This place isn't plastic." She didn't know what "plastic" meant and I can't now remember the Serbian equivalent for it, but she flung her arms round my neck and wept. "And you *were* so sympathetic," she blubbed.

I admit that such incidents may seem merely an interruption, a sordid adventure, no more. But taken in the right way, one is either beaten by or one rises above such experiences. They form the shadows of travel. To the untrained, visual shadows have no colour, yet most people will agree that feelings have a mental colour of their own. I look upon the moments of physical suffering that we have gone through as stimulants to our capacity for realizing life as a whole. Our natures demand contrast and it is good to know all sides of life.

THE QUEST FOR A BETTER LIFE
AND A BETTER SELF

Peter Freuchen

I AM a Dane. Mine is a country where, ever since ships have sailed and foreign lands been accessible, travel has been the high road to riches and adventure.

In the age of the Vikings Denmark was over-populated. Farming, mostly confined to the land near the coasts, was able to support but a small population; while fishing and hunting the large forests that covered the rest of the countryside could not provide enough to feed the growing number of mouths, and so people were forced to be off and away, outward bound in search of what they could not find at home.

The joys of travel and the chances travel gave of proving one's manhood and ability appealed to the imagination of those young Danes. Many of those who thus left their country never returned; a few because they had fallen in battle with their enemies, that is those whom they tried to deprive of their property, the others because they found life easier in foreign lands. Reports of their good fortune and success would reach their homeland and set the young lads dreaming and send the young men forth to follow in their path. So, before very long, to "go off as a Viking" had acquired almost the significance of passing an examination. It was the able ones who went, those with energy and courage, who were prepared to risk the fate that might await them: a safe return, or death perhaps, or a new life abroad. They ventured and they experienced adventure; they won fame; they created tradition.

The lazy ones stayed at home, the stupid and the pusillanimous, those in whom ambition evaporated the moment they were required to hazard anything to accomplish it. Alas! that was the beginning of my country's decline, for those stay-at-homes were our forefathers, the ancestors of those who live there today. Now, it is only in the individual that the urge to journey forth is still sufficiently strong to make him break his ties and set off, outward bound.

148

Denmark, however, is not alone in this respect. Wherever I go I come across people who want to hear about travel and far journeyings and who themselves say that they personally have always had an extraordinary desire to go to foreign countries and see strange peoples and visit distant climes. After listening to their confessions for a while, you involuntarily ask: "But then why don't you travel?" And always the answer is that one has a family, another an examination to pass, this one's mother would not allow it, that one is afraid of not being able to stand up to it, etc. There are always excuses enough and they merely show that that person's urge is but vaguely felt, or at any rate not felt so strongly as to make him indifferent to all other considerations.

Another explanation often given is that the person cannot afford it. It's only the money he lacks, so he says. Yet those who *want* to travel, who live life more intensely on a journey, never wait till they have the money in their pockets. They earn it as they go along, making travel a livelihood. There are many ways of doing that. Think of sailors, of business men, and of the host of people science sends to the outermost bounds of civilization and beyond the bourn of urban bourgeois ease. Women travel as stewardesses both on the seas and in the air, as nurses, or sec-retaries: they all have that restlessness in their bodies that is the hallmark of the true traveller and so they must be up and away.

People still do find their way to all the different parts of the world: it can only be the travel urge that drives them there, that mystical joy men find in the unknown and in the not-yet-tried. For such people a life of travel is never empty or dead. They have their dream and it keeps them young.

Many have found themselves forced to journey out into the world. Migrations have but seldom been due to mass sugges-tion, to a people's listening to tales of how beyond the frontiers within which they were born lay fortune and happiness; though in earlier times, even kings, princes and great leaders have had to lend their ears to such whispers and be up and away, taking their followers with them. Most often, however, it was the search for food or other necessities that drove people from their lands. Over-population meant that they had to struggle for their livelihood and that made them anxious to move on to other parts. To do so they often had to overcome and drive out those already in possession, who had themselves previously done the same when they occupied the lands the newcomers now wished to inhabit.

The scientists tell us that the Lapps of Northern Scandinavia once lived on the shores of the Caspian Sea. That tough little people has been constantly on the move, that is to say, in continual flight, and today they are still subjected to the pressure of farmers moving northwards into places which the Lapps had hoped to have for all time as a refuge for themselves and for their reindeer. Today, the Lapp is *right* up in the North. He can go no farther. His journey is at an end. He won happiness and enjoyed it for a few centuries. Now, his feeding grounds have shrunk and shrunk; political frontiers have set barriers athwart the path of his moves from place to place. His journeys have grown shorter and shorter. The sweeping prospect over unknown expanses that once was his alone, is so no more. The Lapp's travels were forced upon him, but each time he broke camp and moved on, he hoped that he would reach his goal, and so long as he was on the move, the prospect was bright. Now his dream is over, its light extinguished.

But the Lapps, like other travellers, can still perhaps take pleasure in movement itself and in the adventure of seeing what is new. The Jews are the most famous wanderers in the world. Some have told me that it lay in their blood to feel at home wherever they were, no matter what language was spoken around them, or whether they had come down into the plains or gone up into the mountains. But even the Jews strove for two thousand years towards the goal that they have reached now, however modest; they wanted a country of their own.

It is different with the gypsies. They journey and wander haphazard. Their mentality is that of the born artist. Be they great musicians or talented in other directions, they still delight in the vicissitudes of the road and its ever changing public. Most gypsies I have known were content with a waggon fitted out as a dwelling, with a wretched screw to pull it, and a few baskets to weave, knives or axes to grind, or fortunes to tell for their livelihood. They might even live by begging, but seldom were they thieves or dishonest. They knew, of course that dishonesty was punished with incarceration, the terror of any gypsy. They are lovers of freedom whose joy it is to be ever on the move, preferring to starve as a knife-grinder rather than to take a permanent job with a wage every week, a pension after thirty years, and never a day's excitement.

It is the excitement that drives men out on their travels, when happiness is what they are after. It makes the eternal quest for what one suspects to be there all the more tempting, because everyone harbours within him the hope of something better, though he knows not what it is. He merely knows that he could not see it there at home, where the Great Adventure came to none; that it was only in the fairy-tales of childhood, which we all would so gladly have happen to us, that the unexpected happened.

I have felt all this myself. My family were seafarers on the one side and merchants and farmers on the other. It was the lot of the seafarers that captured my imagination.

My childhood's best friend became apprenticed to a saddler, another friend became a postman, yet another went into the office of the mayor of our little town, a great stroke of luck that. Later, I saw them as self-satisfied people interested in the doings of that little town and with a great respect for each other and for themselves. Whenever I come home and look up these friends of my childhood, they look at me with gentle compassion: "We've managed better than Peter," they seem to say. "We haven't had to travel all about the world just to get our daily bread." And they are right, for they are the settled type of person on whom a Government can depend. They never long for anything revolutionary or world shaking, and one knows that they will never shake any worlds themselves.

There were others of my friends who went with me to the university. When they came down they became clergymen and magistrates, some doctors or engineers, and nearly all of them good citizens who have been a credit to their country. Nor did they suffer so badly from imagination that they were always requiring a new stimulus for it. Their lives went the way of officialdom: each time a superior died, they moved one step up. In the end they will move on and out to the cemetery and, if they have been sufficiently long in the service, their graves will be given a fine smart headstone. Some people are like that.

Others are driven out into the unknown. It is travel that lures them out. They are not all of the same kind these people. Some go out into the world to find a job. If they arrive in the right place and find one, that is the end of their travels. Such are the majority. Others journey forth so that they may come back home and show that they have achieved what they would have been unable to get for themselves had they stayed. Others again never find peace in their own minds; they always have some new goal in sight, are always setting forth again on some new journey. No sharp distinction can be drawn between these groups; they inevitably overlap. And even the stay-at-home will go with them in imagination. There is something inside the saddler that tugs at him to be up and off, but he forgets it when it is time to knock off and he washes the blacking from his fingers and sits down to his evening meal that never fails to appear on his table to the minute. Thank God for order and comfortable slippers.

And yet those whose whole life is a journey, are also happy. They know nothing else. It is because they must follow the animals they hunt that the Eskimoes in Thule, the most northerly people in the world, are continually on the move from place to place. One year they will live on Melville Bay to get bearskins for the men's trousers. At other times they must go north to hunt the narwhal whale which provides the thread with which their women sew. Or they must live for a while by the birds' breeding grounds to get birdskins for shirts, or they must winter there and catch foxes in their traps so as to have warm furs and something to trade in the shop. Always they are on the move, travelling. Early in the spring the whole tribe gathers up in the north to catch walrus on the new ice. They live in tents, in houses of snow, or in their permanent cabins in the ground during the short autumn before the ice is passable and during the dark winter night that is four months long. During that time they are unable to hunt, yet they travel far to visit each other, which visits are occasions for tremendous banquets at which they enjoy themselves listening to news from distant settlements.

No sooner have the first shafts of light from the sun forced their way in through their gut window-panes than they are all thinking of being off again on their travels: just to see lands emerging over the horizon and to feel the motion of the sledge.

Once distemper came to the Polar Eskimoes and when the epidemic was over that little isolated community had only four dogs left. That was before I ever came to Thule, but the old women would tell of how long their journeys took in those days when they had had to march and drag their own sledges.

"And we had more enjoyment out of our trips then, for we kept warm and walked and walked; now you just sit and freeze on the sledge while the dogs pull it."

That was all very well, I told the old woman who had said that, but with dogs to drive behind you travel farther than when you walk. "Does that matter?" replied old Arnaluk. "All travel is just moving on and away from a place where you have spent too many days at rest!"

With my late wife who was born up in those parts, I once went hunting musk ox in Ellesmere Land with a sledge and dogs. Another family had been across there and had had the misfortune to lose most of their dogs, and so they were having to walk behind the sledge and were making but slow progress.

We came across the tracks of their sledge at a place which they had passed a few days previously. In the snow we could see the tracks of the man and his wife, of their half-grown sons and daughters and the impressions made by the boots of children of four and six years old. I told Navarana that I hated to see small children being forced to walk all those hundreds of miles and suggested that we should turn round and go after them and offer to take some of them on our sledge.

"No," said my wife, who was both wise and good, "for don't forget that these small children are brought up from the time they are quite small to travel and to surmount difficulties. Our life here is one continual journey and it is better to begin as early as possible."

And that evening, when we had built our snow-house and the lamp was alight, she told me a tale of a real life of travel.

Once upon a time there were two married couples who were the greatest friends. Always they chose the same place in which to live and the two men always went out hunting together, while their wives helped each other with their household duties and to prepare the skins. Eventually people began to laugh at them and to tease them, saying that neither could catch a seal unless the other were with him. And so, the young couples decided to part company for a while, each going his own way.

It was agreed that they should travel round the world in

opposite directions and that they should go on till they met again.

And so they set off. Things were often difficult when they came to places where the hunting was bad, but even though they often had to stay over the summer or spend a whole winter in the one place, they never forgot that they had promised to travel on till they met the friends of their youth.

In the end they became so old that young people had to support them as they walked along, but they would not die, nor rest either, until they had met their friends.

In their hand each held the horn cup they used to dip water up from the streams when they were thirsty. Each of the men had carved two such cups out of musk ox horns, and given them to the other couple as a keepsake. Now the cups were so old and had dipped up so much water that only the handles were left So worn were those drinking cups of theirs.

Finally, they came one day to a dwelling place at which another aged couple had just arrived. And that couple too was unable to walk unaided.

And so it was that the friends met at last having been all the way round the world.

"You two seem to have aged a bit, but we have lasted well," said the one man, for he and his wife really did believe that they were still like the young couple they once had been.

"Those are words that should have been spoken from my mouth," said the other man, for he and his wife had had the same thought.

"Did you experience anything worth the telling?" asked the first man.

"Each day we hoped to experience strange things never yet seen. That kept us on our feet as we journeyed. That and the hope of reaching our goal," said the one man and so died.

The other then said that it had been the same with him. And then he too died.

And that is the end of the tale of the two aged couples who spent their lives travelling and never saw what they hoped to see.

Several years passed and then I went to Alaska. I was there with some film people from Hollywood. They were able men in their own jobs, keen to do what they had come to accomplish, and accustomed to travel in many lands.

We wintered there and our ship was frozen in by the ice and they used her as a background for the story of the film they were making. A number of the people who lived in that place where we were, were given employment with us. Among them was a friendly old soul called Billy Geisler. He was very old, so old he could remember all the famous gold rushes and he would tell us quietly and dispassionately of all the times he had run or driven behind a team so as to arrive on the scene among the first. Always he had been on the move, and he still was, even now that he was an old man, for the dream of his youth was still within him. His journey was not yet ended.

Billy had a hard time of it that winter, so we had him come aboard and give us a hand with different things. Billy was the sort of person to whom there is nothing unusual in the unexpected, so he accepted our offer with the condescension that comes from being uninterested in everything but your own plans.

One day I was standing on deck when Billy came out from shore across the ice to his work. There was a ladder from the ice up to the ship's rail and this we all used. Billy, however, who was eighty-four, went on up to the bows and clambered up by the hawse.

"What's the meaning of this, Billy? Why don't you use the ladder, it's perfectly good."

"No thanks, not for me, Captain," said Billy. "My grandfather was eighty-nine and he fell off a ladder and killed himself. My father was one hundred and three and he fell down a ladder and killed himself, so I'll keep away from ladders, thank you. I don't want to die yet!"

Billy told us of his own desire for travel. Many of us came from Hollywood and he knew those parts well. He and his father had lived in Los Angeles once, but then so many people had come there that Billy had ceased to like it and so he had moved on up north. How many people were there there then? we asked.

"Oh," said Billy, "Los Angeles was already a large town. That was in 1873 and I don't think I'll be lying if I say there must have been about a thousand people there. It all became far too ordinary, so I left."

With the coming of summer Billy disappeared. Then one day

a gold-digger came down for provisions. He had been several days on the way and he had come across Billy Geisler.

Billy was up one of the creeks washing for gold with a "Long Tom," and he was quite alone. Unfortunately he was stricken with gout and had a job to get up in the morning, so he had asked the other to bring him some liniment on his way back so that he could rub his aching old limbs and rid them of the rheumatism.

The gold-digger did not want to go back at once, and as I had to take the motor-boat up the lake, I offered to take the medicine with me and to walk up to Billy so that he should have his gout remedy as quickly as possible.

We anchored at the mouth of Swan Creek and I walked up the stream until I found my old friend. It took me several hours to reach the place, but there he was standing waist deep in the water. He had dug himself a large pool from which he shovelled up gravel and washed it. He was evidently getting a little "pay dirt" every now and again.

When I called to him, he straightened up and waded in to the rock where I stood waiting.

Billy complained of his pains which made walking difficult, but there was his little tent properly pitched and with his tools outside it. You could see that there was work being done. But all the same he was in pain, and it was all he could do to get up to me.

"Now listen," said I to Billy, "Why do you insist on slaving like this? You've done enough in your day. Surely you can come down now to the 'Pioneers Home' in Sitka and live in peace and quiet. You've not the slightest need to labour away at this."

Billy managed to force a grin on his face that was twisted with pain.

"Well, you see, Captain, I just want to wash here for four or five years to get some cash. When I've got enough to buy some machinery, I'll get going properly at a place up in Alaska that I found forty years ago. It's the best spot in all Alaska and just right for large-scale mining, gold from the roots of the grass down."

"That's all right, but what will you do with all that gold, Billy?"

"Well, you see, Captain, I had a girl back there in Connecticut. I couldn't get her then because I was poor. So I went off on my travels and I've been at it ever since. But one day I shall go back to Connecticut and show her something that will make her eyes pop out of her head. And then she may well think that Billy Geisler's good enough for her!"

I was younger then than I am now, and a bit of an arrogant fool, for I began trying to talk sense into Billy.

"Listen," I said, "You've told us that you left home in 1871, so perhaps your girl's dead by now. Either that or she's a great-great-grandmother. Anyway, she's not the same girl you left. You'd much better go to the Pioneers Home."

The moment I had said that I regretted it, for it made Billy great and me very small.

He took my medicine bottle and smashed it against the rock. He roared with anger and swore in heartfelt contempt.

"What the devil do you think? Do you imagine that I don't know it's all a dream? But it is *my* dream, and it is what I have lived on these many years and it has brought me through such bad times as none of you can even conceive. You young puppies are so damned clever. But you don't understand what it is to live alone with an idea and a dream. Get to hell out of here and mind your own business!"

With that, Billy waded back out into the stream that he had widened into a large pool so that he could dig out the gravel which he washed to get the gold he wanted for the girl he had loved in 1871. And I walked shamefacedly back to my motorboat and sailed away. I never saw Billy Geisler again.

Billy was one of those who had kept their dream. His life was decided from the moment he was unable to win his girl. He had managed to get it into his head that it was only the money he had lacked. Perhaps, deep inside of him there had been a doubt, but he had silenced it and had clung to his dream. That was why Billy had had to be continually on the move. Had he settled down anywhere, ordinary, everyday life would have grown up around him and demolished his dream.

I have met others with the same hope. As a rule, they are young men who have met with some disappointment at home. One had been unable to buy the farm that had been his father's and his father's before him; another had been refused by the girl he loved; some had been unable to get a start in life, others had just felt a longing to get abroad.

Those I am thinking of were dreamers, often people who took a delight in nature and loved plants and animals, which made them experts in many things that belong to open-air life. They had been disappointed and, as was right and reasonable, had looked for something they thought they would be able to tackle.

Some decided to go to Canada or Alaska and become trappers in the immense forests there. Behind that choice as often as not lay the books they had read in their boyhood, books in which the trapper's life is described as a series of adventures and wonderful experiences, where hardship always ends in a great junketing or is rewarded with due applause for the courage, ingenuity and kindness of heart that they all believed themselves to possess. Also, being familiar with guns and having spent many a long hour sitting waiting for birds or beasts, whiling away the time with day dreams, it had seemed merely natural that they should try to take up as a career what had occupied their free time so pleasantly. So it was that they set out for the forests of the north and became trappers.

During the months, or years, needed for their preparations, they would read all they could about the life they had chosen. Some would stick to novels, others got hold of magazines and periodicals for "hunters, fishermen and those interested in furs," all unknowing that most publications of this kind are written by people who have never seen a pine-marten, fox or otter except in a zoo. Some of these would-be wanderers went further and studied the biology of the animals in learned books and thus well equipped they made their appearance in the townships on the fringe of the great forests, ready to start.

Their aim was always to trap skins to the value of a million dollars a year. They were going to show that this could be done; you see, they knew, they had their methods.

The story of one is the story of them all. They knew exactly what provisions to buy, what sort of cabin they would build themselves, that they must catch white fish to dry for the dogs that they had to have. So, they got together their equipment and went off into the woods, filled with high hopes and with plenty of courage. They were free men, kings in the forest; now at last they would be able to live just as they had always wanted to live all these years; yes, it would suit them down to the ground.

Then the snow falls and the hunting season begins. They set their traps and snares and their life soon becomes a routine. The real trapper sets out on the Monday morning with his dog which pulls a toboggan. He himself walks the soft snow of the forest on snow shoes, a rifle slung over his shoulder and the dog following in his tracks. In the evening he camps, felling a couple of trees for his camp fire, and so he sleeps in the open until the next morning, when he is up and off again. His traps are so arranged that in his rounds he describes a great loop and returns home on the Thursday or Friday. Then the animals he has caught must hang up in the cabin to thaw, on the Saturday he skins them and stretches the skins. The Sunday is his day of rest which he can devote to rejoicing at his open-air life, pitying his friends at home and wishing they could see him. And on the Monday he starts all over again.

The upshot for them all is that at the end of the first year they come to the Trading Post and have to admit that they haven't had quite the success they had expected.

"But, of course, you have to learn first. There are certain things where you need experience. You'll see next year. I'll make you gape."

And what he has caught brings in just enough for a "holiday," that is some ten days' or a fortnight's hard drinking, after which his money is so reduced that it just suffices to fit him out for another year: ammunition, flour and tea, sugar and salt, some dried fruits and vegetables. He has to get back while it is still summer, for he must catch white fish in the river and dry it on long racks to feed his dog during the winter. That done, the long winter can begin.

Next spring he reappears out of the woods.

The trader can see at once how little he has brought.

"Yes, there were two ways of setting about it. I chose the wrong one. Not that my method isn't all right, but it has proved unsuitable for these parts. But next year, you'll see. I've got the experience and now I'm going to reap the benefit."

And so a third year passes and the result is still as meagre as ever.

"Yes, of course, there are years when there just isn't anything in the woods. We all know that. And this last winter was one of them, at least in my district. I can assure you, I'm surprised that I've caught as much as I have; for I don't believe there was one more living creature in the woods than these I got. But luckily, as we know, a bad year like that is always followed by one of the really good ones. So I shan't miss the boat again."

And so it continues. Year after year. As he goes his solitary round he has plenty of time to discover why it is he doesn't catch more than he does. Too late he realizes, as so many have before him, that the only way to make money out of skins and furs is to trade in them. He who sets the traps can make no more than suffices for his daily fare and that "holiday" of two or three weeks before he must return to his woods.

He never achieves the huge catch he expected. But his life is spent in constant movement, eternally travelling even though merely in the one forest. He has adventures and he dreams dreams. Assuredly he wins peace of mind, for I have visited such trappers in their cabin and know that that is so. Calm, friendly people they are, men of few words. They are glad to see a strange face, but never seek one out for themselves. And always they have their day dreams. What they think about, I don't know. But perhaps by travelling out and away from the place of their birth they have developed into truly "decent" people and have acquired real peace of mind.

I came once to a trading post up in Canada where people were talking about a trapper who hadn't been seen for a couple of years. At first they had thought that he had moved farther east and so was trading at another post, but when they got in communication with it he hadn't been heard of there. Another year passed, and then the matter was reported to the Royal Mounted Police, the finest force of its kind in the world. A patrol went out to look for the man. They found his cabin in ruins, his bones were scattered all over the place and had been gnawed by foxes and gluttons. That has been the fate of many who have disappeared in the deep forests. No one heard of their journey's ending, but it may well be that their travels brought them to their goal and that they found peace with themselves.

You must not confuse these men whose desire is to get away from all others, with the ordinary emigrant, the person who moves with his family to America, Australia, or some other country, just to get away from the "restrictions" of life at home.

That was an expression we often heard in Denmark when I was young. These "restrictions" were vague and indefinite, but a thing to which we could not submit. And it was always the best who went away. I can remember how, when I was a child, agents from the shipping lines or railway companies in U.S.A. and Canada used to go round the country districts. They would tell tales of the huge fortunes that could be made, of how there were new towns growing up over there, and that whoever went could not fail to share in the growing prosperity. These men appealed to the imaginations of the young people and it was those who were the most daring whom they won over. Plenty of young men and girls decided to break away and go.

It was often difficult for them to collect together the necessary money for the journey. I can remember many who spent years scraping every penny together. They spent nothing on amusements, never went to the fairs or markets in the towns, never came to the pigeon-shooting or to the cattle-shows, but put their money in the bank. And one fine day they would leave.

Later, I used to come across them out in the prairie. Many of them well-to-do, others had had nothing but toil and struggle, from which only their children would benefit. They, who had left home and country to make a better life for themselves, would have their proud hopes fulfilled at least for their children. I have seen old men who were rusted and bowed, and their wives too were marked to show that they had in truth borne their share of all that labour.

Yes, I remember a young couple from my boyhood days. A fine couple they were and so confident that they would get on. They saved up for three years there at home in our parish. I remember how they would sit together in the servants' hall poring over their savings books, and how they gathered together their kit for the journey. When one of them, as though it were his greatest task in life—which perhaps it was—carpentered two wooden chests and covered them with yellow wax-cloth fixed with brass-headed nails arranged in the shape of their monograms, we all came and admired the masterpiece. An old cow-man who was my hero and a man whose word carried great weight in the village because he could show a huge scar from a sabre cut dealt him in the 1864 war, gave the young emigrant a few words of warning.

"Those chests will catch the eyes of the Indians and robbers. They're the first thing they'll pull off the post-waggon."

Those mystical words and the fatal significance behind them gave me a deal to think about.

Some fifty years later I met the two again. They were both aged and looked quite different from what they would have had they lived in Denmark. The fierce summer heats had dried them up, and hard work had bowed them. They talked about the market-town at home, the cattle shows and the old people in the parish most of whom were then dead. The two chests had long since been broken up and burned.

They had never had enough money to be able to afford a trip home to see their families. And, besides, they had given way to the same temptation as so many others, and in their letters painted rather too rosy a picture of their life and circumstances. But at least they had had the satisfaction that their one son was still farming the land they had brought under cultivation; one daughter was a doctor, and two other children were in good positions but so far away that their parents had not seen them for many years.

Whether those two got anything out of going abroad is an open question. They themselves would say that they had achieved that at which they had aimed, but one must always remember that ideals and goals are constantly changing. They were happy after their own fashion and in all probability had never realized how the fires of their youth had been gradually extinguished by their struggle to tame the land for the benefit of their offspring.

I have met many emigrants and seen so many of the different lives that have been their lot, but the truth of the matter is that once they had reached their destination they stopped travelling just as effectively as though they had gone back home.

There are individuals who retain the feeling of being on a journey. I have come across many of them, too. The majority stint and save to be able to travel back and visit their family. As a rule such a trip is a disappointment.

The emigrants, of course, just save enough up for the fare. At home, they say to themselves: "We can stay with nephews and with brothers and sisters. We know so many who have been missing us all these many years, for haven't they said so often in their letters." Then home sickness makes them set out a little before they really should, but all the same they buy their tickets and home they go.

And so the news reaches Denmark that at last they are on their way: "The rich uncle from America is coming." And the nephews and others buy tickets to Copenhagen to go and meet him. Not return tickets, of course, for uncle can pay the fare home, and also for the hotel and all the rest of it. Money means nothing to him.

It's not that they are all intending to sponge on the returning relative, but they just assume that he can buy a pair of new horses, pay off a mortgage, or have a new roof put on the house without its affecting his pocket in the least. Gradually both parties discover that things aren't at all as they had imagined, and when the trip is over, the emigrant is the poorer by a dream. He had dreamed of that trip home, and found happiness in doing so. But the whole trip lacked any foundation and now he does not rightly know why he went where he did, or why he did what he has done, or what his aim was when he first left home.

However, emigration can scarcely be called "travel," or at most only until one has made up one's mind where one can live and has settled down in the new community. The day that happens there is an end to travelling, and it is only resumed when the emigrant makes the trip back home either for good or on a visit to show his relations how right he had been to leave home. On these trips many discover that the "restrictions" of conditions at home could have been overcome If they had but put as much hard work into doing so, as they did into the prairie, they would no doubt have achieved the same.

And then there are the eternal wanderers. Are they happy? Those who travelled much between the two world wars will remember the desperate young Germans who could never settle anywhere. These were young people born during or just before the First World War. During the four years of blockade when Germany was on short commons they were kept alive with "ersatz" foods of all kinds. I don't know whether it was lack of vitamins, or just that they didn't get the right stuff, but whatever it was that generation was neurasthenic from childhood. They were thin and looked undernourished, and either need or unconscious restlessness had driven them from their country. I came across them in many places in South America, I met them in Alaska, in New York, everywhere you would find these poor wretches always travelling and taking small jobs of any kind but never staying long at anything. As workers they were not conscientious, and they were always having to be off again.

They just travelled on and on towards a goal without knowing what it was, and always they died young. They are of little interest to us here, because from one point of view they were travellers by necessity, forced to journey by their troubled minds.

Is travel a specific for that? Yes, there are perhaps many who feel a certain pleasure in moving, or being moved, from place to place. You can see many queer people travelling and what their quest is, is usually difficult to discover.

Economic conditions have changed greatly all over the world, but there once existed a certain class of Englishman who travelled without any obvious motive, at least as far as others could see. I have met them, too, all over the world, both men and women. As a rule they were tall and thin. They were always most pleasant to those with whom they had to deal, and, although there was a certain contemptuousness in their manner none could take offence at it, for it was really no more than their way of saying that any place which could not provide them with their eggs and bacon in the morning, just as they were accustomed to have them in England, was to a certain extent uncivilized. They were no doubt in search of something, but now you will meet them no more.

Some years ago a French count went on an expedition to the north coast of East Greenland. He told his polar skipper to make for the most northerly bit of coast possible and there they wintered. He had no dealings with any of the crew and himself was never once ashore or even on the ice. He spent the entire winter in his cabin playing patience. He had people to wait on him; he was kind and pleasant, seldom seen and never had much to say. His patience cards engrossed him.

What he wanted up there, no one has any idea. For him the pleasure in his travels consisted in playing patience while wintering in the Arctic. A queer man! Was it delight in travel, or an attempt to experience something and so acquire knowledge of the world?

I don't know.

Personally, I have spent my life travelling. I began before I went to Copenhagen University. I suppose I was born with the urge to tackle the new and untried.

I had noticed early in life that those who had spent a good many years abroad had a certain advantage over us others. It was as though they could see the outlines or main features of a person behind his many small details.

I heard a bit of gossip and talk in our village at home: tales of others' little failings and interest in their private lives and alert watchfulness that none overstepped what in that part of the world was the accepted behaviour. Those who had been abroad overlooked that sort of thing. They knew that you could have different table manners and still be a decent person. They understood that even though you dressed quite differently from others, it was still no proof of mental deficiency, nor even meant that you were impudently contemptuous of your fellows. And those people had my sympathy. Since then I have learned that those who take a narrow interest in their neighbours are often charitable and helpful in both small things and big. Now I often feel uncomfortable when I find myself driving past thousands of my fellow beings and realize that I am indifferent to how they are faring. However, I went off on my travels. My first expedition to the polar region taught me that I was of the right type, that the life there suited my temperament. To leave that and go home and to the university seemed far too tame, for I was neither clever enough, nor sufficiently imaginative to find in books and studies the great adventures my heart desired. Instead, I went off again and I have never regretted it since.

Chance took me to the most northerly inhabited place in the world, and there I settled down. I married into the tribe and became a polar Eskimo myself, for—that was during the First World War—I was alone up there and was forced to live in the old-fashioned Eskimo manner. A harpoon and a spear were the weapons with which we hunted; we travelled from place to place and we were happy in our lives. In the first place I had the great luck to be with Dr. Knud Rasmussen, a man who has known how to combine the superior cleverness of the white man with the Eskimo's ability to shift for himself. We were young and poor, so we had no goods to sell, in fact we didn't even have provisions or equipment. But we got them. We travelled up and down that tremendous coast-line following our game; we undertook trips of a length that none before us had covered with dogs and the same equipment. We lived by hunting, and we crossed the Greenland ice cap at a speed that none before us or since has been able to equal with a dog-team. That was a life of travel and a carefree life as well. My wife, Navarana, was the finest person I have ever met; with no other qualifications but her understanding of herself and her fellows, and her intimacy with nature, she helped me during the eleven years we were married, as no other wife has ever helped her husband. She taught me the fundamentals of travel so well that although I learned them under those special conditions, I have been able to base all my other travels on them, wherever I have been. She taught me the joys of being in a new place every day. We saw a promontory ahead of us, we had no idea what lay behind it. There was adventure and excitement in that, and it never left me.

Navarana died whilst we were on a trip. Our children were both born whilst we were travelling. Travelling became my life. But it was only later that I understood the danger there was in that. I had believed that mine was an honest and an entirely conscious desire to get away from civilization with its —for me—too circumscribed regulation of everything and its predetermined methods for every one of our actions. Yet that civilization, I discovered, was after all the result of the experience of generations, and every man I have come across who had done as I did, began at once to introduce just those things he himself had abandoned.

I myself taught "my" Eskimoes. I introduced new instruments and tools, I sold them things to make daily life easier. In other words, the primitive forms of living by which I felt attracted were the very things that I immediately set about reforming. Of course, I never thought out properly what I was aiming at, but it can only have been to get life in North Greenland to resemble that of Europe. And it was from just that that I was trying to get away.

Now, there is this great difference between life, that is to say travel in North Greenland and life in Europe, that up there your "job" is at the same time a struggle merely to maintain life. When things are like that, life can't be dull. If you slacken off, if you take things too easily, it won't be long before you are a dead man. There is no need to say that excitement and absorption in what you are doing are never absent from your travels. And up there your whole life is travel.

But there were many other dangers in living among primitive people. Remember that I was alone up there, the only white man, and being white I knew a little more about many things than any of the others. I was, besides, the possessor of a number of commodities that were greatly desired. Every year, except during the war or when the ice would not let them through, ships would bring me things that for the Eskimo were treasures of hitherto unimagined worth. That gave me an exceptional position and it lent weight to my words. Because of that they listened to me, and because of that my every wish was fulfilled, my requests were law.

Possibly I am a person of weak character, in any case I succumbed to that, and when I came home to Denmark after spending ten years in Thule, I was first astounded, then filled with righteous anger, when anyone even began to contradict me. I had certainly not been accustomed to that. Soon, however, I was forced to accept the possibility that not everything I said was right. That went a long way towards breaking me in.

Life in the arctic regions, "far from the madding crowd," is not without its dangers. Many people suppose that the period of darkness is burdensome to people there, especially to whites. I have never felt that, because I always had plenty to do. The worst thing about the Arctic is its monotony. It provides excitement and novelty of new conditions for a few years, but then things begin to repeat themselves. It is not easy to learn to drive a dog sledge, but even that is a thing that can only produce a certain number of situations and when you have been through them all, there comes repetition and that gradually makes you more and more sure of yourself, till you begin to feel the lack of novelty even here. Walruses, polar bears and seals are big animals to hunt. They can be dangerous and at any rate have acquired a certain notoriety, but they do not have large brains and their

ability to think is restricted. They know only a certain number
of tricks, and when you have seen these and know them, the
hunting of them calls for little more than the physical effort involved. It can become monotonous and those who cannot bear
a little monotony ought to go home in their first year. For them
polar life will not be the right one, if only because it is a wandering life and not everyone is born to that.

And yet it can completely fill your mind, become part of your
very nature. I realized that when I thought that I had lost it
all. That was when I had the bad luck to become buried under
the snow during a snow storm. When I had dug myself out one
foot was frozen and later had to be amputated.

I was more unhappy then than I ever have been in my life.
I thought that that was the end to all my travels.

I was so distressed and beside myself that I began to write
novels. My great worry was that all my experiences would go
for nothing. The great travels I had planned could never be carried out, or so I thought. And that was why I took up writing.
I knew that no one except the specialist can be bothered to read
tedious travel journals; but I knew too that if you put real
travel experiences into novels, the reader can feel whether they
are genuine or not. The reader is sufficiently sensitive and per-
spicacious to do that. He will notice at once when a novel about
the backwoods has been written by a country schoolmistress
who has never been abroad. So, I gathered together all my experiences and all that I had seen and heard and I put them into
novels which have had a good sale all over the world.

And then I discovered that a man who only lacks one foot
can travel just as well as anyone else, provided he himself wants
to. Since then I have done long and arduous trips. I have lived
to see new ways in which man lives his life; I have known the
joys of being able to set off outward bound, and of coming back
again.

The time came when my books had sold sufficiently for me to
go on writing, so that I was able to combine both forms of excitement. Thus, I became both traveller and author, and I
daily feel how close to each other are these two forms of
emotion.

Through this I have been brought into contact with numbers
of people. For many years I had lived with very, very few,

knowing exactly what they would say to me and exactly what I would say to them. The contrast of seeing and being able to talk with many was so great and wonderful that it made me discover the charm of contrast. That is why I go out on my travels and come home again. I live my travels over again in my lectures, articles and books. Life has arranged itself rather wonderfully for me.

Being all made so differently, as we are, what possibility is there of arriving at a formula for travel and for the pleasures and delights man can get out of it? Very slight, I am afraid.

When I lived in Greenland my best friend from my student days was my "neighbour" for several years. He was doctor in a district some five hundred miles from Thule, and each winter I went down and visited him. He himself drove round seeing his patients and hunting bear, and he loved the life.

After that he took a practice in Denmark. He lived in the country and visited his patients in a motor car. Not even he came across anything very new. He had been too long at it and life was just a succession of repetitions. It was a godsend to him when during the war he was able to help English parachutists and hide them from the Germans, and to take part in the underground struggle against the Nazis. But, before that, he had been feeling the need of change and variety, and he had to get out and away.

So, one fine day, he called in another doctor to replace him. He himself took a job as a ship's doctor and there he was outward bound. He was round in the tropics, out East, and he experienced all the joys that a bath in new worlds always is for those who are wide-awake. Not everybody has the courage to do what he did; nor the strength of character to realize that there are things more important than doing what others can also do and equally well.

But, to travel in search of happiness, is there anything out of the ordinary in that? I don't think so, nor that those who cannot help such travelling come to misfortune by it. And this makes me think of that huge section of mankind that travels in thought, those who read the tremendous travel literature that exists in all languages. What do they experience? Personally, I can't say, for when I have read such books, it has always been as the professional traveller. For me they were reference books,

books I needed in making my preparations and to learn of contrasts.

Now, it is a lamentable thing that so many—ah, how many— of the great travellers are such bad writers. Their imagination led them into the great fields for travel, but it did not always put a pen in their hands. You can often see how they have set about their writing with a certain reluctance, at any rate without inspiration. The result is a collection of dry facts that the reader must himself clothe with flesh and blood before he can get anything out of them. And he does it. It is unbelievable how well people travel in armchairs. Perhaps they come to the land of happiness while they are about it, but then it is such a short time before dinner is ready or they must go to bed and leave off. A deal of imagination is required of these people, for when a book is dry their personal contribution is quite different from what is required of them when an author has the talent to make a situation real and to describe its background and setting.

The armchair-traveller has at least the advantage that he is not disgruntled with the life, government or cooking of his home. He only knows that he can well imagine himself going off travelling, but he just can't bring himself to incur the trouble of breaking up, nor does he dare risk such a leap into the dark, for he is not the type to risk his own person. All his dashing about is done in imagination. There are many like that.

Let me name some of the great travellers who were also inspired writers: Fridtjof Nansen, the famous Norwegian polar explorer, Knud Rasmussen, the great Danish student of the Eskimoes, Stanley and Livingstone from Africa, Humbolt from South America; yes, there really have been many whose writings could capture the imagination. This is not the place to discuss whether they have kept people from travelling or have invited them to do so. That, too, depends on whether their readers feel the urge to emulate or surpass them, or merely come to realize that the joys they themselves are seeking can be found in other parts of the world, and through that they escape from the tedium of their lives in which there is no excitement. We humans differ, if in nothing else, at least in this that we have the strangest conceptions of how one can best and easiest live happily.

I once had a young secretary. He was quick and efficient. Then I went off on one of my trips and he took a job in an office, and I didn't see him for several years. When I returned home the young man came to see me. He wanted to borrow some money. "What do you want it for?" I asked.

It appeared that he had a mighty thirst for adventure and he badly wanted to travel. He had been offered a job in an office in Buenos Aires.

I asked him whether he thought he would find more adventure working in an office in Buenos Aires than in an office in Copenhagen, and his reply was: "Well, at any rate they speak Spanish!"

In Denmark we are rather far away from Spanish-speaking peoples, but one's boyhood's literature with its pirates and Indians and pioneers in the virgin forest always speaks "Spanish," so that young clerk felt that that in itself should be enough to give romance and mysticism to his new surroundings. He got his money and he overcame his family's tears and lamentations. Then I had another visit from him to warn me of the impending call of some relatives who intended to come and curse me for helping him and generally for giving him the urge to travel in the first place.

I came across him later in the Argentine. He was not living a life of great adventure, for he was working in a dairy, but he was satisfied and his pleasure lay in writing home and portraying his life out there as full of dangers and privations. He figured in these letters as a hero, the unvanquished victor of countless battles with brigands, cattle-thieves and fearsome beasts. He, I am sure, had achieved happiness.

Later on he will quieten down, his ideals and ambitions will change, but he will still be able to surround himself with a mystic glow in the eyes of his friends and relatives at home. And herein lay much of his happiness, that he wanted to go on being the great man in the eyes of his people at home.

Yes, but that is in no way different from what you can find in circles much higher and among those much more famous than he. I have met Danish and Norwegian artists who had achieved great success abroad, singers, actors, authors and others. They had their public in America or elsewhere about the wide world, but their real happiness lay in having it known in dear little Denmark or Norway. They dearly loved a mention in a Copenhagen or Oslo paper, but any report of a fiasco in the same place would make them fly into a rage. That shows how impossible it is to travel away from oneself and one's origins. That is why emigrants are never entirely happy, as long as they can remember the joys of childhood in their home, the friends and spirit of their youth in the land they have left.

It is only physical travel that can fully absorb people, for while journeying they forget what it is from which they are fleeing. Some feel indignant at the wickedness of people in the place where they are living, forgetting that people's reactions are often the result of their own clumsy behaviour—often they leave home and go abroad because their business is not doing so well, or because their harvest was worse than their neighbour's. It is so easy to find excuses, but what is usually overlooked is that the person whose shop has the most custom, or who harvests the best crops, is the one who in everyday language is the "most capable."

For failure there is always an explanation to be found. In this man's inventiveness is enormous. He can go on and on finding reasons just why things went wrong, but he who is unlucky once, twice or ten times, or always, the world calls incompetent. Yet perhaps a person who has once been unsuccessful may find it difficult to make his neighbours realize that he is turning over a new leaf. The mere accustoming of one's immediate fellows to the idea that henceforward things are going to be different can cost all too much effort. The answer is to get away, away from those things and persons which are making life difficult and keeping you back, right away to new conditions where you will be able to make good. However, it is only the few who do that. You always take your self with you however far you go; you may be outward bound, but your brain and body go with you. What really matters is to hit on a part of the world where your personal qualities are just those which are in demand. Do that, and you are assured of success, for things will turn out as you have hoped.

Yes, travelling helps one to forget. There was a man in Thule whose three small children were playing a game he himself had played innumerable times when he was a child, for his father had taught him it. The game was to slide down a steep slope of snow on a sealskin. The real excitement came at the bottom of the slope when the one who was guiding had to turn to one side, for below was roaring water. There was a violent tide-race right at the foot of the mountain there, where the sea was never covered with ice, and that was what made it so exciting and alluring. The boy was steering for the two small girls and what happened no one knows. All three disappeared into the roaring sea right in the middle of winter. The parents heard a shriek and that was the last sign of life from them. Their bodies were never found.

After that, Qolugtanguaq journeyed south down to the civilized Greenlanders. He travelled alone, just with his dogs, making for the bad hunting grounds for he wanted a spell of difficult conditions to help him to forget his grief. As he said, travel was the only thing that could offer you new thoughts. Life had taught him that.

Qolugtanguaq was away a whole year. When he came back he moved in to his family. The children were never spoken of again. His grief was forgotten.

There is something in that of the mentality of the Vikings. They went on expeditions to strange lands, some because they wanted renown, others because they were resentful of some little wrong suffered at home.

Travel, travel, travel. It has cured many who have been persecuted by their thoughts. It puts things in new lights and transfers responsibility to other shoulders. People like that should travel. They are the ones who will find happiness in it— perhaps. At any rate they do not have it at home.

I often think of that wise line from the Icelandic saga:

"God punished him for his evil deeds most grievously, for He gave him a bitter mind."

That is true and, if nothing else helps, a man or woman whose heart is full of bitterness, ought to go off and travel. It can't make things worse and it is at least easier to live where you are unknown. All over the world man adjusts himself to his place. I have been in Alaska and met many capable people there. Many were hardened by the tremendous difficulties of those grim winters, but they were all wonderfully understanding and all were tolerant of others' habits, broad-minded and gentle in their criticism.

It took me some time to get to know them for I was a stranger, but one day a wise old gold-digger told me that one of the most important rules in Alaska and elsewhere on the fringe of the world's circle, was never to ask anyone about their home, family, name, or why they were there. Observe that rule, and you will become friends with many of them, he said. If anyone wishes others to know more about him than he himself has already told them, leave it to him to tell it.

That was because in those days there was no one in Alaska who was not a traveller. Now there are farmers there. The Arctic has been opened up to those with quite different intentions to what the old adventurers had. Alaska still has its travellers, but it also has its settlers, people whose journey is at an end.

Many have found happiness there, where they were beyond the reach of the curiosity of neighbours which they had found irksome. It requires strength of mind and character to be transplanted, yet surprisingly many stand it successfully. However, the mere fact that they broke loose shows that there was something in them that they never got from their homes. Travel stimulated their minds. They sought happiness, and even though they often did not themselves consider that they had found it, the thing that mattered was that they searched. Our task after all is to develop the man in us, as a person, and I never saw anyone who had become less of a man by travelling. But that is no reason to regard those who travel as better than the others who stay at home.

Everyone surely knows that large class of people, the amateur yachtsmen, who spend half the year sailing about in fine boats. They have excellent equipment and handle their craft with such efficiency and ingenuity in making the most of conditions as few professional seamen can equal. For them sailing is a sport and there is a tremendous gulf between them and the poor devils who do it for money. Both have a deep contempt for the other, and both try to imitate the other. Are not these amateurs all dreamers? Do they not, I wonder, day dream of mighty voyages to distant seas during which they will encounter and, of course, overcome endless dangers and unexpected difficulties? I know them only from the tales they tell ashore. They will describe how they weathered the most dreadful storms; how they escaped that uncharted rock. In their talk they relate over and over again horrible things that we others with a

greater respect for ease and comfort are only too glad not to
have experienced. Yet those are just the things that for them
gave the summer its charm. It is the sea they love, and they
miss it all through the winter. These people are travellers at
least in spirit. Their bodies never get very far away from their
elegant cabins or out of their well-cut clothes, but they do have
adventures and experiences, they take an active part in moving
from place to place, and are far nearer to being "traveller"
than the general run of tourists.

Let me say here and now that to be a "tourist" has always
seemed to me the worst fate than can happen to anyone. I have
only tried it on few occasions and never for long. The last time
was in my own country, Denmark, in company with a number
of famous authors. We were led round by a guide who in a
furious gabble gave us much false information about many of
the places we saw. We forced him into a church about which
he had no patter prepared, and inspected the skeletons of some
old kings. They were in glass cases and each had his name on a
plate, so that he couldn't go wrong there. But he wanted to tell
us something more about them, so that he could show off his
languages. So, pointing with a long finger at the skeleton of one
of Denmark's rulers, killed in 1086, he said: "Il est mort!"

And no one protested.

I have seen tourists in many countries. They are hounded in
herds from castle to church, from church to picture gallery, and
on to famous views. After a few days they surrender to their
grim lot and trudge along apathetically without a word to say,
or the desire to look, their mental faculties so low and depressed
that they cannot even remember their delight in travelling,
nor their faith in the adventure that would come their way, nor
the things they had hoped to learn, not even all the money they
had wasted on that ghastly enterprise. Touring is not travel.

And yet you cannot define the difference between them. At
least not in a few words; there is too much, too many things and
too great a distance separating them.

Some have set off outward bound in order to win honour and
renown, as in the days when kings wanted colonies. Then there
were scholars whose happiness consisted in knowing more than
others about the earth and distant places. There still are, and
their numbers grow from year to year. Every returning expedi-

tion breeds with its results the germs of others. The purely adventurous excursions to places that "Had never before been
visited," are now no more. There are so few places like that
left. The aeroplane has revolutionized discovery. The camera,
films, wireless and competition have put an end to the exciting
fairy-tales that used to curdle the blood and inflame the
imaginations of the young and inexperienced. I remember myself my boyish almost adoring admiration for polar travellers
who came back and told tales of starvation and suffering, of
pitiless frost and menacing death. A little later, I began to
wonder how it was that they always wanted to go back up there.
Then, when I myself was able to sample polar life, I never encountered any of their great sufferings. I have lived a happy
life travelling, and I have still not settled down for good.

A certain frugality is also necessary in the traveller. Do not
think that happiness lies in having much money, fame whether
scientific or military, or in having an unsurpassed travelling
technique. Happiness is to be found abroad and at home in the
worth of what has been achieved. That will vary according to
the goal you have set yourself, the point of view you have taken.

A scientist can return home after several years' travel abroad
and be happy because he has found a hitherto unknown
northern limit for a single flower. Others aim at unravelling
the geological complexities of some mighty chain of mountains.
Others have even greater aims. Happiness does not lie within
the limits of the definable. Happiness dwells inside us.

I still believe that travel caused me to develop into quite a
different person from the one I would have become had I stayed
at home on my little island all my life. But has it made me
better or worse? That question can never be answered. However, the nice thing about us all, is that we have such fine
opinions of ourselves. So, we are inclined to think that what we
did was absolutely the right thing to have done.

That being so, I cannot refrain from adding in conclusion,
that you will find happiness if you only travel on and on until
you believe you have found it. If it means that you have to go
on till the end of your life, you have at least gained something:
you have had the pleasure in advance.

IN SEARCH OF ADVENTURE

Negley Farson

IN the first place, let me say that I do not like the title for my section of this book; I have never deliberately *searched* for adventure, and I hope I never shall. That would be too self-conscious. My quest, let us call it that, for an exciting and satisfactory life began in the gutter—where most adventures usually end up. That was the frightening thing that I learned very early on. I think of it now, when I read Eugene O'Neill's *Moon of the Caribbees* or *Bound East for Cardiff*, or Conrad—a superb example of what I want to prove—and think what was the eventual end of the men he described in *The Nigger of the Narcissus*. Down-and-outers, it's a three to one bet. That was the thing that scared me early on: I soon learned, from my passion for prowling around the docks, that the adventurous men who had quite obviously seen the most of this world had, equally obviously, got the least out of it. An acquaintance with the world does not necessarily enrich a man's mind; not unless you have the mental capacity to realize what you have seen, or been through. Logan Pearsall Smith has described perfectly what I mean by the "recognition of adventure" in his *Autobiography*: "This . . . *receptivity* (my italics) to experience, and a complete surrender to it, combined with a patient effort to grasp its deepest meaning. . . ." That was the life motif of Conrad, and probably the one thing never thought of by the crews he described, and their like.

Even so, as you see them hanging around the East India Docks, or shuffling along the icy sidewalks of lower New York, coat lapels pinned over (to hide a chest that in some cases has no shirt); heads down against the wind; hands in the pockets—except when one is thrust out to you asking, practically demanding, the price of a square meal—as you stare up at night at their stoic backs outlined in the steaming windows of the doss-houses along the Bowery, waiting for the time for lights out so that they may lie down on the floor and seek sleep—and forgetfulness—above the slush and the desperation of the dirty streets—you would think that these men, who had known the glory of blue days when they scudded before a Trade Wind; who had enjoyed to the last swig of whisky, fight, or paid-for kiss all the unmitigated hell the white man used to be able to raise in the ports of the Far East: those days (and aren't we paying for them now!) when you could kick every sanguinary Wog, Chink, Malay or what-have-you off the sidewalk—you would think that these men would have *some* memories to live upon, *some* Golden Treasury of personal experiences and achievement; something, call it what you like, that would bolster them up in adversity.

But it is not so. They are empty men. That's why hopeful young authors burrowing about the East End, or the waterfront of New York, or the *cantinas* of Valparaiso, so seldom get a story. They are sitting at the same bar with men who have had experiences that would take a man's hair off: yet, unless they are bragging or arguing in a drunken mood—when it often comes out unconsciously—they think there is nothing to be said. All that world travel has added up to is exactly nothing. Spiritually as well as materially they are no better off, so far as seeing the world is concerned. They are empty men. Either they are like dud photographic plates which will take no impression—or they all have a leak in them. Empty men—just as empty as the rich, pompous banker next door.

So, early on, the first thing I decided that a man must have if he is going to pass up security and/or mediocrity—is a brain. He must know all that he can learn about the place that he is in, or is travelling through. He must understand its history, before he can get to know its people; if it is the uninhabited woods, then he must know a lot more about the trees and animals and the plants of the forest or jungle he is in than just their mere names. Though most settlers don't even bother to learn those! If he has that real interest in his surroundings, then he is nine-tenths along the road to being safe in any country or situation he might get himself into. The next most essential possession, I would say hurriedly, and I am beginning from the top down, is a profession, or a trade, or some skill that you can sell, or *use*, so that you will have some instrument to live by wherever you land. The final thing, of course, is a certain amount of determination, being able to stick it. Given these things, the world ought to be yours—that is, if you have the proper curiosity.

This all sounds a bit didactic, and I am afraid that I shall have to use the upright pronoun, the first person singular, from now on in this essay, because, as I see it, each contributor is asked to give his or her personal summing up of what travel has meant. So, before I return to my gutter, let me give a personal example of exactly what I mean by this profession business: I studied Civil Engineering deliberately to get out of the United States. Not that I don't love my country—I get so homesick now and then for the Chesapeake Bay, the glorious reedy vistas of Maryland and Tidewater Virginia, that I could almost cry—I just didn't like (and I hate it now more than ever) what the rest of the Americans, or the great bulk of them anyway, were doing to it. Those up-and-at-'em Americans, the go-getters, who were turning our rivers into industrial sewers, our forests into tree stumps, our flowered prairies into dust bowls—men who always wanted to move into a bigger house as soon as their salary was raised, who believed that fifty weeks in an office every year—grabbing all the material things you could get—was the natural way of life. From the very day that I ever heard of such a future I was terrified of it: I just knew that God had never designed man to be like that!

So I didn't go to Yale and take the Arts course I had been headed for, or study Forestry, which I often wish I had, although I had been to Andover, its prep. school: I went to the University of Pennsylvania, which I (and a great many other people, some English) think has the finest railway and bridge-building school anywhere in the world. It was Prussian in its fierceness of study. I learned a lot of things; one of them being that I would never be an orthodox, run of the garden, engineer—I hated mathematics too much. Nevertheless, I thought I'd plug through. And then one day, with my degree in my paw, I would light out for South America, and perhaps, who could tell? build bridges in the Andes. At any rate, I was daily learning *useful* things that could keep me alive wherever I went. With me in spirit, a friend I made there, was a red-headed lad, who had been kicked out of the U.S. Naval Academy for hitting a "Jimmy-legs," a Marine guard, when, rather the worse for beer, he had fallen off the wall while trying to sneak back into the Academy grounds. He, too, now that his Navy career was smashed, had this idea of going to South America. English boys would have of course thought of going to the Colonies, or to India, Africa, or to any other of hundreds and hundreds of exhilaratingly strange places, and lives, you once had in your wonderful Empire. We had just the Tropics: Mexico, Central or South America. And, of course, Alaska.

Neither of us finished our course. We were nearly always down the bay, in a beautiful little two and a half ton yawl Jo-Jo Graham had, when we should have been studying differential calculus. In 1912, I (and his weeping mother) saw him off on a ship for the U.S. Canal Zone. In the winter of 1912–13 I received a letter from him asking me would I join him and an ex-officer of the Zone Police, in a gold expedition down in Ecuador. I didn't answer for some time—I didn't like this wild-goose chase prospecting for gold, when so many U.S. mining engineers had already covered the same ground—but, from the New York Athletic Club, I sat down and wrote him. I said this: "Yes, I will join you—but on one condition: we will take just one year, and I will go anywhere you want, trying anything—if at the end of that year we have not hit it, then I'm going to come home. I've got a good job in the Vacuum Oil, and I think I can get it back if I want it." (I had been half-offered a job for them in Madras.)

He never got that letter. Instead, in his foolish way, he sat on the dock at Colon and met two or three boats from New York (why he should have done this I don't know, except to say it was just like him): then he pushed off, the ex-officer of the Zone Police soon quitting, and got himself into the one and very thing that he had dreamed of—a South American Revolution! Jo-Jo got himself into the middle, literally as he was at one moment between two sets of Maxim guns, of the fight between "Bloody" Benevides and the "Blockistas," in Peru. He saw "Machine-gun" Smith, an American Tropical Tramp, spray the square from a church tower in Lima. He lay on the floor of his hotel bedroom while bullets chipped the window sill and pocked the opposite wall. I can hear him exulting (for he was a rabid Romantic): "My God—what a life! What *luck* to be here!"

In the meantime, I had gone to England, then to wartime

Tsarist Russia. The why of it all is not important here. Suffice to say that I went to Petrograd to spend three weeks and stayed three years. In 1917, I came out to join the British, the R.F.C. In London, I went to the Embassy to ask if there was any mail. They handed me, among other letters that had been chasing me for some time, an old one from Jo-Jo Graham. It informed me that he could not wait for America to get in, so he had volunteered for an American ambulance unit with the French Army. Would I join him?

I stuffed the letter in my pocket, intending to answer it when I had the time (one virtue, or vice, that certainly I have not got is writing letters). And in Egypt, when I was lying in hospital myself, I got a letter from my father: "I wonder if you ever heard, if anyone has told you, what happened to your old pal Jo-Jo? He was killed, as a captain in the American Army,—no trace ever found of his body—in an advance at Chateau Thierry. So, I suppose, he had the end that he hankered for. He would never have settled down. But while he was still in the French Army, with an American ambulance unit, he got the *Croix de Guerre*, for evacuating the wounded under fire . . . at Bar-le-Duc. . . ."

So that was the end of the man I was going to "chance one year" with. I was just as hell-bent to see the world as he had been. But I wasn't going to do it in a damn-fool way, or so I thought. I was burned up with remorse for not having stayed to get my degree (I was yoicked out of the University at the call of Love) and I had the idea, until, in 1914, I sailed for England, that one day I would go back and eventually sit my degree. I had only one year to go. I felt that I just must have that one instrument—a profession—that would entitle me to earn a respectable life, by that I mean a position of worth, wherever I went. I disliked and distrusted myself for what I considerd would be my most monumental failure in life: not having the guts to stick four years at that University until I won my degree. I did *not* intend to become either a genuine or bogus beachcomber or a Tropical Tramp, picturesque as some of those desperate characters are made to be in the stories of Jack London, etc., or Russell's *Where the Pavement Ends*.

That was a hard-and-fast rule with me, and I have never deviated from it one inch (otherwise I would be lost): have *some* means of making your living wherever you go. Writing turned out to be that means to an end. Although, as I hope, the end is not quite in sight yet. And I also saw "Bloody" Benevides. I talked with him for two hours in the Palace at Lima. With that *terrific* bronze statue of Pizzaro, with his sword upraised, sitting on his horse before the Cathedral: that statue which makes all Peru tremble—for the Andes still reverberate to the echoes of the Conquistadores, surely the toughest body of men this world has ever known. Adventurers beside whom even the Elizabethans must take their places respectfully. And remember this one cardinal thing (nearly always ignored) about both of them—they did it for *gain*. The Spaniards plundered the Americas for gold: the Elizabethan adventured for territory and trade, and astounding personal profits— though some lost their heads on the block instead.

Pizzaro promised the Inca that he would give him his unconditional freedom, if he filled a certain room up to the ceiling with gold. From all over the Andes the Incas came bearing llama- and back-loads of gold as his ransom. When the gold was about knee high in the Palace, Pizzaro, evidently believing that there just could not be any more gold in the Andes, killed the Inca. The Indians heard, threw their gold off the cliffs, into foaming rivers, buried it. They are still searching for that Inca gold in the Andes. And in Ecuador I met Captain Erskine Lock, British Army, who had found some of that Inca gold over in the Oriente, headwaters of the Amazon. Three fish-hooks, made of gold, aside from some stream-worn objects (not nuggets)—found at the foot of a falls. I have held those fish-hooks in my hand; I took a photograph of them, and the other gold, placed against a dollar bill in the Bank of Ecuador. I spent my last night, coming down the Andes, at Riobamba, with Captain Erskine Lock, dead now.

Well, there was quite a lot of adventure—that I never looked for—between 1912, when I saw Jo-Jo off for the Panama Canal, and 1937, when I sat before "Bloody" Benevides in Lima—and I had actually done the very thing that Jo-Jo and I had intended to do: seek our luck in South America. For I was free-lancing when I went down there. On my own, if I ever was! I have to laugh now, when I recall my paramount thought when I found myself in the high Andes, for I crossed them from Popayan in

Colombia to Quito in Ecuador, passing one or two still smoking volcanoes, and through the town of Ipales, just flattened by an earthquake, and staring 10,000 feet, straight down, into gorges. I was thinking of Philadelphia, when I went to the Dean of the Engineering School, Edgar Marburg, to make my apologies for leaving, possibly one of the most brilliant bridge-engineers then living. I couldn't tell him I was in love; that my girl had just been cut dead in the street by my family; that that was the reason I must get a job at once—so that I might marry her. But I have an idea he guessed, for he smiled and said—

"Negley, make me a promise, will you? A real promise. I want you to promise me—for the sake of humanity!—that you will *never* build a bridge." One of the few promises that I have had no trouble in keeping.

But to return to my gutter—where all of this started.

You will see how, as the phrase goes, as the twig is bent the tree inclines. In other words, why I did some of the idiotic, or very sensible, things that I did do. And in none of them was I deliberately looking for adventure. The gutter was in a little New Jersey town, beside a dirt road, in that wonderful era before the days of the horseless-carriage, where the clop-clop of a horse's hoofs were the only sound to be heard on the sultry summer nights, above the constant whine of the mosquitoes or the dull boom of a bull-frog in a pond across the way. In the torrential thunder-and-lightning storms that periodically lash New Jersey, shaking our little, old-fashioned white clapboard house, with its old slate mansard roof (and a cupola a-top of that, from which you could look out over the surrounding country, which still was country then)—the deep gutters in our street often became rivers—swirling, muddy, like the broad River Plate. For the road was high-crowned, so that the rains of summer would run off quickly; as well as the winds of winter blow the snow from the top crown. In that gutter, I launched my first boat—and immediately capsized.

This was a canoe made from half barrel hoops, a pole (for the keel) was stolen from our clothes line; canvas, shrunk tight as a drum-head by pouring boiling water over it, after it had been tacked and stretched into place; painted with my grandfather's precious carriage enamel. Its ribs stuck out like those of a starved horse. A cross-section of it was as cylindrical as a clipped cigar. But that was the first of many canoes, which, as I began to build them over frames, took on the flattish, seaworthy bottom that a good canoe should have—like those of the Maine Indians—and then I fulfilled the object that I had been building them for. I and another boy transported the best of them on the handle-bars of two bicycles to Newmarket Pond, some six (it seemed a thousand) miles away. And there we had a glorious summer or so, paddling in and out among the bullrushes, watching the turtles fall off, plop by plop, as we came up to them sunning themselves on some old grey tree branch protruding from the stagnant water; putting up surly blue herons, with their protesting harsh *craake!* emptying their insides in a long white stream as they left the water: catching an occasional catfish or a pickerel or two; wading into the tussocked solitudes where the red-winged blackbirds nested and sang. . . .

Beauty—the finest thing in life?—yes, we felt it; we knew that we had it. No use for our fathers, school teachers, or anyone else, to tell us that we were meant to be taken away from *that*. Here luck entered in, for I happened to have a grandfather (who had adopted me) who was not at all in love with, or a believer in, what is commonly called the "American way of life." On the contrary, he detested it. And with some reason. He was one of Sherman's four generals (see *Gone With the Wind*) who had burned Georgia "from Atlanta to the sea." He will be chiefly remembered, if at all, for a cavalry charge he made at the battle of Stone River, taking the Confederate battery, from which rose the Civil War song: "Who saved the Left?" Very little was said, certainly by him, about what he did to the Right on another day. He was breveted, on the field, by the order of Lincoln, from a Brigadier to a Major General—but what he did in that other battle blackened his military career and the rest of his life. Eighteen years in the U.S. Congress could not make up for it. Embittered, he became an idealist, and tried to fight Bills through Congress to build a huge canal system, thus incurring more embitterment—for the powerful railway lobbies broke him out of even Congress. So he had retired, full of hate, to this little New Jersey town, where I first saw the light of day. And I grew up, therefore, with almost a prenatal hatred of all politicians as such, plus an instinctive contempt for the people who had too much money—and not much else.

But there was another thing which "bent the twig." My grandfather (than whom I was certain no greater man had ever lived) who had run away at the age of seventeen to fight in the Mexican War, had turned to that country in his latter days, *faute de mieux*, as a sort of consolation. Therefore our little New Jersey house was often full of strange characters. Uncivilized people, my grandmother declared, because they smoked cigars in bed and burned holes in the sheets. "*Spiggoties*," as most Americans, who had never met a real Mexican, called the gentlemen from below the Rio Grande those days. My grandmother was afraid (and quite correctly) that my grandfather was going to lose what little was left of his once comfortable patrimony in his Mexican ventures. (The money he left me in his will vanished like a puff of the Mexicans' cigar smoke.) And there were other strange people at our table: Americans—but "out-size" men, to whose tales (usually from the hall) I listened pop-eyed: "Oh, yes, yes, yes,—ha, ha!—Hunt, you remember that morning . . . when we came out on the verandah, and they started shooting at us! Ha, ha—had to run for the boat that time, didn't we? Damn good thing, too, that there was one of them lying there. I've always said . . ." and then, a little later: "But we did put that one (Revolution) over. We put our side in and we got the concession to build that railway . . . though God knows what they'll do with the damned thing, now they've got it . . . ha, ha, ha! . . ." Years later, one of these very men, said to me in the Waldorf-Astoria Hotel in New York: "Come down with me, my boy—and I'll make you a general." That was "Haitian" MacDonald.

Well, with talk like that and the background of hate that I had, even if it wasn't mine—yet—it was small wonder that I grew up with ideas for life that were not at all connected with catching the 8.15 up to town every morning. I don't think that the idea of adventure, as such, ever entered into my head until long, long after I had left the United States. It was just that I wanted to find an active, useful, and interesting life—a life, in short (and it is so hard to find), that would make me glad just to be living it. To enjoy being alive.

Another home entered into it: my father's. I visited him occasionally. He was always admonishing me (though I knew that he didn't believe it himself) that "life is cruel" and, e.g., I would have to work that fifty weeks out of every fifty-two in an office of some sort, and for somebody else—"That is, until you can make enough money, if you ever do, to stand on your own feet." He opined that that did not seem likely. He took his consolation out in a succession of boats that he owned, usually decreasing in size and importance, and in duck and reed-bird shooting down the Delaware river. And I saw that though he may have been an habitual failure in all the material things, he was a far more worth-while man, had more real substance to him, than the town's richest banker (a most infuriatingly self-satisfied man) who actually did live in the next house. He, I saw, was stupid. And I only laughed when he admonished me, which he did on every occasion: "What!—Negley—been down the river, shooting, have you?—don't you ever go to school. Well, well, well,—I suppose you know what you're doing . . . just enjoying yourself, eh?" I'd rather have had my Old Man, any day! During one period of two years, the longest that I lived with him, I bought a second-hand gunning-skiff: decked her over: put in a centre-board and rigged her for a sprit-sail—and spent the next summer down the Delaware and Chesapeake Bays, the part of this sorry world that I seem to have always had a real blood-love for. It must have run in the blood, for it was only "down the bay" that my father ever found any of the sure satisfactions.

So you can see—to dispose of the need for any forced philosophy—I, for one, have never been animated by the urge to search for adventure, as such. On the other hand, I have met only too many people who have done just that thing—and, with very few exceptions, they have always ended up by stunting themselves. They became publicity hounds. Anxious to make the first page of the newspapers. Or to have some hysterical publisher's blurb on their book jackets. And nearly always as I have come along in their wake I have found that they have left a bad taste in the mouths of the indigenous inhabitants, the local white people they met along the way. They may have done everything that they claimed they did, but—"Well, you know he's rather *not* the chap I'd like to be with on safari. Always trying to make an *impression* on you . . ."

And I'll ask any reader, if they can't think of a good dozen people they know—writers, most of them—who are just like that. It is a form of prostitution, to my way of looking at it. Most people who have had great adventures, or wandered much, know that the best things you bring back from travel— you never sell. They affect you too much, they're too *personal* things—and, you can't offer these things in the market place. (And if you were in the habit of doing *that*, you would never have such adventures.) Very often you are full in the middle of a sticky adventure, something really awkward in life (and I don't mean just physical risk: really the lowest form of adventure) before you even know you are in a tight spot. I was in that position during most of the three years I spent in Tsarist Russia. And (this is rather amusing) just as I did when I was on one of the battered Arctic convoys coming down from Murmansk in the spring of 1942, I read books like a fiend—so that I could forget all the rest of the world—to read myself out of it. I read most of the Russians (English translations, of course) between the end of 1914 and the Kerensky revolution, in Russia itself. *Anna Karenina* first came into my hands then, and Gogol's wonderful *Taras Bulba*!

Where did the adventure come in?

Ho!—did anyone ever think of the Adventures of Ideas? That is the title of Alfred North Whitehead's book: philosophical, I know, very tough to assimilate, for it deals with the sort of history that *ideas* can have in the life of humanity—abstruse, unconscious ideas: not political bigotry—and the high importance of Adventure for the promotion and preservation of civilization: the mutations of human experience, the concept of the clash of thought and the clash of political interest, and of the "senseless agencies," which drive mankind from its old anchorage—"When mankind has slipped its cables, sometimes it is bent on the discovery of a New World, and sometimes it is haunted by the dim sound of the breakers dashing on the rocks ahead." Consider such a conception of the adventure of ideas in the experience of the human race—and the thought that you were there, on such-and-such a day; say, that you were lunching in the *Hotel de France*, Petrograd (as I was), the day the March Revolution broke out—and you will have some conception of what I meant when I said that physical risk was probably the lowest form of adventure. Because, for any foreigner, an Englishman or American or a Frenchman, unless he really wanted to get into trouble, there was very little danger in the Kerensky Revolution. A vivid account I read of it afterward by Isaac Marccoson, the fabulously high-salaried American political commentator (who was not there) terrified me far more than the Revolution itself. Yet to have been present in those "days that shook the world" was, certainly, one of the greatest adventures of our times. (John Reed, by the way, was a great friend of mine: I spent my last night in Petrograd with him.) Consider this whirlwind we lived in, the last years of the Romanoffs, and you will see why the stunt-merchant adventurers, doing risky things around the world, so as to direct its attention to their own self-conscious selves, always strike me as being cheap. You will also see another reason why I did not like the title given to my section of this travel book—I never deliberately went out to look for adventure, in which case it would almost certainly have eluded me; I have had, on one or two occasions, Adventure literally seize me by the throat. And I was fascinated by my own predicament. *There* is where the real adventure comes in—in the ideas that pass through, or come to stay for ever—in your mind, when you have been in the centre of some epic trouble. Not always your own trouble.

Let me explain that. During those three tragic years, from the end of 1914, when starry-eyed journalists and blind statesmen were writing and orating about "the Russian steam roller" (which never had an engine), to that ill-fated day when Nicholas II signed his abdication, I don't know how many Russian Ministers of War I saw—there seemed a new one almost every day—but I do know that, before any war supplies were ordered, each of the above swindlers (who were really the cause of the immediate downfall of the Romanoffs) had to get his "cut": we estimated, as we always had to deal through one or the other of two smooth and millionaire middlemen, that it was 2 per cent. on every order. Meanwhile heroic Russian soldiers at the front were facing the enemy with empty rifles and no munitions for their artillery. Stanley Washburn, the American who was the London *Times'* correspondent, returned from watching the Germans take Warsaw, and told me with tears in his eyes that the Russians had only one or two shells left for each gun: they fired those, then tried to take their pieces out of action—to save them for another hopeless battle. "Why," he said furiously, in the dazzling splendour of the Hotel Astoria's dining-room—"the Germans marched across *with their bands playing*! Don't tell me that retribution is not just around the corner for *these* people." Meaning the corrupt Russians that we had to contend with.

We, the munitions men, knew that it was hopeless. The graft was too colossal, too overwhelmingly widespread, for us ever to hope that we could find some *other* Russians—and the Grand Dukes were notoriously honest, courageous, and inefficient—who could ever allay it or put it down, or even get around it. Russia was being sold out, right before our eyes: *we* knew that she was losing the war in Petrograd, not at the front. In desperation I went to the Grand Duke Sergé Mihailovitch one day, in his palace on the Millionayia, then head of the Artillery Department (the Bolsheviks made him jump down a mine shaft at Perm, so it was reported later), and told him I could give him the name of one Russian who was killing more Russians than any ten thousand Germans could—every day! The lean, Borzoi-like Grand Duke, who had the immense height characteristic of the Romanoffs (Nicholas II, did not have it) sighed, spoke with shame of the almost impossibility of circumventing the corrupt generals under him, and said that if I made my charges specific, in writing, four copies—he would see what he could do about it. Why the four copies I could never understand: perhaps that, too, was a sign of the Russian nobility's unworldliness. Anyway, something happened, he was removed from office within the next few weeks, left Petrograd for his palace in the Crimea. And that hope was gone.

And the reaction? Well, during the winter of 1914–15 I became a balletomane. I saw the Imperial Ballet in all its glory. I only wish that Sacheverell Sitwell had written his *Valse des Fleurs* then. For I lived among the splendour he describes, saw the end of it. I loved going on the nights of that first Russian ballet, *The Humpbacked Horse*: a gay little piece that the great Diaghileff considered too primitive, too lacking in classic art, to let the incomparable Nijinsky dance it. Both of them were out of Russia at that time: Nijinsky was either in Hungary or Vienna—though I saw him dance in the Metropolitan Opera House, New York, when, in 1916, I returned to the United

States for an operation—it was in *Scheherezade*, I think, for I seem to have a recollection of him as a faun-like figure cutting other people down. As a compensation for a morning spent in the gloomy War Department the Mariinsky Theatre provided a dream world, a momentary vision of ethereal tenderness, in which we could live—before wrapping our fur coats around us, we went out into the snowy night. But not to bed! Oh, no, we told our *isvostchiks* to drive out to The Villa Rhodie, one of the all-night resorts on the William Island. There we bought sweet champagne, and listened to the gypsies sing—wept, perhaps, as we listened to that sweet-sadness of old Russia, the Russia that was passing. On Sundays I went out on the William Island and shot live pigeons in the company of Count Schuvalov and Count Shermietoff (for whose family history, in Tsarist Russia, read *War and Peace*); and I took bets with Kazanskov, one of the most expert pigeon shots in the world, famous at Monte Carlo. I played baccarat in the rooms of a Russian princess who was living in the hotel, and played poker till dawn at the New English Club, alternating between periods of destitution and comparative affluence. And as I said, I *read*: in the gloomy mornings or afternoons, when I had not the inclination, and very often not the money, to go out for another bout of wild dissipation, I lay in bed and read. I read all the English translations of Russian books that I could get hold of: for I wanted to *know* Russia—and what had led up to what was happening around me. And sometimes I would sit at my window, as the night of Russian winter closed down in its cold green light, stared at the painted church domes, and thought about how Russia, Holy Russia, really ended in Asia—and of the tribes of ugly little horsemen, the Golden Horde of Genghis Khan, who raided all the way to Moscow from the far-off Amur River. Perhaps—who could tell?—I might even go out there. The tents of Tartary.

All this was adventure. During those three years I, several times, came as close to a nervous breakdown, a complete collapse, as ever I hope to be. I got one order. But it was months and months, over a year, before I ever got another. New York, which knew less than nothing of the all-round incompetence and corruption of the Russian War Department (and hardly knew where Russia was on the map) wired me to return to London.

I wired that I would remain in Russia at my own expense: please forward back salary. They wired me the shocking information that I had no back salary: the London manager, with whom I shared a flat on Great Portland Street, leaving him the right to draw part of my salary to pay my end of it (as I have said, when I first came to Petrograd it was with the intention of spending only three weeks) had skipped. He had taken my back pay, along with the firm's cash account. . . .

In the spring of 1915 I went up to Archangel, while the northern rivers were still frozen, to wait for a ship, bearing some test-machines for me—a ship which never arrived. But I had seen the Far North of Russia, the Samoyede and their sleds, the frozen tundra; and the fact of getting an order began to lose its importance to me. After a month or so of Archangel, I suddenly packed up and went all the way down across Russia: from the snows of Archangel to eating dinner at night by candlelight, outside the Naval Club, Sebastopol, on its terrace beside the luminous Black Sea. I fell in love with the Crimea. That spring of 1915 was the most enchanted of my life. I flew (merely as ballast) with the young hydroplane pilots of the Russian Navy, flirted with their wives, played tennis, swam in the Black Sea—went up into the Crimea to visit the fortress of the old Tartar Khans. I have seldom experienced such beauty. And beauty, of both what I saw and felt, was beginning to be about the only thing that I cared about—and would, I knew, place above all things, for the rest of my life. As it was in the beginning, when the lonely heron rose with his harsh *craake* from the rushes of that silent swamp in far off New Jersey. . . .

I think I have said sufficient, if only by induction, of what the term "adventure" had come to mean to me. It means a heightened functioning of all the senses, in some instances even an emotional ecstasy. The adventure lies in the idea. This takes it away from the flesh. If this sounds a bit precious, then I had better explain by example. During those three years I saw history being made in the streets of Petrograd. And history means nothing if it does not teach us something. Some of us knew that we were seeing the end of an epoch. Its basic theme being, really, the folly of living for material things. And some, our own countrymen in particular—strutting around the Hotel Astoria with American flags in their button-holes, always cursing about "These damned stupid Russians!"—didn't have the faintest idea that a Revolution was on the way until it burst right in their faces. They hadn't the faintest idea of what Russia had been; or was, as they badgered the War Office and boozed themselves about in the cabarets; they did not even have any interest or curiosity about the Russia that was about to be— when the Red Flag came out again. (In this respect they were like some recent U.S. Congressmen, at least one of whom, on a "fact finding" tour of Europe—did not even know that Sweden had a King: Senator Elmer Thomas, from Oklahoma—one of our Elder Statesmen. See *Time*, Dec. 12, 1949: you will see that I am not exaggerating the ignorance nor slandering the American big businessmen in Tsarist Russia, between 1914 and 1917.) But some of us knew, and aside from being apprehensive, were overwhelmingly curious about the new Russia that lay ahead of us. We had seen enough of Romanoff rule to want another one. I, for one, as by 1916 I had made up my mind to live in Russia. I was in love once more (unlucky fellow), and had every intention of marrying and settling down to live in Petrograd—set up an export business. That was one of the reasons why I had been back in the States in 1916: to get the agencies for the American companies that I wanted to represent in Russia. And if the terms "adventure" and "business" may seem a paradox, let me remind you of John Company in India, or the Merchant Adventurers of Elizabeth's day—or the early Scots who went to Ivan the Terrible's court in Moscow. Yes, the idea of settling down to set up a business in limitless Russia, for the ultimate end of the Nevski Prospekt ran on and on and on to the very gates of Peking, was an adventure in itself. I arrived in Stockholm, on my way back, the day the Grand Duke Dmitri and Prince Youssoupoff killed Rasputin. And, even before I took the train to go up, through Finland, back to Petrograd, I needed no one to tell me that, as the phrase goes, the jig was up. I knew I was about to lose every material thing, and prospect, that I had in the world.

Strangely enough, I did not care. I felt no sense of loss. The excitements were too intense. One's own personal losses and deprivations dwarfed in an instant into utter insignificance. The editor of this book gave me, as one of the leading questions that he thought I might like to expatiate upon: What does it

feel like to be in an "adventure"? Well, here was one And as
I took the train that led up through the deep, snowy forests of
northern Sweden to Torneo, I remembered how, three years
before, I had made the same journey where we crossed the river
in sledges, and with what expectations! Now I was going back
to save what I could from their wreck. I had no other feeling
than what could be truthfully described as an awful curiosity.
Therefore, when a young Englishman and I (he was in the
uniform of a Russian officer) came out from our lunch in the
Hotel de France, and saw the shopkeepers on the Nevsky hurriedly
rushing out to pull down the steel shutters over their show-
windows, saw that the Cossacks, riding along the snowy sidewalks, were merely shaking their steel-tipped whips, the
dreaded *naigkas*, and not using them on the people; when we
sat, stymied by a growling, angry mob, where the Leiteny
crosses the broad Nevsky, and watched a squadron of Uhlans,
their lances down, charging down on us, snow flying from their
horses' hoofs—when, instead of being spitted, as we suddenly
began to fear at the last instant, we saw them throw their
lances up and merely smash the crowd up by charging their
horses through it, leaving dozens of black bodies squirming on
the snow—and the Englishman said to me: "This is IT. This is
the Revolution. This is the end of us!"—by which he meant our
business, personal possessions, even our future in Russia—I did
not care.

There was one real adventure in life. I, a foreigner, could
afford to have no feelings, or, to put it rightly, could afford to
feel a vivid interest in the new Russia that, for a couple of
months, I watched in the making. But many Russians, some in
the very highest places, and with immense wealth to lose, also
felt the same keen interest in the making of a new Russia,
sympathized with the millions of people, who firmly believed
they had been suddenly liberated from the rule of a police state,
and, even if stripped of their own wealth, were eager to join in
the work of building a great, new, and joyous Russia. For the
last years of the Romanoff were really the worst of them: they
were getting worse, not better. But we soon saw that the Pro-
visional Government of Prince Lvov, honest, hard-working, and
well-intentioned men as they were, was really a body that was
given to organized indecision; that it was only feebly holding

the door against the real revolution—the real revolt, as Romanoff Russia had no Middle Class which could accept the other,
the Kerensky Revolution—the Revolution of the Proletariat. I
had my hand on the back of a huge guardsman from the
Preobrajensky Polk, one of the crack regiments of the Imperial
Guard, the day he was shot (between July 3rd and 7th: I can't
state which one exactly), as a handful of soldiers were haran-
guing a demonstration of some 30,000 workers—at whose head
was being carried the Jolly Roger, the black flag with the white
skull-and-crossbones—and the blood curdling slogan: "WEL-
COME ANARCHY!"—in that human volcano of 1917.

That day was the "peak of the pass in the eight months between the March and the November Revolution," as Trotsky
later called it. For the regiments in Petrograd made no organized opposition to the workers—The Dictatorship of the Proletariat—after that. Soldiers mutinied, shot their officers, came
streaming back from the front. I met officers whom I had
known—one from those happy days when I was flying with
them down on the Black Sea—whom I even met in civilian
clothes. One even asked would I give him a suit of mine; then,
he was a funny little chap, he suddenly roared with laughter:
"Yours!" he said, the difference between our size suddenly
striking him—"why I'd look like Charlie Chaplin!" I never
saw him again. I left Russia with just the clothes that I wore.
So when I turned up at the gates of Blackdown Heath, Alder-
shot, one night, to put on the old maternity jacket of the R.F.C.,
I was just as bare as I was when I came to England in 1914.

As so very few foreigners have ever read the document that
Nicholas II signed when he abdicated, I would like to give the
last paragraphs. They are pathetic.

"Not wishing to part from Our Beloved Son, We bequeath the
heritage to Our Brother, the Grand Duke Michael Alexandrovich.
Blessing him on his accession to the Throne of the Russian Empire,
we adjure Our Brother to rule in full and unbroken harmony with
the people's representatives in the legislative assemblies, on principles which they shall determine, and to take an inviolable oath
that he will do so.

"In the name of Our dearly-beloved country We call upon all
faithful sons of the Fatherland to fulfil their sacred duty to it by
obeying the Tsar in this time of grave national crisis and to help

Him, together with the representatives of the people, to lead Russia into the path of victory, prosperity ond glory.

"May the Lord God help Russia. NICHOLAS."

That was the end of an epoch. And anyone who had passed through it would be a curiously insensitive person if he paid too much attention to himself from then on. At any rate, for some time after. For me, flying in Egypt meant the end of a numbness. A picking up of interest in life again. An interest in my own future. Those who can remember the aftermath of the 1914–18 war, the anxiety, or perhaps hopes, with which we began to "begin life again," as most of us then called it, will realize the personal adventures that we all had. For starting once more, from scratch, is also an adventure. A very real one.

Mine began in Chicago. And for some eight months, vainly trying to sell motor trucks, I led about as disenchanted, disgusted, and distressed a life as ever I want to know. I *loathed* the people, the potential customers, that the accepted rules of good salesmanship made me be polite to, when I would much rather have told them to go to hell. It was with joy, one morning, that I saw that the leg I had smashed in a crash in Egypt was breaking down again. It was with joy that I rushed up to Canada, to an operating table, to have some more dead bone chiselled out. I had been "on the table" so many times that I had ceased to count them (though I was still afraid of it); but I knew that after *this* operation—I was going to "take life by the ears." I was going out in the woods to live. Do the one thing I had always wanted to do. And, by the grace of God, after the third try, I had at last married a girl (English) who loved the same things that I did, and wanted to live the same life. People thought we took chances! We never took a *chance*: we merely got out, went to another phase of life, when we saw that the going was good.

We will always see that little cabin of ours out in the woods of British Columbia. For there began two years of adventure, as sweet and as satisfying as ever a man and woman could have. We had the large sum of $30 by the time we reached Vancouver, which was less than the hotel bill we ran up there before a Medical Board finally made up its mind not to hospitalize me again (which I had refused) and, with a sudden impulse of humaneness (or a sense of fun) gave me three or four months' out-patient's pay. That was all we needed.

The cabin, really a log bungalow, stood in the shelter of an immense wall of forest. Douglas fir, towering a hundred feet at least before their branches began. Before it lay the lake. The lake was 20 miles long. The autumn that we came there, there were only five families living on it: the original settler; an Englishman, who would inherit a peerage if all his four brothers died (and they were very healthy: he always said jokingly—"I had the damnedst luck that none of my brothers was killed in the war!"): an almost indigenous Scot, whose flea-like ability to live on the backs of everybody else, who had practically no cash themselves, both puzzled and pleased everybody (the storekeeper told me that the Scot's bill there for a year was never over $85); an eccentric German settler, ex-officer in the Kaiser's army, who had "done something queer" out in German East Africa, or so the story ran: the Game Warden, lean Englishman with a French wife, who lived as comfortably and as casually as a pair of woodland animals in their little ten by eighteen feet shack, built on a cedar-log raft—and ourselves. The man who had loaned us his log bungalow for that first winter, my wife's Irish uncle (the dead spit of Bernard Shaw), had been a Colonel in the Indian army, and he had built this log house India-fashion—against the *heat*! Result, we crouched before the fire of evenings, our faces being blistered by the flames, our behinds acquiring icicles. But what a life!

Now here was Adventure that was sweet to the muscles, satisfying to the senses and a challenge to one's wits. What more could one ask, so far as adventure itself was concerned? To me, it was like going all the way back again, to the days when I built my first canoe. I love working with my hands. I liked the idea of having to look out for ourselves I loved the *independence* of it. Swinging an axe, or taking one end of a crosscut saw—the old German, and he was a tough one! took the other end—I had the tang of real achievement. Immense stacks of kindling wood, piled up against the oncoming winter: far more tangible to me than any money (say, that I had lost in Russia) in the bank. Cooking, washing up, drying the dishes, making beds; this was a gratifying form of team-work that we

went through every day   With my dud leg, I could not go very
far into the bush—the salal brush of B.C., and the immense
fallen timbers, make one of the most impenetrable jungles I
have seen anywhere in the world, even in tropical Africa. But
I usually managed to collect a couple of pine grouse, if I spent
a hard day going after them; I had a half hour or so flight
shooting ducks nearly every sunset; up on the first settler's place,
where their original log cabin still formed part of their present
log house, his youngest son and I shot some deer back in his
clearings: and in the spring when the trout fishing began—why,
we tried every way you could think of to cook rainbow trout.
One, when we had a couple that were around two pounds, was
to fillet them, dip them in a batter of egg and bread-crumbs, fry
and eat with mayonnaise. And my wife makes a mayonnaise as
firm as a school-girl's breast. The other was to bake them,
stuffed with parsley and bread-crumbs, with plenty of butter.
We bought these eggs and butter from the Hudson Bay Co., the
eggs being ordered by the gross. We paid for them by the newspaper articles and short-stories that I was (after making one of
the largest collections of rejection slips in this world) at last
beginning to sell. That spring we had our own home: an un-
painted shack, just built, on a cedar log raft. I made all the
furniture for it. We moved it around into a little lonely bay
where we couldn't see anybody, just the mallards who were
raising their young in that bay. Two years. We could have
stayed there for ever. (And sometimes I wish we had.)

Remember, behind all that fresh life lay the memory of other
lives: of the dazzle of Tsarist Russia, of desperate Chicago. And
we went back to Chicago.

There, where I was eventually made manager, I had another
two wonderful years. These were also adventure. For nothing
is more exciting than leading a group of men who have some
faith in you. I got so tangled up with my salesmen that I even
became mixed up with them in their private lives: divorces and
such like . . . I was lucky: it was a huge company, and the
Chicago branch had always "been in the red": I had taken all
the salesmen off the small stuff, put them on to the big: we had a
good year; one day one of the vice-presidents came into my
office and told me that "Chicago is in the black." This was just

before Christmas, 1924. The company gave me a big cheque, as a Christmas present. And on that day I told the V.-P. (now one of my most treasured friends): "Well, Bob, I'm going to quit." "What—*now!*" He couldn't believe it. "Why, you so-and-so fool, you are right on the crest of the wave!" "That's just the time to quit," I told him.

So in 1925 my wife and I came back to England. After a long search, we bought the *Flame*: she was a little twenty-six foot, clinker built, centre-board, Norfolk Broads yawl. And we sailed her from the North to the Black Sea.

On that six-months' trip, yes, it can be said that we stuck our neck out once or twice. Once or twice we did take a chance, just, if you must have it, for the thrill of the adventure. One was when we refused to let a Hungarian pilot be put aboard her, and took *Flame*—which weighed two and half tons dead weight—down through the swirling Iron Gates and the Gorge of Kazan. It gave us quite a run for our money, one or two scary moments. But we had already been about as scared as we thought we could get, in the *Flame*. This was when we took her down through the rapids at Vilshofen—not having the faintest idea where the rocks lay. We found one of them. It broke our keel.

I thought that in the snow-storms of December, some six months after leaving Holland, when we at last took *Flame* out into the Black Sea—and I cupped my hands and took a big drink of it; as I had promised I would—that we would have *done* something. Got somewhere. Established something that would make us feel more pride (and confidence) in ourselves. But it was not so.

The most astonishing thing about that trip, after it was all over, and we had done what we said we would, was that we both felt a let-down—exactly as if we had done nothing. I suppose that that is what that old saying means: "It is better to travel hopefully than to arrive." I don't know. That over-quoted sentence also holds the implication of disappointments—names, for instance, that have taunted you: names like Samara, Astrakhan, Bokhara and Samarkand. Well, when I did finally come to Astrakhan it did disappoint me. On the other hand, the Khyber Pass, and the green rushes of the Kabul Delta, surpassed even my hopes. And so I have travelled—for adventure quite possibly, for my type of adventure. Adventures of the mind even more than of the body.

In an eight months' wandering through Africa (1938–39) in which I drove my own car from coast to coast, from Dar-es-Salaam in Tanganyika to Duala in the French Cameroons, my wife and I had plenty of exciting moments. One was right at the very start, when the rains bogged us down in the black-cotton soil of Tanganyika, and for mile after weary mile I had to hack down thorn trees to build our own corduroy road. An axe, and some burlap sacks—for my tyres to get a grip on—really saved that trip. My wife did the cooking on all that trip—120 days, or just four months, from the Indian Ocean to the Atlantic—on a 4s. spirit lamp. On which we often had three courses. (And on which we sometimes had naught to cook!) When I gave away my kit at Accra on the Gold Coast, the two things I found it hardest to part with were, not the battered, trusty, heroic old Ford V-8, but the heavy frying pan and that 4s. stove. In fact, I didn't part with the stove: rusted to nothingness now, it lies in our garage in North Devon. I saw it when I was looking for some other things, only the other day. . . .

After two trips into Africa, the last (1947–48) ending in a richly rewarding safari up through the camel country of the nomadic Somalis and the pagan pastoral Boran to the green foothills of Abyssinia, (there were 10,000 thirsty, roaring camels being watered at the ancient wells of Wajir when we got there), I have come to the conclusion that some of the most genuine adventurers that Britain has ever produced were the almost always nonself-seeking explorers and the early administrators who opened up Africa. The story of the naval officer, Hugh Clapperton, in search of the source of the Niger, who died in the arms of his valet at Kano—the servant Richard Lemon Lander, a Cornishman, son of an innkeeper at Truro, then turning explorer himself—his most dangerous adventure being his attempts, finally successful, to escape from the fat widow Zoma, of the city of Wow Wow, who wanted to marry him—"She'll get you!" smiled Clapperton, with almost his dying breath. Lander, ex-servant, did explore a large part of the Niger from below the bend to its mouth; returned to England and was given the first Gold Medal of the Royal Geographical Society; back to Africa, he was wounded in a treacherous attack by the

natives at Angiama on January 20, 1834, and died at Fernando
Po, which he managed to reach, a few days later: "A victim,"
wrote one of his companions, "to his too great confidence in the
natives." Captain Cook was like that.

James Bruce, Mungo Park, Hugh Clapperton and Richard
Lemon Lander, David Livingstone, Richard Francis Burton,
John Hanning Speke, Samuel White Baker, Henry Morton
Stanley (American): one ought not to dare step foot in Africa
without knowing what these men did. And what they stood for.
Determination, courage, sacrifice. Their story, so little known
by the average Englishman, can be read, in compressed form,
in a fascinating book called *African Discovery*: by Margery Per-
ham and J. Simmons. To anyone who wants to know what real,
nonself-seeking adventure is, I heartily recommend this stirring
book. It is an experience itself to read it: it stirs the blood like
reading *Moby Dick*.

Enough of myself. I have made it clear, I hope, that adventure, for me, has always been the mental satisfaction I have got
out of strange countries, scenes, and situations. A fabulous adventure was when, in the spring of 1929, an old eccentric
Englishman, Alexander Wicksteed, who had tried to go hermit
in Red Moscow, and I tried to take two horses over the Main
Range of the Caucasus and down to Sukhum on the Black Sea.
We set out from Kislovodsk, that old Tsarist watering spa described in the stories of Pushkin and Lermontoff: went along the
northern face of the Main Range, crossed the streams high up,
usually on a level of about 8,000 feet, small torrents that
eventually made the wild Terek River and the broad Kuban.
For three of these weeks we never saw a road, and, for many
days, not even a trail. For part of them we travelled with a
band of nomadic Turco-Tartars, on their spring migration with
their cattle in search of grass. I have written this story elsewhere. Sufficient to say that Wicksteed never got up to the top
of the Klukhor Pass, and that I was frozen in there on the night
of June 27, 1929, at 9,000 feet—it was too early in the year to
get around the last 50 yards: the rains of spring had made the
snow faces too dangerous. "It is better to live!" said the
Karachaite mountaineer who was one of my porters. We had
got quite a way out on that dangerous face, and it took us about
a quarter of an hour to get up the nerve and make the turn, just

to turn around, in the treacherous snow; and even those cat-like little men of the mountains grinned when we got back to what I would call "hard land." But it was with gloom that we made our way down, retracing our steps into the glacial valley. It was an uncompleted adventure that has occasionally reproached me ever since.

I have an idea that mountain climbing is probably one of the purest of adventures. I know practically nothing about it, having never climbed with a rope. And when I have listened to Alpine climbers talking, or read their accounts of it, I have often been struck dumb as to their almost orgiastic passion for taking insane risks. Yet, in a small way, I have scrambled about some tricky places that have amply let me see the thrill of it, also to understand a definite reticence that you meet in conversation with these men. I knew Frank Smythe slightly, and if you could persuade him to let himself go, even if ever so little, he soon forgot you were there, and you could see from a certain rapt expression in his eyes that he was again "hearing the silence between the spaces," as I think he himself actually described that awe one feels in the high altitudes. And I met L. S. Amery, for the first time, when I was down in the Dinaric Alps, and he was having what was for him a very cushy climbing holiday, with no real risks. Small in body, great in heart and mind, he amply fulfils what I meant when I said that adventure takes place in the mind, and that a brain is an absolute essential if the adventures that you have in life are going to mean anything lasting. Little Leopold S. Amery: one time First Lord of the Admiralty; Secretary of State for the Colonies; Secretary of State for the Dominions; Secretary of State for India and Burma—has three mountain peaks in this world named after him. He was the first to make the ascent of what is now known as Mt. Amery, Alberta, Canada.

In those two enchanted springs and summers that we spent down in the mountains I was writing books. It was there that I wrote *The Way of a Transgressor*, by the simple method of never putting my trousers on until I had done my ten daily pages. There was an adventure for you. We were broke. The little chalet-like hotel we lived in was run by a religious order: food and lodging was the large sum of 4s. a day. The book was a large gamble. But those mountains all around us made it a thrilling risk. Our breakfast was served us each morning, in our bedroom, by Minka, the huntsman's daughter: for this fabulously beautiful region had once been the hunting reserve of King Alexander of Yugoslavia. His hunting lodge was right near us: I poached his trout streams quite regularly. Also, as this part of Slovenia had once been under Austria, a certain White Horse Inn atmosphere still flavoured our chalet. It was noticeable in the coffee, with whipped cream such as you get in Vienna, the crescent-shaped fresh rolls and the honey and butter we had for every breakfast. And Minka, with her rosy cheeks and gay smile, made each day a delight to get started on, no matter how hard the chapter or particular ten pages that lay ahead of me. As luncheons were equally delectable (usually being trout that I had caught the previous evening) I usually finished my ten pages and put on my trousers by lunch-time.

In the afternoons we either fished the mountain streams, or we climbed. One day every week we took off completely, when with rucksack on my back we hit for the higher altitudes. And each month we took one stretch of four days off, going for long climbs along the Italian frontier, sleeping in the Yugoslav skiers' huts. My wife, my young son and myself. Sometimes we were lost in the snow fog, and we came down one or two snow-faces much faster than we had intended. On the second year, when he was only nine years old, my son climbed Triglav. It was only 9,000 feet, but it was the highest peak they had in the vicinity. And there were one or two awkward corners, where the old hand-holds had given way, which made us wish that we had not started on that trip. Also between Little Triglav and Big Triglav is a narrow ledge where the wind seems determined to throw you off and hurl you down through space, through the floor of clouds far below you. When we got back to the Alexander Hutte, 8,000 feet, drenched from the heavy rain that lashed us on the way down, and my young son and I, wrapped in nothing but blankets, sat before the hut's fire waiting for our clothes to dry, we felt that we really had had an adventure. His mother, I might say, who can't see a mountain without immediately trying to get to the top of it, had just taken Triglav in her stride.

All such things are adventure, legitimate adventures. We had the same feeling, the thrill, around the camp-fires as late as 1948, when I went up on safari in the deserts of the Somali camel nomads to the frontier of Abyssinia. Waking up on some of those mornings, watching the sun rise (for we used no tent) I felt that life was so fresh and joyous that it was almost like being back again in the expectant days of one's youth. The stark hardness of those lava deserts seemed only to confirm my happiness: there was a sharp sense of life being fully lived. The very rawness of it enhanced its reality. I think that is the essential feeling to all adventure: the sharpened validity of all your emotions—and physical discomfort often adds to them.

Down here where I live in North Devon, on one of the most beautiful and lonely spots of this rocky coast, I can still have adventures. Small as you may think some of them to be. In pouring rains, on windy nights so cold that you do not want to take your hands out of your pockets, I go out with a friend of mine and his "long dogs." He has trained these delicate creatures to course at night, so deadly that he will often bring back fifty or sixty rabbits from the sand dunes. It is a far, far more merciful way of killing them than with a trap. They know no suffering—it is over in an instant. And this is one of his ways of making a living for a very happy family that he keeps going. He is an ex-trooper of the Royal Horse Artillery, and began life as a colt-breaker—and I have not laughed so whole-heartedly in years as I have listening to him talk about men and horses as we have lain on the sand dunes waiting for the dawn to come (and sometimes it seems as if it never will!), waiting for the dawn flight of ducks.

The other night we were flight shooting. As he remarked, about the time when everybody else is going home is just the time when we go out. We were crouched there, keeping our hands covered and our faces down, so that their whiteness would not put the ducks off; it was pouring rain, and so cold that my numbed thumb could hardly slide the "safety" up. He stared across the marshland to where the lights of our local village made their pattern in the night. We discussed what one or two of our friends were probably doing at that moment. In pubs, probably. The rain was lashing at our backs, trying to get down our necks. He, who seems to shoot more at the sound than at any sight, the mere smudge, of a duck in such total darkness, got three teal that night. I got one. As we stood up from lying in the mud, he looked at the lights of the town and said exultantly—

"Bless you, sir, there's not a dozen men in that town that knows there's a life like this!"

In that jubilation lay the note of pure adventure.

IN PURSUIT OF KNOWLEDGE

John Garstang

"Longtime in search of knowledge did I range
The field of human life, in heart and mind
Benighted."

. . . WORDSWORTH. Prel. XIII.

YOU can acquire knowledge for its own sake easily enough among your books at home, or by making a short journey to the nearest library; but the pursuit of knowledge involves travel. You have only to dip into the pages of the ancient historians and geographers, such as Herodotus and Strabo, to realize that it has always done so and always will. The pursuit and search for the buried treasures of knowledge calls for a unique combination of abilities, for the explorer-excavator must be traveller, detective and scholar all at the same time. It is, perhaps, the most exciting of all intellectual pursuits. I, certainly, know of no more thrilling or rewarding adventure than the discovery of some ruined city or monument, long lost to sight, at some point where modern and ancient pathways cross.

Where does the pursuit of such knowledge start? Usually in ancient writings. The location of Hazor, for example, centre of the organized power of the Canaanites as described in the Book of Judges, followed on a study of the roads leading to the scene of the epic struggle narrated in the Song of Deborah. Theoretically there could only have been one such centre, the Huleh basin, in which all routes available for chariotry converged; yet that did not detract in any way from the thrill and excitement of following up this clue to a successful issue. This method of approach resembled in miniature the process of reasoning which ultimately restored the lost Empire of the Hittites to its place in History and upon the map.

Mine has been a life of travel, mostly in pursuit of knowledge. What I have to tell must necessarily be somewhat autobiographical, for which I ask the reader's indulgence.

My first travels did not take me far afield, only, in fact, about ten miles, but being at the time a schoolboy, it was rather an adventure to catch an evening train which put me down at nine o'clock within four miles of a well-known observatory, whose kindly director allowed me to spend the night with a five-inch telescope among the stars in space. This happened several times. It came to an end when the luggage train that I had previously taken to get back in time for morning school broke down. But those solemn hours left an indelible impression upon my attitude to life. They taught me the relative sizes of the planets, the fourth-rate magnitude of our sun and solar system in the depths of space, and reduced to their proper proportion the problems of human life upon this earth. Now at the age of seventy-four, I am firmly convinced that the teaching of the elements of astronomy to the youth of our little planet would not only inspire individuals with a truer sense of values and proportions, but might contribute radically to a better understanding between nations. But I am digressing.

The way to this observatory passed the old Roman station at Ribchester. This soon attracted my interest, and in my undergraduate days I frequently tramped the six or seven miles that separated it from my father's home. Then, with the encouragement of Professor Haverfield (one of the great friends of my youth) I undertook a modest excavation. What an adventure that was! It lasted through two long vacations, and disclosed the outline as well as some of the internal buildings of a standard fort or Castellum, one of the units in the net-like system of forts designed to protect Britain from inroads of the northern tribes. There was found the fine bronze helmet or headpiece of a statue, which has long been a feature in the British Museum.

One item of knowledge leads to another, whetting the appetite. I had now learnt how to walk and think.

In the autumn of 1900 I joined an excavating party at the Egyptian Abydos, and there learnt about camp life and surveying. The next year saw me farther afield, exploring the western deserts mostly on foot in company with a Bedawi guide. During those three years I learnt to understand the Egyptians of the upper country, and to speak their language, which is purer Arabic than that of Cairo and the bigger towns. Thus prepared, I transferred my activities in 1904 to Beni Hassan, site of a well-known necropolis of 2000 B.C. A famous row of decorated tomb-chapels halfway up the cliffs overlooked the

Nile from the eastern side, and provided admirable accommodation for myself and occasional friends, as well as for my work-people when they arrived by river boat from their village in the south. We soon found that a goodly number of tombs below the gallery had escaped robbery, having been filled up in antiquity with great boulders which were difficult to move. Inside these tombs we found the contents exactly as they had been placed originally on and around the painted coffin, and in one of them there remained in the sand the actual imprint of the bare foot of one of the ancient Egyptians who had arranged the offerings and finally closed the tomb-mouth with cement and blocks of stone.

The ancient Egyptian religion required not only that the body of a dead person should be preserved, but that provision should be made for its nourishment; and to this end wooden models of work-people and servants engaged in domestic operations, such as bread-making, beer-brewing, fetching birds from the market, the ceremonial killing of an ox and so on, were placed within his tomb. Scenes of a similar character were painted on the walls in the great gallery above. Naturally, these models and paintings mirrored the daily life and occupations of the members of the community centred around the feudal lord and gentry of the locality, and were faithful illustrations of the domestic practices of the day. Thus, a permanently well-filled granary was represented by a model, with figures of basket carriers climbing up a ladder to pour the grain in through a hole in the roof, while a scribe or teller would be seated conveniently near recording the quantities on his tablet. These offerings were mostly conventional and almost standardized. Their quality varied in different tombs, presumably with the wealth and social status of the deceased, but occasionally among the models would be some that were real masterpieces of wood-carving. These offerings were not merely symbolic, for, as a result of some magical process that followed incantations and prayers, they were supposed actually to provide for the material sustenance of the dead during the long period of waiting until the soul returned and the corpse revived. The essential fact is clear that the ancient Egyptians, from first to last, believed not only in the immortality of the soul, but in a future life on earth with an actual reincarnation.

I found all this strange at first, and pondered it not a little. The amount of work involved in directing an expedition employing sixty men with no other assistance than that of those few natives susceptible to training, the daily routine, the surveying, photographing, developing, printing, and recording, the keeping of a diary and accounts, this all kept me on the run from early morn till late at night, and I had neither time nor eyes for the glories of the sunset seen across the broad valley of the Nile, as the sun descended behind the western hills to plunge us into another night. Then an artist friend came out and stayed with me a full season there. By re-arranging my time-table I was able to snatch half an hour for tea—at sunset. To this day I feel grateful to my departed friend for pointing out its glories, for that put me on the way to the explanation of the problem I had been pondering.

In Upper Egypt each day and every day (with rare exceptions) you can watch the sun rise. All day it blazes down out of a cloudless sky, and then you can watch it disappear behind the hills in the west. The actual setting is so clear that nearly every time you can see the last ray turn green. Almost every night is clear and starlit. These elementary phenomena occur and recur daily throughout the year, and every year. It has always been so, ever since the Nile Valley formed. Each year, and every year from of old, the Nile overflows its immediate banks and inundates all the cultivable land between the deserts and the barren hills that bound its valley. The height of the flood-waters varies a little, and to meet that the peasant must be ever watchful, to build up or open his barriers, for these flood-waters deposit not only fresh mud but fertilizing materials from the higher sources of the river. These recurrent phenomena, whether daily or seasonal, dominate and have always dominated the life of the Egyptian people, for all depend ultimately on the soil which constitutes their land. To the ancients, it is clear, the fundamental impression Nature implanted in their minds was that of continuity and repetition. Reflection will tell you, as it did me, that there was nothing in these primitive experiences to suggest an end of any kind. The fundamentally vital matters, such as the ever-flowing Nile, the ever-shining sun, the yearly inundation, and the duties they engendered, were all recurrent or continuous. There was thus no reason to suppose that Death was not also part of a recurrent or continuing process like night and sleep. The idea that Life could end finally would not arise. Death could only be an interlude, and so they made elaborate preparations for the period of waiting (including the preservation of the body and a complex ritual) and did everything of which they could think to ensure corporeal and spiritual completeness when the long wait was over.

This sense of continuity is still illustrated in the burial and religious practices of the inhabitants today. From our vantage point upon the rock terrace we saw their festivals and processional visitations of the tombs with the same wailing of women as of old; and we learnt that widows often secretly bury bread and other food in the graves of their departed. In ancient tombs I have frequently observed among the usual dummy or imitation supplies, the remains of real bread and olives or dates placed upon a plain pottery dish. The conclusion is that the provision of real foodstuffs points to an inherent belief in a return to life; and that the use of dummy and symbolic substitutes grew with the development of ritual under a priesthood that preyed upon the popular belief. This is, however, only one aspect of the effect of environment on the thoughts and life of the inhabitants of that unique land.

With the sun and the Nile controlling and providing the primary necessities of life any ancient Egyptian who was at all observant became habituated to repetition by the unfailing and visible recurrence of the leading natural phenomena, while any inventive talent he may have possessed remained dormant. The recognition of this fact is what I gained by my stay in the cliffs at Beni Hassan; and it added a hundredfold to the interest of all my further travels up the Nile. There is abundant confirmation of it. In all the old religious centres it is illustrated over and over again in the rows of columns and statues, long avenues of sphinxes, hall after hall added to older temples, always to this same model; grandeur and prosperity expressed by aggrandizement resulting in stupendous columns, colossal statues, etc., in which can be found little or no originality of design or thought. Even the Pyramids evolved by slow process of repetition and enlargement over a thousand years from a simple form of grave and cover, the earliest developed type being the Step-Pyramid of Sakkara. An artist will probably find a more interesting illustration in the wonderful technique and amazing realism of Egyptian sculpture as early as the pyramids themselves—again the natural consequence of a thousand years of uninterrupted watchfulness upon which the ancient inhabitant depended for his very existence. It is not that the vital phenomena which dominated his eye are not represented in other countries, but here they stared him in the face day after day, while the isolation of his strip of land beside the Nile in the deserts of North-East Africa restrained the infiltration of fresh ideas from the more varied experiences of Syria and contemporary Babylonia.

My earliest travels when exploring upper Egypt were mostly done alone with my Bedawi guide, and at other times accompanied by a working party and light camp outfit. It was thus that I re-examined at Hierakonpolis the royal tombs, and recovered a corner missing from the oldest recorded hieroglyphic inscription upon a small ivory plaque. It bore the name of Mena, traditionally the earliest monarch of United Egypt. The fragment was triangular in shape and not more than half an inch in length. It was recovered after sieving about forty tons of debris that had been exposed to the weather for eleven years. At the same time there came to light a duplicate of the same plaque almost complete, and nearby a similar process recovered a small head in lapis lazuli, missing from a figurine in the Ashmolean Museum at Oxford. Later, I took these prizes to Cairo and showed the corner of the ivory tablet to the learned keeper of the national museum, who promptly declared that it could not belong to the tablet because the restoration should read differently. After a little argument he consented to see whether indeed the pieces fitted, and summoning his chiefs of staff and key bearer he led the way in solemn procession to the show case. He was greatly surprised to find that the "fit" was perfect and completed the plaque; and very soon he was plunged into an excited discussion with his French colleagues. He expressed his gratitude by handing over to the Ashmolean Museum the head in lapis lazuli.

These finds were incidental to my early travels by the Upper Nile, where I was really bent on investigating the possible connection of certain remains in the upper country with the more primitive cultures of Africa higher up. This led me to Aswan and thence by local sailing ships to several places in central Nubia. At Abu-Simbel I saw the giant sculptures and the central shrine lit by the morning sun, and was greatly interested to find even there a record of the Pharaoh's relations with the Hittites and his marriage with a Hittite princess. For my immediate task I established myself in a small chamber in the top of a temple pylon at Dakkeh. From the open window in the evenings I could see the crocodiles disporting in the wide river, which hereabouts resembles a lake owing to the damming of it at Aswan; and I could hear the endless chatter of the village wives as they ground their corn with rubbing stones, or busied themselves at the wash-tub—scenes familiar in Egyptian life nearly 4000 years ago at Beni Hassan and elsewhere. In the old graves of this neighbourhood I found burials resembling in appearance those of pre-dynastic Egypt, though trinkets and scarabs associated with them showed clearly that they belonged to the historic period of the XVIIIth Egyptian Dynasty. Here the practice of placing real foodstuffs with the dead was more clearly in evidence; and here was the same Nile and the same cycle of phenomena, only with less possibility of extraneous influence.

My journeys of exploration in Upper Egypt have been mostly done by rowboat and donkey, and in Nubia by native sailing boat; but the travels of an archælogist involve extremes. Requiring official recognition and permits for his delvings, he is sometimes granted a semi-official status, and travels as do the mighty; but that is rare. If the object of his quest lies in out-of-the-way or forbidden areas, the nearer he draws to it the farther back he goes as a rule in his mode of travel. There now came to me a welcome interlude of the more comfortable kind. While studying the antiquities of Nubia, I was invited by the Sirdar of the Sudan to investigate the site of Meroë, an ancient Ethiopian capital beside the Nile just below Khartoum, well known from writings of classical historians and geographers.

Travel from Wady Halfa southwards cannot well be done by river owing to the cataracts that intervene; but the train service set up by the British after the reconquest of the country by Kitchener is extremely comfortable, and the saloon that bears the name of that great soldier-statesman is relatively luxurious. It

was thus we travelled, thanks to our official invitation. Among
our luggage was a large hatbox. Though we did not realize it
then, it was too big to be got through the saloon doorway or
windows, and at Halfa station we were informed that there
would be a short delay owing to some necessary shunting. Stepping on to the platform during this operation I was greatly
entertained by seeing the saloon brought back to the head of the
train with an empty ten-ton "flat" attached. Into the middle
of this the hatbox was placed ceremoniously by the Sudanese
porters and a tarpaulin spread over it to keep it in place and
clear of sand. The station manager then informed us with great
solemnity that we were ready to start.

About two o'clock in the afternoon we got away; and some
hours later a white-robed waiter came into the little dining-
room and asked whether he should serve tea, and whether we
preferred milk or lemon. In our innocence we voted for milk.
Presently the train began to slow down, and opening a peep-
hole in the shutters we peered out at the glaring sunlight scene.
The Sudan differs essentially from Egypt in that the arable land
is confined to a narrow strip beside the river. The Nile differs
from all other rivers by reason of the fact that for two thousand
miles it receives no permanent tributaries: practically all its
waters come down from its sources in Abyssinia. Lower down
in Egypt, nearly all the normal water is drawn off to irrigate
the wide flat plains that form its banks, and much is lost by
evaporation, so that as one proceeds upstream the river actually
becomes bigger. In the Sudan, however, irrigation had not
been organized, but we found ourselves travelling through fields
and groves of stunted trees forming a green strip about a mile
in width. Presently we heard the brakes applied, and the train
pulled up rather quickly. Through our peep-hole we saw our
serving boy with a cup in hand racing towards a goat which
was browsing some thirty yards away. Catching it with skill
evidently born of experience, he half filled his cup with milk,
and regained the train, which again got under way. A few
minutes later the boy appeared with a tea-tray tastefully arranged, including a small cream jug of warm milk, and having
placed it on the table he said solemnly, "Tea is served, Pasha,"
and retired without so much as a smile.

All that evening and through the night the train continued to eat up the miles, and when we awoke next morning we were crossing a wide stretch of desert without a sign of vegetation. Towards 11 o'clock we found ourselves again near the river, but were astonished to see through the window on the other side a succession of shimmering lakes on the banks of which appeared groves of trees, while in the water there seemed to be islands and boats. We had not expected any luxury of the kind. We gazed and gazed, but then, while rounding a bend, all trace of what we had thought we saw disappeared completely, yet fresh pictures formed each time we came into the same angle of the sunlight. These were, of course, mirages. This experience made me realize how easily they might have lured a thirsty traveller or animal to death.

Arrived at the site, we pitched our camp in a grove of palm trees beside the Nile. I was disappointed to see no trace of the ancient city. In the distance, however, on the gravelly desert some three or four miles away, were two groups of small pyramids, which on the analogy of Egypt presumably betokened the burial place of the potentates whose city must have been quite near. The strip of cultivable soil was hereabouts overgrown with prickly acacia, and difficult to explore, as the spikes of these trees were two to three inches long and very sharp. However, near the edge of the desert, half a mile away there appeared a mound containing masoned blocks of stone, and here our workmen began operations. It proved to cover a sun temple, presumably a later one than that which Zeus is stated by the historian Herodotus to have visited "to feast with the Ethiopians."

The central feature was an altar on a raised platform surrounded by a terrace bordered with sculptured blocks, and approached by a ramp sloping upwards from the East. As Lord Kitchener told me on one of his visits, the great sun temple of Java rises in similar fashion, but on far greater scale, in a series of ambulatories diminishing in size and culminating in the central altar at the top.

Nearby we found a necropolis of primitive tombs with unusual contents which we ascribed to the pre-Meroitic period, though they may prove to represent the native civilization after the fall of the mushroom capital for which we were still seeking. Our search for the city was ultimately successful, though it took more than a year to find the clue. By cutting away some shrubbery just within the cultivable area we exposed traces of masonry, which we at once proceeded to clear. They took the form of a series of rooms which became larger and more elaborate as we proceeded westward, until finally we uncovered a central sanctuary with the high altar in position and a number of inscribed reliefs on the surrounding walls. We had exposed the local temple dedicated to the Egyptian god Amon, mightiest of all the Theban deities; and this at any rate was older than Herodotus.

The back of this sanctuary abutted on a stout ashlar wall which looked like a portion of the ancient *temenos*—the enclosure of the temple. Following up this clue in the next year, we were led into a forest of prickly acacia trees, through which we had to cut our way. After tracing it for two hundred yards we found it turn not in the direction that would have enclosed the temple, but into the heart of the forest, towards the river. It proved in fact to be part of the defensive wall of the city we were seeking, which we proceeded to uncover—not without hard work and nasty wounds.

In one of the older palaces, under the corner of a wall, we found two pottery vessels of the period filled with gold dust and small nuggets together with three plaques inscribed in Egyptian hieroglyphics with the names of Ethiopian Kings and other trinkets. It was an uncomfortable find to make in so remote a spot, even though the natives of the locality out of a respect for their "Sid Ahmed"—a Moslem saint—were peculiarly honest. I opened the sealed jars late at night in our darkroom in the presence of Professor Sayce and a stalwart German member of our staff; and having made the inventory placed them empty in the store-room after pouring the contents on my camp bed under the mattress upon which I spent a troubled night. Fortunately a government official arrived very promptly in reply to a cryptic telephone message from our temporary station to railway headquarters, and relieved me of further responsibility. The gold was recognized at once by a London expert as Abyssinian river siftings, and was valued on assay at nearly £2,000, which was devoted to further excavations and the needs of the Sudan Antiquities Service.

Attracted by the brilliant starlight and the new aspect of

stellar space which the latitude of Meroë provided, I had set up observing posts and brought out from England a four-inch telescope with accessories, for to me it is always delightful to spend a night with the stars and nebulæ. I was to discover that in pursuing this hobby of mine, I was but following in the footsteps of an earlier traveller. In a courtyard of one of the northern palaces we found the mud-plastered walls to be inscribed with graffiti drawings and calculations representing (as it seems to me) a seated astronomer making observations by means of a primitive apparatus rather like a movable telegraph pole which was manipulated with ropes and a sort of "Hooke's handle" by an attendant who stood behind him. The figures upon the wall doubtless registered his results, spread over a period of time. I believe these drawings, of which a full account has been published, to record a calculation of the latitude of Meroë by one of the earliest astronomers, who counted the days the sun took in passing from its vertical position at midday to its maximum northern elongation, checked by similar observations of its return. The figures registered show a slight discrepancy, but would involve only a relatively small error of latitude calculated on that basis. Some such method of computation is known to have been employed from the writings of Pliny, who also records how Eratosthenes calculated the latitude of Aswan in the third century B.C. The date of our graffiti, however, would be nearer to that of Hipparchus, about 160 B.C., who is credited with the invention of several astronomical instruments. The observer at Meroë, or his scribe, initialled these local records in the Meroitic script with the letter A.

This discovery was somewhat obscured by the outbreak of the First World War; but even so, it is curious that, though published in detail, so far as I know no astronomer has been able to reconstruct the instruments depicted or to offer an explanation of the calculations. It has been left to my schoolboy knowledge and experience to attempt the solution. At Princeton in 1943 I showed my published material to Professor Einstein who, with great kindness and concentration, studied it for half an hour. He then asked me by what means any person sufficiently educated to use such instruments might have reached the spot at the date indicated. Once satisfied on this point, closing my volume with the gentleness and humility characteristic of his nature, he remarked: "I cannot understand how any scientific man can fail to be interested in the origins of his subject: I think your explanation is probably correct."

My pursuit of knowledge of Meroë led to one other striking discovery, that of a full-sized bronze head of the Emperor Augustus when a young man. It is a glorious work of art. His characteristic "great gleaming" eyes are successfully represented by a yellow-black iris of faience enclosing a pupil of glass, the whites being of alabaster. This head may have been carried off with other loot from Aswan which the troops of Queen Candon are known to have raided about 23 B.C. It was found buried by intention face downwards in a pocket of fine sand and was quite intact. It was set up in my work tent and high officials of the Sudan, including the Sirdar and Slatin Pasha, assembled to inspect it. Kitchener of Khartoum wanted to keep it in Khartoum as an attraction to visitors. My reply was to tell him the story of a dealer in Omdurman from whom my wife had bought some ostrich feathers for which we had not cash enough to pay, and to whom I had offered an English £5 note. Turning this over somewhat contemptuously he said "What is this?" To which I replied indignantly, "A £5 note of the British Government." Giving it back to me he said, quite seriously, "English Government! Here today, gone tomorrow; give me your cheque, Englishman's cheque always good." Having gained a hearing I then argued that in the British Museum this prize would be permanently secure, and that for every person who might see it in Khartoum at least a thousand would see and appreciate it in London. A dead silence followed: "K. of K." was reputed to be an autocrat, and the officials present looked as though they expected an earthquake. But Kitchener saw the point, and asked Slatin Pasha what he thought. The latter to my great relief supported my view, as ultimately did the Sirdar.

Now, the bronze head from Ribchester, where my work began, is exhibited in the same gallery as that from Meroë—personal souvenirs from the opposite poles of the Roman Empire.

The excavation of the city of Meroë was practically completed and the work of conservation begun, when disaster overcame the project with the outbreak of the First World War. I had proposed to consolidate the mud brick walls of the buildings and enclose the whole area during the following winter, and the Government had begun to make plans for encouraging tourist traffic. It was not to be. The heavy rains of successive seasons (during which I was in France) defeated our intentions; our camp home was pillaged and most of my instruments disappeared including the telescope I so greatly treasured.

During the armistice I was summoned to London, and asked to undertake the organization of a British School of Archæology in Palestine. With the necessary documents I travelled with military facilities to Marseilles and thence on a hospital ship to Port Said. I was carrying dispatches of a confidential character; and on presenting my papers to the port officer, he rang the bell and summoned a young naval officer, who was instructed to convey me by the Canal to Kantara "with all possible speed." Never shall I forget that journey. With barely time for a hasty meal, I found myself on board a fast launch driven by compound diesel engines which had sixteen cylinders a side, and away we went. The young officer had his instructions, and evidently meant to fulfil them. All was well in the broad water of the harbour, but when we entered the Canal proper it was quite a different matter. Regulation speed is four knots, but we were realizing fifteen or twenty. Sitting in the stern I noticed that the water in front did not rise in foam but was drawn down as a hollow by the powerful screws, giving the impression all the time that we were falling or going downhill so to speak. Looking behind I saw that two waves, separating at our stern in a V-shape, were following us and washing each bank with a steady roller about four feet high. After a little time, during which I tried to explain something about "more haste less speed," I saw abreast of us a peasant woman bending over the calm water washing clothes. I had hardly shouted a warning when the wave covered her completely and all that could be seen was a pair of wriggling legs and floating linen. The wave passed on, leaving the poor creature "high and wet"; we stopped to assure ourselves of her safety, and so learnt what she thought of us. The young officer did not understand Arabic, but he reduced speed to six knots and I arrived comfortably at Kantara, and from there went on by rail to Jerusalem. I had never seen the Holy City before, and little thought that I was destined to live there for seven years as a Government official.

Like many other Englishmen at that time I was not fully aware of the political situation. It was all the more disturbing to find the place in military occupation, and to sense a growing feeling of unrest that seemed likely to become perilous; though before I left the Service finally I had learnt and demonstrated that an international brotherhood was still possible.

I was now no longer actively in pursuit of knowledge, for my task was to help in formulating a scheme for the protection of the ancient monuments of Palestine, which include many of the religious buildings of the country. This, too, involved travel, and I went by car to Jericho, deep in the Jordan Rift, an impressive and, at that time, a dangerous ride: and to Ascalon where are the remains of a great Roman "Free-city," with traces of its Forum and other monuments, all girt with a semi-circular wall fronting on the sea; and eventually back to London with my reports. It became clear at this stage that my duty lay in Palestine, and with profound regret I resigned the office of Adviser to the Sudan Government to which Lord Kitchener and General Wingate, the Sirdar, had invited me before the war broke out. My regrets were compensated by the stimulus derived from my first glimpse of the Holy Land; and I returned there the same year with my wife and daughter.

Finding that there was little to be done immediately, I went on a first reconnaissance and so had my first glimpse of those historic areas in the north of Palestine, the Plain of Esdraelon, Megiddo, Mount Tabor, Bethshan, Tiberias and the Sea of Galilee, which I was to visit time and again during the next seven years; and I learnt something of the realities of racial hatred that turned the blood cold and menaced civilization where all should have been peace.

My new duties were to organize a department of Antiquities under the new Civil Administration, and to direct it conjointly with the British School. There were advantages in this scheme, for both were relatively modest undertakings, and I was fortunate in finding a suitable building in the vicinity of the Cathedral. There, with the devoted collaboration of my former student and life-long friend W. J. Phythian Adams, as Keeper of the Museum, we began the threefold task of preparing for the reception of students and the excavation of Ascalon, while gathering together a small group of inspectors to register all the historical monuments of this country and take steps for their protection. We enjoyed from the first the collaboration of the American School and of the French archæologists of St. Etienne. To forestall any political pressure and to give due consideration to conflicting claims, an International Advisory Board was formed to advise the Director of Antiquities. It comprised representatives of all the bodies, whether scholastic or religious, interested in the ancient monuments and archæology of the country, including Arab, Jew, Greek or Latin, French, Italian, American and British; and I am happy to recall that notwithstanding the material or traditional conflicts of interest involved, our meetings were always cordial and all questions were ultimately solved by mutual concession and without division.

Within two or three years no less than a dozen archæological expeditions began work under permit of the Department. Some of them became major excavations, notably the American investigations under Dr. Clarence Fisher at Beisan (the Biblical Bethshan) and at Megiddo, and those of Professor MacAlister in "the City of David" at Jerusalem to which the Palestine Exploration Fund now transferred its activities. Keeping in touch with such work and with our field inspectors involved me for some years in frequent journeys, mostly done by car. Fortunately the country is very small, not much bigger than Lancashire; but the roads at that time were bad and sometimes dangerous. In the course of these journeys two trains of thought took root in my head. The country was underpopulated and undeveloped: the historic plain of Esdraelon, the most fertile position of the land, was almost uninhabited. It seemed to me that the policy of intensive colonization was fatuous because uneconomical, there being few natural resources to develop, and dangerous if pressed with undue speed in view of the Arab fears that their homes were menaced. I visualized a peaceful Palestine, where the population could revive on natural lines, backed by the resources of civilization, without the shock of sudden political or social change. The Rothschild colonies, long established under the Turkish Regime, were respected organizations assimilated to the social order, where Jew and Arab worked together in friendly relations. They were established illustrations of possibilities that might have been developed with restraint and respect for human rights without injury to the feelings of others. The Arabs on the other hand were backward because unaided, and had no backing or voice in world affairs; yet we were bound by the terms of the mandate to assist in their development and to respect their rights. I saw the possibility that a moderate, just and sane policy on these lines might secure for the world a peaceful Palestine, where the nationals of all races could enjoy the fruits of their labours and visitors from all countries could travel freely to see the Holy Places and historical monuments and perform their devotions in quiet, and so leave the country with an imperishable and delightful memory. So I devised a scheme of routes and tours, of guards trained in courtesy, of well conducted hotels and other features of an ordered Service that would ensure these ends, and provide from tourist fees for the upkeep of the monuments if not for the whole administration of the country—but all in vain. The scheme was swept aside, together with the fair name of Britain, by the pressure of dollar politics and Zionist territorial aspirations. Instead of a peaceful Palestine in which to wander, we stand today as it were on the edge of a volcano that will sooner or later shake the world with violent eruptions.

The second thought is happily more durable, and will surely survive the threatening disaster, for it is a matter of history. My frequent visits to the historic sites, at first those under excavation, Jerusalem and Shechem, Megiddo overlooking the plain of Esdraelon, Beisan and Jericho in the Jordan valley, Ascalon and Gezer in the Philistine plain, then the southern deserts and the less known areas of northern Galilee, including Nazareth, Hazor, and the plain of Acre, awakened in me long dormant memories of the Bible stories heard in my youth. As the excavations continued and historical materials were brought to light I became intrigued, and re-read those stories, but I was perplexed. Some of the descriptions of sites and places seemed so real, while others remained obscure and out of focus. It was not long before I realized that the descriptions of the sites and cities which investigations proved to be historically old were found in precisely those passages in the Old Testament that critical scholarship had decided to be in general the oldest portions of the text. So, after resigning my official post, I devoted several years to following up this clue. With my old colleague, now Canon Phythian Adams, and my wife as companions, I

returned to Palestine and revisited every identified place mentioned in the older sources of the books of Joshua and Judges
and examined two key positions, Jericho and Hazor (which I
had located the previous year) more thoroughly with the spade.
The impression of material reality underlying the narrative was
confirmed; indeed no radical flaw was found in the topography
and archæological indications of those documents. Examination will convince the reader that they contain, in spite of later
additions, the core of the historical narrative, relatively free
from discrepancies while giving a fairly continuous account of
the sequence of events. Their chronological framework also,
which had been a source of constant controversy, will be found
to fit without strain and with advantage, into the known history
of Egyptian activities in the land. This vital factor is overlooked
by most students of Bible history, yet under any scheme of computation the Pharaoh ruled over the country during the whole
period covered by the narrative, with an organized administration backed by police posts at various points. Though no direct
allusion to the fact is made in the Books, it is historical and in-
contestable; and no student seeking truth can afford to neglect
its implications.

During the seven memorable years of our sojourn in Jerusalem, my wife held open house for welcome visitors and her
Friday evening parties were attended by friends of all races and
religions, for discussion of politics was not encouraged. There
we frequently had the Grand Mufti (a much maligned patriot)
and the Zionist representative, seated in amicable conversation
or in discussion which was always temperate. Among our frequent guests was the Emir now King Abdullah from beyond the
Jordan, who loved to watch the stars through a new telescope
I had taken there. He knew the names of all those visible, for
most of them are in Arabic; and he told us many Arab folk-
tales concerning them. I visited him frequently, for the opening
up of the antiquities of his country, which included the fine
classical city of Jerash and the rose-red rock city of Petra, fell
also to my lot. At first Jerash had to be approached by a five-
hour ride on horseback: then a track was cut into the sides of
the hills so that a car could travel, albeit perilously, along it. It
was a difficult and dangerous feat; but now a good road exists.
In all this work the Emir, though not controlling it, took a lively

interest; and after my retirement from official duties I several times enjoyed his hospitality.

A growing interest in the Hittites, known at the time only from Biblical and Egyptian sources, took me early to Asia Minor towards which Professor Sayce's comparison of some widely distant inscriptions already pointed as their homeland. There travel from railhead was almost invariably done on horseback. It is true that my earliest exploration in that hospitable country was done on foot, in 1904, with the Phrygian country and monuments as the principal objective. The pine-clad valleys of that area left me with an indelible souvenir of their romantic beauty, and the monuments provided fresh interest every day. Most impressive was the so called "Midas tomb," the entrance to which was guarded by rampant lions carved in high relief on the solid rock. The resemblance to the famous Lion gate of ancient Mykenae on the opposite side of the Ægean has led to an illuminative discussion as to their possible connection in origin. The identity and coming of the early Phrygian warriors present, indeed, problems which only extensive exploration can solve. They seem to have overrun the Hittite capital about 1200 B.C., and in Homeric legend were allied with the Trojans.

The quest for knowledge about the Hittites led me far afield. I had already searched in local museums of Italy for Etruscan antiquities that might link that field with Troy, as suggested by Virgil's story of the migration of Æneas, and I had found seventy points of resemblance in details of Anatolian art. But few of those were local products of Troy. The Hittite monuments, once they had been recognized, were traced over an extensive field, through the heart of Asia Minor, as far as northern and central Syria. Pictorial scenes upon the walls of Egyptian temples of the fourteenth and twelfth centuries B.C. bore witness to a long period of conflict between the armies of the Pharaohs and the Hittites for the possession of the then rich Syrian provinces. The struggle came to a head in a pitched battle at Kadesh on the Orontes, in which both sides were crippled, and it was concluded a few years later by the signing of a treaty of peace, the text of which in Egyptian hieroglyphics was already translated. The immediate problem was to localize and examine the centre of Hittite power.

In pursuit of this objective, I found myself with three companions in 1907 in Ankara, then a small town, where we bought horses and organized a caravan with guide and guards, and set out on a journey of exploration which was to examine all the accessible known Hittite sites and gain an insight into their setting and environment. It was a grand journey, each day brimful of interest, and entirely free from unpleasant incidents; it took us zigzag through Asia Minor in a general south-easterly direction, across the Taurus Mountains to the southern coast, then eastwards over the Amanus, until we finally disbanded at Aleppo in northern Syria.

Having crossed the Halys river, on the third day we reached the village of Boghaz Keui, the Village of the Gorge, lying at the mouth of a deep continuous glen, its slopes thickly covered with trees and shrubs with here and there a contrasting patch of bare rock or red-brown soil. Beyond were heights of seven thousand feet. Near Boghaz Keui is the ruined city of Pteria, at which I had been planning to make excavations, but we found a German expedition already at work. It is an imposing site, on high ground girt with a wonderful rampart pierced with stone-built arched doorways adorned with sculptures, and further protected by fortified positions on the rocky eminences which formed the pillars of its defensive system. On the top we found, seated at the entrance to his tent, Hugo Winckler, a distinguished philologist, pondering over the fragment of a baked clay tablet inscribed in cuneiform. He was greatly excited, and without asking whence or why we had come, he burst out with: "We have here the names of Rameses and Hattusil; it must be the Hittite copy of the famous treaty between the Pharaoh and the Hittite king, and this tablet is part of the state archives," pointing as he spoke to several groups of similar broken tablets piled on the ground; "this place was indubitably the capital of the Hittite Empire." That was great news, indeed. As he spoke workmen appeared carrying more baskets of tablets which they poured out incautiously on to the ground. He complained that he was single-handed and that the work lacked supervision, and accepted my offer of help. We stayed three weeks, doing what we could to save the other tablets from damage and to develop the excavation methodically. (The next year I received in Liverpool a visit from the great historian Edward Meyer, who invited me to undertake the direction of further excavation on a share and share basis. My backers agreed; but unhappily the negotiations broke down when we were informed that the publication of results must be entirely in German, whereas we desired parallel publication in both languages. Had we gained this equitable concession Hittite studies might well have received earlier recognition in British Universities as a subject of academic importance, particularly to students of Greek origins and the Homeric background.)

The tablets came from a large palatial stone building of elaborate technique and plan on a lower terrace at the foot of the Acropolis, and this was only one of the many features of this long forgotten capital. Three miles away, in a natural outcrop of rock in the shape of a roofless grotto there is also a unique ancient sanctuary, wherein doubtless were performed many religious ceremonies. The leading *motif* shows the chief Hittite deity, the storm god, borne (in effigy) on the shoulders of his priests to confront the leading goddess of the land, who like her son (later called Tammuz or Adonis) is represented as standing on the back of a lion. In the retinue of the god are the leading deities of the Hittite pantheon; and in that of the leading goddess are the local versions of the same deity indigenous to the land. The whole scene represents a *Hieros Gamos* or divine marriage between the paramount Hittite deity and the time-honoured mother goddess. It is a grand scene, alive with features of interest and stimulating to thought and speculation.

Our journey continued, here, there, and everywhere, over mountains and across rivers, following up rumours which rarely materialized, but, when they did, provided ample compensation and called for cameras and copyists. I wish I could do it all again.

We reached Tarsus by way of the Cilician Gate, that famous defile through which have passed peoples destined to form nations, the armies of conquerors engaged on continental struggles, Eastern religions bound for the unthinking West, St. Paul with the Cross of Peace and the Crusaders with the Sword. Few passes can have such a historical record, few compete with its scenery. If you could acquire all the knowledge that has passed this way, it would make up a lifetime of pursuit. The steep slopes of the valley are thickly covered with pines, oaks and cypresses; in places the bare rock protrudes and towers aloft in almost vertical pinnacles that sometimes reach the snow-line. Here are the clear dark waters of the Kara Su bursting out of the naked rock to change the colour of the whole river. On and on you go, hemmed in by wooded highland landscapes of wild grandeur, and in the distance the dark green slopes of rugged Taurus and the white crest and crevices of Bulghar Dagh. And then you reach the gorge, the veritable Gate of Cilicia which an ordinary double-door would close, and so emerge into a fantastic world of crags towering upwards for a thousand feet, of peaks and heights wooded with a myriad trees glowing softly in the sunlight, a valley riven here and there by great protuberances of red and grey rock. From the pathway you can look down into peaceful glades alive with flowers and creepers through which the river winds its way. It is a place of incessant beauty and surprise.

From Tarsus we went to Adana and thence eastward, with a caravan of thirteen animals, over the Amanus range to a tiny village called Sakje-Geuzi, in the broad marshy valley lying between the Kurd Dagh and Giaour Dagh. Here I found several mounds which invited excavation, and I began work on one of them in the following year. Last year, forty years after I had first attacked this site, I had the great joy of revisiting it on horseback and seeing excavations there resumed by archæologists of the newly formed British Institute in Ankara.

By far the most rewarding aspect of all my travels in Turkey, both these early ones on horseback and those later undertaken with my wife's companionship by train and car, has been the recognition of the immutability of the main road-lines of the country, which are entirely determined by dominant physical features. Slight variation there may be, of course, over small sectors; but in deep valleys there is only one natural route, while mountain passes and river fords are also permanent. This has become a prime factor in determining the topographical outlines of the Map of Anatolia under the Hittites, on which I have been at work for thirty years and which has now (I believe) reached a useful form, at any rate as a basis of discussion and research. There can be no doubt about the advantages, if not the necessity, of studying historical geography on the spot, and such a map might provide the pointers to problems and possibilities of great interest.

The Hittite capital was not a natural road centre, but was connected locally with two very ancient trade routes, the one north–south from the Black Sea to the Mediterranean, while the other can be traced from the western coast at Miletos, Smyrna and Troy, eastward through Phrygia towards the Euphrates by way of Kangal. Here this one bifurcates, one branch heading up the river by Erzingan and Erzerum to northern Persia, the other crossing the uplands that border the Euphrates basin southwards to descend on Malatia, where fords and bridges give access to Biarbekr and the basin of the Tigris. These ancient routes cannot be radically altered; they were in use in Roman times, and are followed today by the Turkish railways. In the west also the ascent from the coastlands to the plateau, after leaving the river valleys, can hardly avoid the track defined by a series of parallel ruts scoured out by the carts and chariots of antiquity in the rocky outcrops through the Phrygian highlands. These uplands, with their verdant valleys, are among the most attractive parts of Asia Minor; the bracing air is filled with the delicious scent of pine-woods; the pastures are well-watered by clear streams, and the meadows ripen under a glowing sun. Being ready made, this road was followed from the middle of the sixth century B.C. by the Persian postal service between Sardis and Susa, though a shorter route might have been developed by way of the Pisidian highway or the Cilician Gates, to cross the Euphrates at Carchemish. The track to the Cilician Gates from the Hittite capital can also be traced in similar fashion by a broad series of ruts heading due south toward Eregli. This is less well known, but I have followed it for miles, on horseback, though too late in the evening to obtain a satisfactory photograph.

These two natural routes, which crossed at right angles near the Hittite capital (more precisely near Yuzgat), were utilized and developed by the Hittites as four trunk roads radiating from their capital city. They form the main lines on which to reconstruct the historical topographical map of Asia Minor in antiquity. Thus, when the empire builder with the unpronounceable name Sabbiluliuma (abbreviated by the Egyptian scribes to Saplel) crossed the Euphrates to descend upon the Mitamian capital and Harran in Mesopotamia, he can hardly have avoided the main road by way of Kangal and Malatia.

So, too, in his expedition to Kumakhu (the classical Camakha, now Kemak) he must have descended from Kangal to where the road crosses the river, and followed the left bank as far as his objective (where the route returns to the right bank) because the gorges of the river and the features of the neighbouring country admit no alternative, as I have learnt in my travels. So too, again, when his son Mursil, who had been trained by his father and was endowed with the special genius of leadership and military tactics displayed by Alexander and Napoleon, led the Hittite armies towards the west to the conquest of the rival state Arzawa, he cannot have avoided using the established highway towards the coast. Setting up his headquarters at Sivri Hissar, where numerous secondary routes converge, he broke the enemy forces into three groups which he proceeded to demolish separately. This task was arduous and he was obliged to camp through the winter at a strategic point to prevent them from re-uniting. In the sequel he descended the Meander river to Milawatas (classical Miletus, now Milet), and also entered the Arzawan capital, possibly (but doubtfully) near Ephesus. The full story of his exploits would fascinate the reading public and thrill schoolboys, if only they could be set out in English with appropriate maps. They are replete with episode and incident; but I only mention one. After crossing the Sekeria River, Mursil and his army saw a vivid meteorite, which passed over them from behind, therefore going westward. (The date would be about 1330 B.C.) This fire-stone is said to have descended upon Apasas, the enemy's capital, where it wounded the king. Is it a mere coincidence that an object from heaven was revered in Ephesus conjointly with the goddess Diana, as we learn from the Acts of the Apostles (XIX. 35)?

This incident is however irrevelant to my present purpose, which is to illustrate by concrete examples how important is travel not merely to appreciating the present, but to a fuller understanding of the past. Here in Turkey the latter aspect of our enquiry is exemplified to a unique extent by the permanence and visibility of the ancient road systems, owing to the peculiar configuration of the land itself. By applying the principles illustrated by the examples outlined above, cautious examination of all the campaigns and boundaries defined in the Hittite texts will surely enable us to assemble and fit together the numerous small kingdoms and districts with which they deal. As in a jig-saw puzzle, the straining of any joint will distort the picture; and any part into which no element fits naturally must necessarily remain blank. On these lines the map of Hittite Anatolia can be reconstructed, tentatively at least, and with it a whole new literature describing the social structure and development of a great though short-lived empire will be made available to our schools and colleges. It is well worth studying, for then as now it was the people of Anatolia who resisted the ambitions of superior powers with alien customs whose success would have changed the course of history.

SEEING THE WORLD—I

Lord Dunsany

TWO good ways of getting education are to get it from books or from travel. But there is one curious difference in the process, which is that when it is got from books it is only from the printed pages that one gets it, nobody ever getting any mental sustenance from the blank pages at the beginnings or ends of books; but with travel it is not only from the great galleries of pictures or sculpture, or architecture of foreign cities, that education comes to one, but from the empty spaces of deserts and wide plains that have never known a road. The education from the galleries and cathedrals is obvious, but when one remembers that nearly all religions and philosophies have come out of deserts one must see that there is something of value also in the calm of the desert. Such calm may perhaps be found here and there on the moors and hills of England; but, as our island becomes more crowded, and as swifter and swifter transport makes our crowds more and more pervasive, the calm of such places as the forest of Arden in Shakespeare's day has shrunk to a narrower area, and for the calm in which one is thrown perforce on one's own thinking one usually has to travel. And, if I were asked where, I should say for choice the Sahara, going south from Dover until one comes to El Kantara, the Desert's colossal gateway, through which one enters the Sahara as through the gates of a university, to receive that education that the absolute silence can give one. And how, I may be asked, does that vast silence teach? To begin with there are no events or objects, that civilization does or has built up, for thousands of square miles round one; no news to read, nothing that man has made to look at; and one is forced to think, as children thrown into the water are forced to swim. One need enquire in a city the purpose of nothing: all is running smoothly and has been all thought out. But in the Desert nothing is happening at all, and in that stillness and silence one can, perhaps for the first time, think. I did once come on an object of interest in the Desert, before I had got very far in, an object of interest

229

to men, the sort of thing that would be shown to a tourist in any city, the tomb of a prophet. But he was a prophet who had died before the birth of Mahomet, after which, as the man who was running my camp informed me, there were no more, and would be no more, prophets. And this object of interest served to emphasize for me how rare news was in the Desert. It also reminded me how that calm bred prophets, even though only one in every thousand years; and, though that is not many to have come out of deserts, it is a good proportion of all we have had. Perhaps the dwellers in deserts come on content quickly, and then have need for little more. So the Arabs, having given their names to the stars, and taught Europe the art of writing, may have thought that those inventions that make our cities, and provide us with the means of so rapidly leaving them, were not really required. Wonder about anything in a city, and there is always someone to tell you the answer; but in the Desert you do your own wondering, or rather your wonder has to find its own answer. I think the first realization I had of the enormous calm of the Desert, when I was going into it once for only the second time, was when I raised my wrist at the edge of the Desert to look at the time by my watch, and realized as I raised it that for the next few weeks time (such as is shown by watches) would not matter, and I lowered my wrist before I looked at the time. If you want water to drink in a town you turn on a tap, if you want a bath you turn on two. But in the Sahara thought is needed even for this, and down there at the foundation of life and its needs, and with ample time to do so, one cannot help reflecting about the way of it, and perchance finding out something that was not clear amidst the noise of our cities. While things rush by us all day, to be condensed into news that is served to us almost immediately, they move too swiftly to be watched with attention, and the news that they make is too much for our minds to grasp, which can separate the realities from the dust of the trivialities more easily in the silence under stars that the Arabs named. So that, whatever may be the quest that has lured us away from the cities, we return to them with some knowledge of their affairs that we should never have had while we stayed where those affairs, some important, some trivial, were pouring over each other in one noisy flood, disturbed by the rush of time, as the Desert is never disturbed. Of course a book might be filled by the reflections of any man in the Desert; and then at the end of the book would come the blank pages again, pages that represent the content of the Arabs, among whom speculations cease, for the last of the prophets has given them the Koran and there is no need for more.

As one goes northward out of the Desert of the Sahara one begins to find, half buried in sand, fragments of things left behind by the ebb of the tide of an empire; and just as one finds small shells left at low tide by the sea one may come on coins bearing the head of Constantine, large numbers of which the nomads find lying there, and melt the copper down and use it to mend their kettles. And farther northward still, where cultivation slopes down like a beach to the edge of that dry sea, one sees grander ruins of empire, carved marble with beautiful lettering, broken and upside-down, graven with the forgotten commands of emperors, or calling upon all future years to remember what none of them heeds any more.

And any traveller here must begin to get some inkling of the treasure with which the past has stored the world for us; for not only fragments of carved marble are to be seen between the desert and the coast, but here and there a whole city. Timgad, for instance, with its triumphal arches still standing above paved streets grooved deep by the wheels of chariots, can set for us, even in its ruin and even in that lonely waste, a certain standard of dignity. For the dignity of the Romans, that overawed and governed all of the world that they knew, cannot fail to be shown in everything that they did, and a grace that they got from the Greeks shines yet in their marbles, which though deserted are still resisting time. In the British Museum one can see such things if one cannot travel; but there are certain contrasts that one cannot see there, as when one sees the wild land from skyline to skyline, much as it ever was, and right in the midst of it that relic of a wonderful civilization, and Time triumphant over it all, and hears the jackal saying at night, "Ha! We have returned to our own," and the owl saying "Who has ever disturbed us? Who?"

Our laws and much of our language came from Rome, as we can see without travel, as though we read of it in a book written by a magician; but travel wherever Rome has left her cities behind her, and it is as though one saw the magician with his

great pen, writing still. That empire that Rome left as it were
by the banks of the river of Time, while her emperors and senate
and people drifted down it, is to be found flashing its ruined
marble to great distances, so that travellers may meet it upon
far journeys and in many directions. By the borders of Turkey
her pillars may yet be seen, white and surprising upon lonely
hills, where once some palace stood; some pillars of hers in
Algeria help to support mosques, whose builders knew no more
of the Romans than that djinns or genie had once dwelt in those
hills and built; and in Tunisia stands one of their amphitheatres
more perfect than the Coliseum in Rome. Or travel up the
Nile and one may see in some of the temples the figures of
Roman senators painted upon the walls; for long before the
story of the Pharaohs was over Rome came to Egypt, and by
coming provided a romance for Shakespeare, and by going
ended the grandeur of Egypt's history, and the Egyptians rested
awhile from building mighty memorials.

One cannot infallibly tell travellers what they should go and
see, even when fortunate chance should give them a free choice,
for they may come on famous things that fail to impress them;
but one can certainly say this, that any traveller whatever will
now and then, and probably often, come upon things that will
amaze and delight him, sometimes things little known, like the
round huts of the Zulus in forests of Mozambique, sometimes
things that have awed the ages, such as the Parthenon, with its
pillars shining like pale gold on the Acropolis, watching still
over Athens, for whose patron goddess Praxiteles helped to
erect it, and over the seas that Salamis gave to the Greeks, and
half surrounded by mountains, whose vast solemnity is not too
great for that work of man to appear as their comrade, when
the sun at its zenith or setting is bright on the faces of both. For
never have I seen the Parthenon inferior to any of its surroundings, sea, mountains or Athens, or to any events that occurred
in the scene around it; and when war came to the hill on which
it stands, there was nothing about the Parthenon that seemed
to be put out of countenance. Indeed why should there be? For
its patron Athene was a warrior goddess.

And another thing the traveller may see that will scarcely
leave him unmoved, and that is the Sphinx. Let him not ask
me why, for fear that I shall be unable to give a good reason;

only—let him look at it; look at it and know that other travellers have looked at it too, and gone their way, for over six thousand years, and among them the greatest traveller of all, the sun itself. Yes, the sun also has looked on this strange inscrutable figure and gone its way, for the Sphinx was set facing the dawn at midsummer, but the sun in that long time has moved away a bit to the right.

What else may the traveller see that will awake his wonder and store his memory with a treasure for life?

The great Pyramid is another of these things. A king who had come from the South wanted a mountain in which to be buried, like those in which kings were buried far up the Nile; and finding no mountains near where he reigned, he ordered one to be built. Five thousand years have passed since this was built, and there are not many things bigger that Man has made in that time, and probably none until recently, so that the traveller, to find any work of man whose vastness is comparable, should go to Kimberley and look at the mine, into which the great Pyramid could be easily dropped.

And while I am naming strange treasures with which the world has been stored I must mention Abu Simbul. It was a bit out of the way for the ancients, as it still is for us, or it would surely have made the eighth of the wonders of their world. Certainly I regard it, with wireless and a few other things, as one of the wonders of the world today, full as the world is of wonders and, rather disconcertingly, turning out more. Abu Simbul is as wonderful as building a mountain, for it was a little mountain, but a king of Egypt had it hollowed out and a temple carved out of the heart of it. Like the Sphinx it faced the dawn at midsummer, but during the ages the sun wandered away, and no longer upon that day looks the four gods straight in the eyes, where they sit by the altar in the heart of the hill. Still, I have been in that temple in the dark when the sun came up over the rocky horizon across the river, and seen the darkness slip from the aisle of the temple and the four gods suddenly blush. After that, as you go up the Nile, that river of wonders, there is nothing more that could well be given a place beside the seven wonders of the world, though the journey is of great interest and one may overtake on one's way great animals that have retreated from what is progress to us, whatever it be to them.

The last stronghold of that progress, on one's way up, is Khartoum, where English gardens are and even roses, and after that only lonely outposts and, beyond them, none of our progress at all, and elephants still survive, wondering, for they are very intelligent animals, whether Man with his firearms and in defence of his bungalows will mow the last of them down before his inventions destroy his own race.

There are not many species of animals in Africa that do not drink at the Nile, and there is one that drinks nowhere else but from the White Nile or its tributaries, a chestnut-coloured antelope called Mrs. Gray's Cob, and I think that the same may be said of the situtunga, an animal that not only drinks at the Nile, but likes to hide in it with only its nose above water, an antelope with webbed feet.

Farther than this the traveller will not go, and scarcely so far, if the reasons for his travel be to see the treasures with which the world has been stored by Man, and reasons for travel are what this book seeks to explore. For the works of Man end here, but for little mud towers on the banks of the river, and the round huts of the Dinkas, with doorways too small for a lion to enter, and the long canoes of the Shillooks, and occasionally a steamer from Khartoum, as quaintly antique as the canoes. But men travel for many other reasons, and, whatever their reasons, acquire the great by-product of travel, which is a wider picture in the mind, when one turns one's gaze inward to those scenes that are lit by the imagination as the outward scene is lit by the rays of the sun. I used to revere the imagination so greatly that I supposed it could build out of nothing, but I feel sure now that, had Milton been born blind, he could have described neither Heaven nor Hell, and that in the calm that his blindness enforced on him his mighty imagination built with material that he had stored in his youth, material much of which he may have even forgotten, and which had sunk down through memory into scenes that lie in the deeps of the mind. And so far superior are the things that a poet may bring up from those quarries, to anything that the intellect may find on the surface, that I greatly prefer Milton's description of Hell to anything that he could have deliberately thought out, even although it does seem something so like a university garden with undergraduates discussing philosophical points.

> In discourse more sweet
> Others apart sat on a hill retired
> In thoughts more elevate and reasoned high
> Of providence, foreknowledge, will and fate,
> Fixed fate, free will, foreknowledge absolute.

That somehow does not picture to me the flames of Hell, and devils just thrown into torment.

So we will go on with our journey, realizing that it is not only Man that has made the earth beautiful, and that even in those great spaces that are empty of all his works there is education and treasure. And few places are emptier of the works of Man than the Nile where it is young and free, although far farther down Man has snared it and set it to work, catching it with the great dam at Aswan. And let us, by the way, not pronounce it as three syllables, merely because the French, who must have come there before us, have no W and have to use the letters OU instead. In those emptinesses, as they must seem to all who are familiar with cities, the Nile flows sluggishly through great areas of marsh occupied by one of the deadliest enemies of Man, whose work it would seem to be to protect the heart of Africa from him. I do not mean the lion; lions would not hold us back: I mean the mosquito. In the long fight, and after tremendous casualties on our side, he seems to be being beaten and to be slowly retreating, yet I do not know what else still guards what is left of the secrets of Central Africa, protecting some of them still from our tennis-courts and our bungalows.

If we go farther still on this journey we do what the storks have done, and discover the other tropic and the temperate lands beyond it. And, as the storks have done this only recently it must be from Man that they have got the idea of that longer journey, probably learning from aeroplanes that there was land beyond the equator; for it is only Man that changes his ways, and from no other creature would they have got a new idea. Going southwards still, one finds the Nile free of its marshes, and this river that knows great deserts as well as the reedy wastes flows, farther up, through solid land and even breaks into laughing cataracts. Beyond the Nile one comes to Kenya, a land to which men travel now to get coffee, or groundnuts, but to which earlier in this century few travelled except to get heads and skins of wild beasts. The purposes of this travel may be to

ornament a room in a house, but the consequences of it are to
bring one face to face with Nature, by which I mean things
untroubled by Man, until one comes oneself to trouble them
and in doing so learns their ways, as one can only learn by contrast. My own travelling, in times of peace, has been almost
entirely with the object of putting good heads on walls, but it is
not the object that entirely decides the experiences of travel: the
object merely starts one off, and then one's opponents, the wild
animals that one is after and the wild lands they inhabit, shape
the course of one's journey. And just as the multiplication table
is a good, and indeed necessary, grounding for mathematics, so
it is a good grounding for any life, even lives lived in cities, to
know how to light a fire, and to take from the wind and the
stars such advice as they can give one about finding one's way.
In such lands the sun calls you, and calls you boisterously, for
nobody sleeps any more after the early rays have entered his
tent; and the sun tells you the time, and, if you ask a Samburu,
Kikuyu or Masai how long something will take to do, he will
point to the part of the sky in which the sun will be when the
job should be finished. And so one comes back to cities from
companionship with the sun and the stars and the wind, somehow enlightened by the great company that one has kept, as
though one had studied under illustrious tutors. All that one
gets from travel it would be impossible to say, for it is more than
one ever notices, but certainly something remains to one in
cities from having learned anything of the wild lands, and the
glare of the streets never wholly effaces from memory the glow
of the little fires that surround a camp to keep away lions, or the
silver-blue of the stars that shine on the great plains of grass and
the forests of Kenya. Roads are now being made through those
forests, which must make travelling easier, but something will
be lost from what travellers knew who used to travel by
elephant-tracks, which until a few years ago were the only way
by which to go through those forests, unless one could get along
the less comfortable path of the rhinoceros.

Beyond Kenya lies Tanganyika, equally wild and, no doubt,
equally being gradually tamed, with a greater mountain to
show than even the one that gives its name to Kenya, the mountain of Kilimanjaro, with its white locks lying over its black
head, while Kenya's head and two shoulders are all white; and

south of that lie the forests of Mozambique, thousands of square
miles of them. And going south one comes on civilization
again and what we in Europe consider the right way of doing
things, and what to Africans must seem sheer witchcraft. One
comes too on scenes that remind one of Tennyson's lines:

> And like a downward smoke the slender stream
> Along the cliff to fall and fall and fall did seem.

> A land of streams, some like a downward smoke
> Slow-dropping veils of thinnest lawn did go
> And some through wavering lines and shadows broke
> Rolling a slumbrous sheet of foam below.

For Africa has great waterfalls to show to the traveller, and the
contemplation of them and of mountains is a thing so inspiring,
that I feel that these two have a great deal to teach us, even
though the roar of the waterfall and the silence of mountains
are languages that we have never been taught. Two such
waterfalls are in Natal, at Howick and Karkloof, and one in
Kenya where the Guaso Nyero flowing idly by marshy banks
goes suddenly headlong down past the trees of a primeval
forest, grey-bearded cedars that seem to watch its passing as
they watch the passing of time.

Perhaps there are three classes of traveller, those that can
look at great waterfalls or at mountains and be unmoved by
them or totally unaffected, those that know what message they
have to give us, and those who, like myself, know their august
and ancient presences have much to tell us, but through ignorance of their language do not know what it is. I should think
that most of us are in that class. It is probably some feeling of
that kind that lures onward the mountaineer. I remember that
when I was very young my nurse told me that people climbed
mountains and were often killed while doing it. I asked her
why then they climbed mountains, and she said that when they
saw them they could not help it. And I think she was probably
right. As for the waterfalls, since Man appeared on the earth
whatever has had ears and been near to a cataract has heard
what I listen to as I stand awed by one of them, and not only all
that had ears, but all things that could vibrate; and if they can
tell us nothing else, at least they tell us that there is something

that was before all the affairs of our cities and will still be there when all our cities are gone; and at least they give us a standard of comparison, lest we set store by some ephemeral or trivial thing and venerate something worthless, as we might have done had we never heard those voices. For those who cannot travel I may say that Tennyson's description of them is exact; and it is one of a poet's duties to preserve for others beauties that the world has to show, which incidentally would have been impossible for Tennyson to do had he never travelled, but always stayed in the beautiful but flat land of the fens of Lincolnshire. For no-one imagining anything falling from a height would ever think that it could pause or be slow, and yet cataracts fall exactly as Tennyson said.

But let us return, as the storks return, to the lands that are more fully stored with the treasures of the human race. And if we should return by land and when winter is leaving the North, we may actually pass those storks on the way, wheeling and slanting up into the sky, where they gather into large flocks, and then setting off towards Europe. If we go by sea it is a lonelier journey, except for those that come with us, and it is only rarely that we will see a bird, for blue things flying away from us over the sea all the way through the tropics are not birds, but fishes. The sea then is beautiful, but with one beauty, the beauty of a single sapphire the size of a planet. It is only when we come out of the tropics and see again part of the Great Bear, though only his hind-leg, with his head still under the sea, that we see the immense variety of the sea's beauty. And let me advise all travellers to look at it, for I think that very few of them have ever seen the sea. Whenever I have travelled in large ships I have always seen all the passengers, a long row of them, sitting on the sunny side, looking out at a sea that is mainly a sheet of glaring brass with the sun dazzling above it. No eyes can see anything in that glare. And when I have gone to the other side of the ship to look at the gorgeous waves breaking like sapphire cliffs, or cliffs of black marble, to show quarries of jade and mines of turquoise pouring out their treasures on snow, I have always been entirely alone.

And so one comes home. But travel is not a thing that is ever ended, while anything of the lure of wandering remains in the heart, and, though opportunities are not always to hand, one may learn from travels which one has had how to travel at all times and in all places. For is not a traveller one who, moving from place to place, notes what he sees and estimates it, using the mind as well as the feet? And the world is stored with so much more than we have the power to notice, that we may be assured that, if we look about us anywhere, we will see things that we have not only missed, but missed every day of our lives. That is one thing about travel, that it teaches us to notice; and that teaching is something that we need never give up anywhere. And another thing that travel does for us is to give us a standard of comparison, whereby we can estimate familiar things that merely seeing every day of our lives may never have enabled us to understand, until we were able to test them by the measuring-rod of comparison. The astronomers would have known little of the distances of the stars if they had always stayed in the same place, but luckily for them they have been given the opportunity of travelling about 280 million miles every six months, which gives them a base for a triangle, very lean and long, but sufficient to tell them something of distance. Similarly our own little travels provide us with new points of view, from which to look again at our fixed ideas. And, strange though it may seem, I have never heard anyone deride any foreign custom without finding upon reflection that we have something very like it here. For instance I used to hear people criticizing the Chinese for deforming their women's feet, which they did for a reason, even though not a good one. But we all deform our big toes, and usually cripple our small ones, without any reason at all, fitting our feet to our boots instead of, what I hold to be much the better way, fitting the boots to our feet. That is only one instance.

As astronomers wipe any mist from the glass of their telescope before they look at the stars, so we before we travel should take care to wipe any prejudice from our minds, not travelling to India so much with the intention of telling people there what customs they should amend, as to look, for instance, at the Taj Mahal by the light of the full moon, and letting it have what effect upon one it will. And one should be very careful not to take golf-clubs with one, for that is exporting some of one's own atmosphere, and also will head one towards golf-greens rather than jungles. Once on a journey from Paris to Calais I was in the same carriage with a couple that had gone round the world, and they had golf-clubs with them. I think one should also avoid going with two other people, because when three Europeans are together they are very likely to look for a fourth, and as soon as they find him they will play bridge. It is better to find your pleasures in the country to which you travel, than to bring your own with you. And, within limits, it is better to look at life in those lands from the points of view that you find there, rather than bring your own. For, sooner than try to teach Africans to have tidy and orderly ways, I would listen again to the simple songs that ring all through their continent, or hear again those pipes that unseen in the dusk will send bars of Pan-like music to float through the gloaming of India.

SEEING THE WORLD—II

Rupert Croft-Cooke

URING a train journey between Cheltenham and London a man once told me his life-story. It was not sensational and he had no dramatic gifts, but it aroused a very sincere sympathy from me. He had gone into his father's well-established business as a young man and because his father had died soon afterwards he had taken over its direction and responsibilities at an earlier age than had been anticipated. Now, approaching sixty, he had decided to retire. He would be in comfortable circumstances for the rest of his life.

"And what will you do when you retire?" I asked him.

He answered without a moment's hesitation—"I shall travel."

"Have you never done so?"

"Oh, I've spent holidays in France and Switzerland. But I mean travel—see the world."

I never saw him again but I should like to know how he fared. For I do not believe that such travelling merits the name. Galsworthy, in the Preface to *Caravan*, points out that a writer who decides to write pot-boilers for a few years because he believes that they will give him the income he needs in order to write the things he wants, is likely to come to nothing. The man who stays at home in order to make the money with which to travel is in the same condition. He will go through the motions, no doubt. He may see the Taj Mahal and the Golden Gate, Rio de Janeiro and the Alhambra, but it will be too late for him to travel in the only way that matters—because of necessity. If you haven't *got* to travel you might as well stay at home.

By "necessity" I do not mean under orders as soldiers are on troopships. I mean the inner necessity which drives a man to travel though it may be against his more facile inclinations, against discretion, against the will of others; to travel when he cannot afford it, when he is not fit for it, when it means sacrifice and insecurity. I have never had much patience with young people who pass their lives in day-to-day monotony only pausing

241

to sigh and bemoan their necessity to remain where they are. "If only I could break away, go abroad, do something else . . ." they say and the passing years see them bound more tightly to the wheel. If they really wanted to break away they could do so.

That is the kind of travel I have in mind, the kind of travel that is done when one can't afford to travel at all, when one is taking a risk of being stranded somewhere. I don't mean necessarily emigrating. It may be the traveller's intention to return when some of his curiosity has been satisfied, when his urge to see other countries, and people has been appeased. But "travel for its own sake," pleasure-cruising or mere globe-trotting are no more than the physical motions of travel. I have myself made many journeys for which I was not equipped or which I could not afford. I remember once travelling from London to Barcelona third class on slow trains, sitting on wooden benches for eight hours at a time, watching the consumption of curious provender by my fellow travellers and finally waking from my own sleep to find an unconscious head on each of my shoulders and an atmosphere of garlic and black tobacco which was so potent as to seem almost gaseous. That journey cost eight pounds, I believe, and I undertook it with no more than twenty pounds in the world—and only that much because I had sold my books to raise it. Yet as we came into Barcelona at night, and for the first time I saw the Ramblas, that tree-lined walk which is as populous and well-lit at four in the morning as at four in the afternoon, I would not have changed my place with that of any Englishman driving up to Barcelona Ritz in a taxi which had been brought him from the airport.

As for being "stranded"—that bogy of the half-hearted adventurer—it is rare indeed, no more probable than that one will be stranded in Edinburgh or Truro. And even if it comes to pass, one doesn't after all starve to death or take to crime or become a beachcomber, unless one was already a potential suicide or criminal or sponger. One comes through this as through everything else by the will to survive it and the intelligence necessary to defeat the forces against one. The experience fell to me once when I was too young immediately to find the way out of it. And even for that, unpleasant though it was, I am not unthankful, for I lost nothing but a pound or two in weight and a few rather silly illusions.

I was nineteen at the time and in Buenos Aires. The combination of circumstances which caused the situation is of no importance. I found myself penniless, homeless, hungry one evening and with no means of support, visible or invisible. I remained thus for three days until I was relieved in a way which also need not be specified.

Three days does not sound a long time. When I read the stories of splendid adventurers who go for weeks through a desert, tropical or arctic, without proper supplies, I am bound to confess that three days of destitution in a hot city sounds a meagre sort of privation. But then it seemed a month, a year— it had no limit in time. Sometimes during those seventy-two hours I felt that I never should escape, that I should die there of starvation, or fever, or mere misery.

I walked, because I have always found it impossible to stand still in a street. The movement of the people about me draws me with it, however tired I am. I walked, I think, through almost every street of the city, out to Avellaneda, to the Recoleta, to Liniers. And then back again, quite pointlessly. During nearly all that time I was hungry and for much of it was literally starving. The very use of that word sounds whining, as though even from this distance I were trying to arouse sympathy. Nothing of the sort. I use it because it conveys the simple truth—I was in a state of semi-starvation.

There seem, now, perhaps, to be a hundred and one things that I could have done. I could have written or cabled to my father. But how would I pay for the cable or even the stamp? And even if I could have done that there would have been a delay of weeks in the case of a letter, and days in that of a cable, whereas it was always *now* that I wanted money and food, now, in that very minute. That, I think, is what accounts for the making of beachcombers. They need so much at that very minute, that they cannot be expected to think of the future. They cannot even think far enough ahead to look for work. They want food, a drink, tobacco, *now*. And they will do anything to obtain it.

That was how I felt. I would, I assured myself, do anything to obtain it. And yet, when I thought of something to do, my nerve seemed to fail, and I slouched away. Quite early in the long agony, on the first morning, after a night on a bench in a plaza, I went to two different Englishmen I knew for help. To one of them I had actually lent money in the past. Both refused it. I do not blame them for that. There were far too many English beachcombers clinging to the charity of the British colony for them to be easily touched. And I suppose that they could scarcely be blamed for disbelieving my story. Or perhaps they thought I should ask for more, either now, or in the future, and that it was best to make it clear from the first that they were not disposed to be generous. At all events they refused, and that broke my nerve, I think. So I turned to the charity of the streets.

In that, I suppose, as such things go, I was as lucky as most, for I was unable actually to ask for anything. Once again, I state a simple fact. Hunger makes one mad. I would walk along knowing that if I was certain to escape all consequence of the act I would have murdered the next passer-by for money with which to buy food. Only the law, and fear of its powers and penalties, restrained me from theft. For hunger wipes out, with an ease which is surprising to a civilized person, most kinds of moral or personal scruple. It turns one into a mere feline scavenger, prowling round for food. And yet, although it did that for me, although I had no scruple whatever left in me, I could not, however hard I tried, enunciate the words necessary for begging.

Fortunately, however, the sort of person who would be responsive to them does not always need to be asked. A bartender—or he may have been the proprietor—of a small café in Leandro Alem, whom I had asked for a glass of water, gave me a packet of sandwiches made the day before. I could always ask for water, because it cost nothing. What absurdities our training and character teach us. Famished, parched, quite blind and senseless with despair, I distinguished between asking for water and asking for bread, because anyone, even an affluent and well-fed person, might ask for water, and only a beggar would ask for bread. Another time, I think it was during the third day when I had stubble on my chin and my clothes were dirty, I awoke from a sleep on a plaza bench to find a large piece of garlic-scented sausage and a hunk of bread beside me.

So that I was not perhaps in danger, in those seventy-two hours, of death from starvation.

And all the time—and I would like you not to laugh—all the time there was something in me which said that this was life, this was experience, this was what I had come to South America to feel. What insight I was gaining! What enlightenment! If ever I should escape from this torrid inferno, I should look back on these days as some of the most valuable in my life. For wasn't I going to be a writer? And did not writers proverbially learn from such suffering as this?

I do not know quite what I learned from it, still less what I gained. I learnt that a hungry man is nothing but a living desire, that all thought, belief, determination, is wholly obliterated by that desire, that he will do anything to satisfy it, and that in all judgments on the actions of hungry men we should take this into account. And I learnt the truth of yet another truism— that human beings are not really ill-disposed or ungenerous, as one might sometimes suppose, but ready enough to help one another when they see the need. As for gain—perhaps a little understanding and tolerance, perhaps a sharpening of that part of my imagination which is concerned with the misfortunes of others. But I cannot pretend, even now, when the agony and misery of it is a memory, that it was in any sense worth while.

Yet in those three days I became, in a very special sense, a *porteno*, a citizen of Buenos Aires. Perhaps there is some truth in the old idea that there is an under side to every great city, seen only by the outcast. Perhaps hunger and wretchedness give a certain clarity to one's vision of streets and people. I do not know. But I do believe that I learnt something about Buenos Aires in that time which I could have learnt in no other way. I woke stiff-jointed and stale from a few hours' sleep and saw morning come up from the Plate and the earliest workers pass. I wanted a bath more than anything, I believe, more even than hot coffee and rolls. Three days without a change of clothes in that heat, without a shave, and with a chance only for a surreptitious wash of face and hands now and again, makes one loathe oneself. And time behaved eccentrically. There would be an afternoon which would seem interminable, for I would pass clocks several times on my walks and find them apparently unmoved. And another day, or a morning, would go by over my head in an hour as it seemed, and I would see that it was noon, and know that although I had travelled that much from the last food I had eaten, I was no nearer to any more.

There was another odd sensation—that of detachment from the rest of the populace. Before, though I might have had no money at the time, I was one with the passing crowd. Now I was isolated. I imagined myself, perhaps, more conspicuously shabby than I was, since I felt so miserably unclean. If I walked along a pavement I felt the passers-by to be of one species, myself of another. Anyone who has gone through a similar experience will understand this, I think. Destitution makes one feel as a leper must have felt in Palestine. One imagines a drawing away of skirts, a stepping off the pavement by a child, a look from another man, to be significant.

I remember, on one of those evenings, talking to an old German. He had been out there twenty years he said, but had lost his job through "intrigue." What sort of intrigue? Oh, I didn't know people as he did. He hinted at infamous dark schemes laid for his ruin, at subtle and unscrupulous people working to bring him low. I have no idea what the real cause of his poverty may have been. But as he sat on a seat in the plaza and puffed at a pipe which he had filled with tobacco from cigarette ends, he looked, in spite of his tattered clothes, most plump and respectable, as though he were sitting in the doorway of a flourishing shop to pass restful evenings. His great regret was that he had not gone to Australia. That was the country, he said. He would have been rich now if he had gone to Australia. And he told me where there was a restaurant at which the proprietor was apt to give a meal to anyone who needed it, so that I set out to walk there at once, and tramped for a whole evening in search of it, but never found its doors. I remember how it took on glorious aspects in my mind, the proprietor smiling blandly from behind his bar and inviting one to have a steak and potatoes at his expense, and filling a demi-litre with beer and talking affably all the time about the inconveniences of temporary distress. But though I walked up and down the street which the old German had indicated I could find nothing to resemble his description, so I shall never know whether in Buenos Aires or in any other city such a Utopian eating-house has flourished.

Except for that old German I made no acquaintances among the men who slept on the seats in the Plaza Retiro, or in that ugly waste land which lay, in those days, between it and the docks. There is little fraternity among down-and-outs, contrary to the sentimental and consequently popular, supposition. I suppose there is recognition among them, but no more. It is by nature a solitary craft, this mere keeping alive in a city.

Three days—it was soon over, and soon forgotten, and it has never seemed quite real. A part of the time—the second evening in particular—I passed in a state which cannot have been far from delirium, for I remember repeating to myself, and once or twice aloud, some crazy phrase or other, and I remember making foolish resolves which I never started to carry out. And I remember a little policeman in the Plaza Congreso watching me for a long time, as though he were debating the advisability of arresting me. And since I knew of no offence I had committed I supposed then and thereafter that I must have said or done something to rouse his suspicion, without being aware of it.

When I had returned to normal life, the whole thing soon became a short chapter, a small piece stitched on to the coloured patchwork of the past. In retrospect it certainly does nothing to lessen my belief that if one wants to travel one should not wait till one can do so in comfort. Counted against the wonders of that early voyage to South America it is less than nothing. To have seen the River Plate, that vast sweet water sea which changes colour with the clouds above it, to know the beauty of the pampas, those rich levels stretching from the Andes to the coast, a separate element, it seems, neither land nor ocean but partaking of the characteristics of each; to have seen the jewelled white city of Rio de Janeiro under its bright emerald hills with islands sporting like porpoises in the deep blue water of its bay; to have lived among the most vigorous and virile people of modern times—all these seem important, not the fact that my improvidence once brought me to despair.

Many other times I have travelled when a more cautious man would have remained at home, and for that I have no regrets, though there have been moments of stress and trial, like the autumn months I spent in a German village in the early 'thirties.

The whole episode, even the discovery of that village, was a youthful, fortuitous affair. I had gone with a friend to spend a holiday in Bruges and though I think now that I could happily spend weeks among the beauties and treasures of that rich town, we were young and wanted movement and new landscapes and changes of scene. So we decided to go to the Ardennes and walk there. We deliberately took no map and followed signposts and stayed wherever we happened to be at nightfall, and suddenly one afternoon we saw a barrier across the road ahead of us with posts painted black, white and red. We had reached the German frontier. It happened, I remember, that some function was ending in the village across the road and the hymn-tune national anthem was being played as we approached it. A customs official gave a cursory glance at our haversacks and passports and we were in Germany—so simple was it once to pass from one country to another.

Next day, still by chance, we came to the village of Monschau. It was very lovely, a fourteenth-century hamlet lying in the valley of three hills, each with a "ruin a'top," and the finest, the *Schloss*, the castle of Monschau, a typical German stronghold with pointed turrets and a fine archway. Through the centre of the village pelted the Raur, a swift sub-tributary of the Rhine. Over it hung timbered houses, centuries old, and plastered in gay colours, pale mauves and pinks and yellows. There were cobbled, winding streets there with houses hanging over them out of which Grimm characters might step at any moment with their curling shoes. If the gingerbread house existed anywhere it was in a wood not far away. Very German—a miniature Nuremberg it seemed to me when I first saw its peaked roofs and turrets. A mile up the valley from the little town, the river had been dammed, and a *Badeanstalt*, a sylvan bathing pool, made. At the municipal expense a large pavilion of changing rooms was erected, diving boards, a boat or so provided, and there, every afternoon, the youth of the place gathered. With deep green mountains and silence about them they dived and swam, then sat for long hours in the sunlight letting its warmth soak into their bodies. And the country around was magnificent. There were steep pine-covered hills sloping down to the tumbling tributaries of the Rhine, the bold streaks of colour made by wild flowers over the heaths, the white, plastered farm-houses. I was enchanted, so much so that I returned with my friend to England, raised a few pounds and returned to Monschau determined to stay there until I had finished a novel.

For weeks I wrote and walked through the forests and swam in the river and ate trout and drank hock with the happy confidence that in another fortnight a sum of money would be due to me from a small firm of publishers in London. Then, as my few pounds dwindled, I began to press for this payment and feel the first pangs of anxiety. Autumn was turning towards winter, dead leaves were blown through the narrow streets of Monschau; the river rose and seemed to roar angrily under my windows. I wrote to friends in London and asked them to visit the offices of the publishers and somehow get me the money I needed to pay my hotel bill and come home. October, November came and still no payment, till I began to feel deserted and rather frightened. The approaching winter and the wind in the pine trees seemed sad and threatening and the little town changed its whole character from the sunlit insouciance of summer. Then I heard that the publishers had ceased to exist and my payment would never be made.

Improvident? Of course I had been. Inconsiderate? I suppose so, but I was in my early twenties and had loved the town and wanted more than anything to stay there. Finally as my hotel bill grew and I saw no means of meeting it, I did the only possible thing. I went to the stout hotel-proprietress and confessed. Her understanding and kindness still seem to me amongst the best things I have known. She lent me enough for my fare to England and I hurried home to see what possessions I had and discharge my debt. I remember arriving in Ostende on a wild night of wind and rain with six hours to wait for the cross-Channel boat and not enough money to enter a café. A Belgian policeman with whom I sheltered under an archway saw me lugging my bag and invited me to the warm stove at his station where I passed the time in happy conversation with a group of *gens d'armes*. There is, of course, no merit in such improvidence as mine, but if I had waited until I could return to Monschau with the backing of a comfortable bank-balance I should never have stayed again in that town.

And so it was always with me. I was prepared at any time to

sell all I had and mortgage what I should earn in order to see more of the world. When, just before the last war, it was the fashion to write books about the European situation which either predicted the forthcoming horrors or lulled their readers into seeing Hitler and Mussolini as jolly, friendly fellows who wouldn't hurt a fly, and certainly not a British one, I hit on the notion of interviewing not the dictators and the publicized men of fate, but the man in the street in Europe. I decided to travel through as many countries as possible spending my time in café-talk and street-talk, trying to understand how the ordinary citizen felt about things. This time a publisher was prepared to support the idea and I determined to set out in winter when Europe would be for the most part free of tourists. I bought an old Morris sixteen-seater bus which had done twelve years' service on the Welsh roads and converted it into a living-waggon with bunks and a stove since my publisher's confidence in the scheme did not extend to the cost of hotels. With two circus-artists, brothers, who had spent their lives in such living-waggons and were infinitely resourceful and reliable, I set out to see life from the road. Through Belgium, right across Germany we went without let or hindrance, though it was the winter of 1937–38. To Prague and down to Vienna, fighting our way through the snow without even a skid-chain, and then to the graceful city of Budapest and across a still almost mediæval Hungary into Yugo-Slavia.

It was the gayest journey I have ever made. We had prepared for it in less than two weeks and into them had been pressed the time necessary for converting the waggon. We had not nearly enough money, but with rum at a shilling a bottle and milk almost for the asking we could sip our hot grog over our stove at night while the snow fell, and eat as much country produce as we wanted and we demanded no more. When we had crossed the North of Italy and reached the Riviera and found our-selves in a new world of English visitors, crowded casinos and expensive sunshine, we felt no more ill-at-ease than we had in the market squares where our waggon had stood in Eastern Europe, and we pulled in beside the promenade at Mentone without embarrassment. And so home after three months' travelling through ten countries. I know no better way of seeing the world.

And no better way of seeing England than by travelling with one of the smaller circuses which rarely stay more than a night in one place and avoid the cities. I first joined Rosaire's Circus at Rye one autumn in the 'thirties. I had intended spending only a day with them but from Rye they went to New Romney, to Dymchurch, to Hythe, and I followed. I learnt how to drive-in a tent stake, and what elephants eat; I began to learn the language of the circus, and, already knew what a *tober* was, and what *Vada!* meant. At eleven o'clock at night, when the good folk in the villages we visited had been asleep this half-hour or more, I had watched the tent hands and Rosaire boys alike "pulling down," till the vast spread of canvas had become a few bundles on a lorry, and seating for five hundred had been packed in piles on another. I lived with some of the men in a bus which was called the Barracks and into its central compartment eight or nine of us would crowd at night to drink tea and eat a late supper before turning in. At first there would only be three or four of us, for the work of "pulling down" would still be going on outside, and shouts would be audible across the field. When the doors opened you could smell the salt air of the Romney Marshes, and our own clouded atmosphere of simmering supper and cigarette smoke would be dispelled. Then one after another the boys would arrive as his particular part of the work of pulling down was completed. Now and again one of them would be late if some village beauty had persuaded him to take her home, for nearly nightly a group would wait in hope of being noticed by the men they had seen perform. But at last they would all be in, and their supper eaten heaven knows how, with plate balanced skilfully on the knees of the crowded eaters standing beside a chest of drawers. The windows would be clouded to opaqueness by the atmosphere within, two or three of us would be "strap-hanging," for the bars still remained above us from the former life of the Barracks, and the wireless set in the boys' compartment would be droning out dance-music. Thus we would squat and talk till long past midnight, and someone would open the door to show the field almost in darkness, every other waggon having long since turned out its lights, and the wind-swept moon showing the lorries laden and ready for the morning's journey. Some nights we could hear the sea beyond the marshes, on others, when the night air was still, there was audible the steady munching of the ring-horses put out to graze.

From Hythe we went to Ashford, from Ashford to Wye, from Wye to Chilham, and still I made no real effort to return to my home and responsibilities. And the next season and the next I went "tenting" with them until the war closed their show before the end of the season.

Yet another way of moving about England without struggling for the mediocre comfort of hotels, I discovered in the early months of the war when I bought a horse-drawn caravan and with a young Romanichal named Ted Scamp as my sole companion lived on the road and among other gypsies. Our journey was not a long one in distance, though we were nearly two months on the road, staying several days in some places and some weeks at Goudhurst because of a fall of snow. It was not as you shall hear a grand trek across England, with nights spent in general encampments or days of journeying as one of a string of waggons. It was long enough to give me the sense of the thing, the feeling of being one of a vagrant people, to see the suspicion in men's faces, and once to know the majestic stupidity of the Law. And it was varied as all good travelling must be, taking us through two counties and most kinds of winter and early spring weather, and bringing us into contact with some nicely contrasted people. But it did not carry us through the summer or to the Welsh mountains. It was a dawdling pleasant journey through parts of Kent and Sussex which ended as unexpectedly as it had begun. It was not made without difficulties, for the house-dweller and the Law have little sympathy for the Romani's need to pull in by a roadside, and once, at least, this was evident. We were sitting by the warm stove of our *vardo* on a cold night of heavy mist when there was a sudden very noisy banging on the door. It seemed that Ted had been expecting this for he signed me not to move, went out, and shut the door behind him.

"Can't stop here," I heard.

"Well what d'you expect us to do? Got no lights."

"Can't help that. Can't stop here."

"You expect us to go on and then pinch us for being on the road without any lights, then?"

There was a brief silence. I found this dialogue out of the darkness to have a certain dramatic quality.

"Where's your horse?" asked the strange voice, clearly a policeman's.

"Down the road," said Ted instantly, but vaguely.

"Well, you can't stop here."

The policeman did not seem to be much of a conversationalist.

"Well, we can't move," said Ted, who was growing tautological, too.

"Been up round that farm, haven't you?"

"So that's who's sent you along, is it? I thought so. All I asked him was if we could put the horse in his paddock. Offered to pay him, 'n' everything."

"Anyway, you can't stop on the side of the road like this. *You* know that, very well."

"You tell me what else I'm to do. Drive on tonight in this mist without any lights?"

"That's nothing to do with it. You'll have to move from here. Why didn't you get in somewhere while it was still light?"

"How was we to know there was a mist coming? We're not doing any harm, are we?"

"You know you're not allowed to pull in on the verge like that. And I'd like to know where your horse is. How many is there of you?"

"Two," said Ted.

"Well, I've warned you. I'll be back again presently and if you've not gone you know what'll happen."

Ted came back and settled down again by the fire.

"Shan't see him again," he remarked, and set about the preparation of rum and hot milk.

"How do you know, Ted?"

"If he could of done anything he'd of done it then. He just wanted to save his face. That farmer must have telephoned down to him. But what *could* he do? He daren't put us on the road without lights. You don't want to take any notice of that. That's nothing. We shall always be getting the mushgros round about something or other. They can't see a vardo without having a go at it."

That was the best hour of each day, when the journey, such

as it was, had been accomplished, the horse unharnessed and disposed for the night, the steps brought from the back of the waggon and set in place, the fire blazing up and the lamp lit. Then we would stretch our limbs as best we might and sit smoking silently while the kettle boiled for tea.

And how we ate! The fresh air, the day's exercise, the quick roadside lunch gave us, at five or six o'clock, horses' appetites. But although Ted ate a great deal he had fastidious table manners and never set a meal on the table unless there was a decently clean cloth on it and polished crockery and cutlery. He told me once that his blessed old daia had taught them, not without a cuff or two, to eat carefully even if the plates were on their knees out of doors. But we never hurried to clear away or wash up the tea-things, for it was over these that we talked, and in exchange for Ted's inexhaustible stock of gypsy stories I would try to answer his sometimes bewildering questions about aspects of gorgio, and particularly of London, life with which he was unfamiliar. That is the sort of travelling for me, unmapped, unpremeditated, comfortable in the most real sense but not without hardships and surprises. Above all showing the land one knew, the familiar people, from an angle entirely new. Viewed from the half-door of a caravan England is a strange country.

Even in the army during the war I found that the will to see more of other countries could overcome many of the more obvious limitations imposed by discipline. Training in Combined Operations took us to Scapa Flow and a story told by a marine that an unauthorized photograph had been taken of our activities ashore got me permission to spend a few nights in the Orkneys to investigate. And an unexpected last embarkation leave after family farewells had been said took me to the Isle of Barra to stay with Compton Mackenzie and see something of the astonishing Hebrides, the islands which have never changed their faith. When our convoy finally left Gourock to make its way to South Africa, so that we lay in Freetown harbour for a night, on some pretext connected with the mail I got myself sent ashore and can still smell that crawling city.

In Madagascar when we had made our landings, it took more ingenuity to gain freedom of movement, but one way or another I managed to see most of it, from the little groups of huts which the timid Malagache calls villages to the fantastic hilltop city of Tananarive, where the castle of the last native ruler is still filled with her barbaric jewelry and baroque furniture, and where outer walls have been built to enclose the wooden framework of the original palace, since the Queen had been told that her dignity demanded stonework but could not bear to destroy her original wood walls.

In South Africa, where we went to recuperate from the feverish maladies of Madagascar, it was a piece of luck rather than any action on my part which enabled me to go up into Zululand. A bout of malaria took me to hospital in Pietermaritzburg and I came out to find that my unit had left for India and that I had two months to pass in Durban before I could rejoin it. Permission to enter the Zulu reserves was granted and I found myself squatting beside the rich old chief M'tubatuba, who presented me some examples of Zulu craftsmanship which are my proud possession to this day. Christmas I spent with an old French priest at one of the loneliest missions in Africa. He had been sent to the place twenty years ago and persuading the Zulus to carry the stones on their heads from ten miles away he had built his own church and home and school. It seemed romantic to me, I remember, that the only way of reaching the mission was on horseback and that I rode for a day across the fresh undulating hills to find the old priest white-bearded and tall like an ancient prophet waiting to welcome me.

The will to travel, which may after all be no more than curiosity, becomes a habit, and a few days at Mombasa during our Madagascar operations were sufficient to send me into the remoter parts of that curious city—the Jewish and the Arab quarters. I remember a little Arab general shop where I would sit during the afternoon noting down words of Arabic, beginning to stutter my first phrases and drinking coffee with the shop-keeper, hot, scented coffee bought from an itinerant vendor.

Then, at last, India. I think now that all the countries I had seen before I went ashore at Bombay might be considered as no more than a preparation for this, as though the thirty-four of them had existed only for me as experiences sufficient to give me a sense of proportion with which to understand "enchanted Hind."

I saw much of it, and no man can say more than that, for
India is a continent rather than a country and one could spend
a life-time learning to understand a little of one of its areas.
Bombay first, a city of great contrasts and glaring colours and
such multitudes upon multitudes of inhabitants that never anywhere in its streets, day or night, could one count less than a
hundred people in sight and sometimes a thousand or more.
That, indeed was my first impression of India—the density of
its population.

South to Belgaum, North to Dehra Dun whence one could go
up to Missourhi and see the eternal snows, West to Karachi,
East to Calcutta—there was no considerable area which I did
not manage to visit. And when I found myself a Field Security
Officer with an area the size of England and Wales to explore
without interference, driving a Cadillac station-waggon with a
couple of sepoys as my companions, I could have asked for no
more. From the borders of Mysore to Ahmednagar, from the
Konkoni coast to the frontier of Hyderabad I went, making
what I deemed it necessary to call "security tours" and learning
every day a little more of the most interesting land of the
modern world.

To see yet another country within a country I persuaded
Southern Army Headquarters that good purpose would be
served if they allowed me to go on leave to Goa. No larger than
a small English county this Portuguese possession is strangely
different from what was then British India, for the tradition of
the early settlers, sternly Catholic and richly civilized, persists
almost unchanged. There is another almost deserted city here,
the baroque shell of Old Goa, once the greatest city of the East,
now a few ruined houses and some vast churches, in one of
which lies the embalmed body of St. Francis Xavier. The
Goanese Indians live in a happy occidental way and cargoes of
good wine were still arriving in the port. I was lucky to have
that experience for it was a closed country to the British throughout the war. There were interned German seamen and a few
Italians who had escaped from prison camps in India to give it
the air of a neutral country though the frontier was a rather
haphazard affair a few miles away.

Later, established once more as a Field Security Officer at
Delhi with all the Central States to drive through, the rose-red

city of Bikaner in the heart of its desert or the great temples of Khajrao standing in solitude beyond the tourist's ken, but certainly making one of the marvels of the world, even my lust for more to see and hear and explore was almost sated.

So as a penniless writer, as a journalist with no expense sheet, as a soldier, I managed to travel a fair proportion of the world's surface, but never in order to escape an English winter or to feel sunshine in February. I went because I could not stay still, because whatever sacrifice was necessary had to be made, because I wanted more than anything to see other lands. And I know now that it was the best way. Such tame travel as I have done since the war has proved it to me. Taking a car across to Denmark and motoring through Sweden and Norway is a pleasant enough way of spending a month, but it is no more. Travelling on a ship which calls at ten Spanish ports so that one had a day or two ashore in Bilbao, Seville, Barcelona and so on, makes an agreeable summer holiday but is not travel as I understand it. Or going, as I did this summer, to work for a month in that strange area of pine trees and nightingales which runs inland from the coast for a hundred miles between Bordeaux and Biarritz may be an excellent way to work and escape the miseries of English diet, but who could call it travelling? No, travel is more than an impulse or an urge, it is a prime necessity and for those of us who feel it there can be no escape. It is a comforting thought that however it may be facilitated and accelerated there must always be enough of the world's surface to last a human life-time.

JUST FOR CURIOSITY

Alec Waugh

WHEN Ken McCormick, Doubleday's chief editor, suggested a few months ago that I should write Lipton's centennial biography, I thought at once "that should mean going to Ceylon."

For over twenty years some such corollary has been for me the deciding factor in the acceptance or rejection of any project. "Is there a trip involved?" That is what I have always asked.

I began to travel in the summer of 1926. In the previous spring, I had read Maugham's *Moon and Sixpence* and *The Trembling of a Leaf*. Were the South Seas really like that, I wondered: I was assured by those who had not been there, that they were *vieux jeu*. But I was not satisfied. I had to find out for myself. I bought a round the world trip ticket that included Tahiti in its itinerary.

I have been on the move ever since. A fiction writer is in a fortunate position. He can work where he likes, when he likes: he carries his own office with him. I have exploited my occupational good fortune.

V.E. Day found me in Baghdad. I had been in the Middle East for four years. I was in the middle forties. But as I sat out that evening on the stone-flagged terrace of my mess, watching the Tigris swollen with the melted snows flow past me to the Persian Gulf, I was not thinking, primarily, of a return to England. For six years I had been under orders, with little control over my own direction. Bondage was ending now and once again I felt the stirring of that long-slumbered curiosity, the fretting of a long stream of questions. I wondered about Malaya, the West Indies, the Pacific. What was to happen East of Suez? The white man had been humbled before Asiatics. Could the Pukka Sahib with his solar topee and his *stengahs*, his *ginpahits* and his *chota hazri* possibly recover his old prestige? Had the British Raj gone for ever?

And what about Tahiti. It had lain, surely, too far south of the Line to play any active part in the campaign. A French island opting for de Gaulle, cut off from metropolitan France since 1940, it had been forced back upon its own resources, without imported fabrics, without canned foods. No visitors had come there, few supply ships. Were hula skirts worn every day —not just for New Year and the fourteenth of July—were native dishes restored to favour? Had it become in fact the island that Loti knew? Then there was Dominica—that lovely and unfortunate West Indian Island that had attracted so many misfits, that had appealed so strongly to the imagination of men and women who in various parts of the world had found themselves square pegs ineffectively trying to fit into round holes. Dominica, lying between two Vichy islands, Martinique and Guadeloupe; with no harbour and no airport, must have been as isolated in that torpedo infested sea as a remote oasis in mid-Sahara.

My brother officers were talking every one of them of their plans for England, their homes and gardens, their careers and offices, their wives and friends, their children and their girls. But the need to know how things were somewhere else was once again upon me.

It has carried me, that need, to quite a lot of places; to so many places that when in World War II, as a rejoining officer, I was asked to complete my dossier with a list of the countries I had visited, I found I could save time by making out a list of those that I had not: so many indeed that the critic may well complain that I have had no time to understand them.

"If you had travelled," I can hear him saying, "simply for travel's sake, I can see your point. There is the excitement of arrival and departure, there is variety, new faces, new scents, new sights, new flavours. That is what every tourist knows. But you travel, so you tell us, to see what a place is like. What can you see of Kenya, by spending a week in Nairobi and six days in Mombasa?"

It is a criticism with which every travel writer is familiar, and which he finds hard to counter. In deference to it, many of us, working on the maxim that in the cities of the blind the one-eyed are kings, visit little known countries where our facts and the conclusion that we draw from them are less likely to be contradicted by residents of lifelong standing. Yet in point of fact it is not a valid criticism; we are unwise to let it worry us. A mathematician can quickly disintegrate a complicated arrangement of signs and brackets whose resolution into a simple equation would occupy a schoolboy half an hour: and the perceptive antennæ of an experienced traveller can recognize within half a week the essential problems and situations of a newly seen community. His instinct guides him. In fact, if he stays too long he becomes confused, he acquires too much information, losing the clear outlines of his first impression. In personal relations we often feel in retrospect that in the first hour of contact we saw deeper and more clearly into a freshly met personality than we have ever since. The trained travel writer, or rather—for training is not the deciding factor—the writer who has an instinct for travel, can learn enough about a country within a week to have at least material for a comparison. I should not for instance consider myself impertinent in expressing my opinion about Russia on the strength of a fortnight's stay in Moscow.

I went there—at what I realize now to have been a lucky time —February, 1935. The political skies were relatively clear. Europe and America were coming out of the depression; George V was about to celebrate his silver jubilee; Mrs. Simpson was not a cause for gossip, outside private circles; the Spanish Civil War had not begun; it was possible to regard the rise of Hitler as German's parochial problem; the Russian purges were some months distant; the world was on fairly good terms with itself; there was at any rate the appearance of a "live and let live" atmosphere; mutual mistrust was temporarily concealed. There was an idea that everyone had something to learn from everybody else—even from the U.S.S.R.

I went under congenial conditions, with a painter, a member of the Upper House, whom I had met first in Tahiti. Politically we should both, I suppose, be Liberals if there were any equivalent today for the Asquith administration of 1910; as it is, he, being slightly more to the Left than I, holds at present a junior ministerial appointment in the Labour Government, while I record a very half-hearted vote for the Conservatives. We went for the same reason—to see what it was like.

We went by train and that is the best way of going. It is a

long journey and it is as well to realize just how far Russia is away. Leaving London after dinner on a Tuesday, we did not reach Moscow till the Friday. There was the Harwich crossing, a morning train journey through Holland, an afternoon train journey through Germany, then an evening in Berlin before taking the night train to Warsaw. It was my first visit to Berlin. To my surprise it looked very empty. The pavements were fairly crowded but there were more cyclists than cars upon the streets. There were few traffic lights. We dined at the Haus Vaterland and only the Rheinesalle was full. The cosy intimate corners were deserted, though the stairs and passages were thronged with dreary bulky men in new but ill-cut clothes who looked like the members of a trade convention. There were few pretty girls. There was an ominous lack of gaiety.

All next day we were in the train, travelling through frost-bound Poland. It was six o'clock before we reached the frontier. We changed more than trains there. One end of a long bare customs hall was emblazoned with a fresco of the U.S.S.R. showing its new cities, the other with a poorish mural of har-vesters and miners. Round the walls in gold lettering, in four different tongues the proletariat of the world was bidden to unite. The customs were dilatory and thorough. The officials were not interested in the usual causes of concern—alcohol, tobacco, silk; they were looking for books and currency. Red tape abounded. Before I could engage a porter, I had to obtain from the Intourist Bureau a permit to employ him; this permit I carried to the cashier to whom I paid 2s. 7d. The receipt I took back to the Bureau who handed a duplicate copy of it to the porter who was then allowed to place his hand upon my suitcase.

On the other side of the customs the Moscow express was waiting. It was like a scene out of *Anna Karenina*, the high train, the snow-capped platform, the station lights blurred by snowflakes, five or six furred figures stamping to keep their feet warm. Indeed it must have been for a very similar train on a very similar platform that Vronsky waited. It was all very *ancien régime*: broad-gauged, high from the ground, the com-partments heated by a vast hand-stoked stove, rep-curtained windows, Edwardian lampshades, one of the lights not working and for the one that did, considerable ingenuity required to find how its switch functioned; the couchettes so narrow that I kept waking with sore knees.

Before I started, I had contacted both the Russian Embassy and the Voks—the Society for Cultural Relations with the U.S.S.R. I had acquired, as had my companion, several letters of introduction. We had taken that is to say the ordinary precautions. Our friends assured us that we should only see what the Soviet authorities chose to show us. They were perfectly right; but the truth of their contention is misleading. The authorities showed us a great deal. Voks was most obliging. It provided cars, excursions, theatre tickets, it arranged meetings with our opposite numbers. We were taken, admittedly, to the "show places," but since Russia was a country in scaffolding, these show places could be accepted as the models on which the rebuilding of the country was being carried out. We had the aims and principles of the experiment explained to us. We were shown how it was intended that the plan should work. We were shown how it was being worked. Voks kept us extremely busy.

No point would be served here, in describing the ways in which they kept us busy. Others have done that, Archibald Lyall in particular in his *Russian Roundabout*. Other writers, again, have explained why independent travel was impracticable and why you had to operate through Voks and through Intourist—the Russian Travel Bureau. Currency was the crux. The local value of the rouble at that time was 180 to the £. But it was not possible for the tourist to buy local roubles except on the black market, which was an awkward operation. He had to change his European or American currency at a gold rouble rate of $5\frac{1}{2}$ to the £. Provided these roubles were spent with Intourist, he received good value for them in the form of car hire, food and drinks. But if he wanted to make an excursion on his own and picked up a taxi on the street, he would be charged at the local market rate; a ten minute journey would cost £2. Equally a visit into an unsponsored restaurant would cost £4. For financial reasons, the tourist was always under official scrutiny, which meant that no unofficial Russian would want to meet him. It was as simple as all that.

I only know of two people who managed to travel independently; one was an experienced traveller, a young Jewish novelist; an excellent linguist who spoke Yiddish; with a great gusto for adventure, a great gift for putting at their ease people of every age and class: short, thickset, with marked racial features, he was able to disguise completely his nationality and status by the simple device of not shaving for two days and not washing for three. He moved unmolested from one village to another, like a medieval friar. The other was a quite young girl, an art student, who hitch-hiked round the country, her canvases serving as a passport, supporting herself by the gradual liquidation of her suitcase—the scarves and scatterpins that would fetch a few shillings in a vicarage jumble sale appealing as irresistibly to the beleaguered Russians as the trumpery trinkets for which in the previous century the South Sea Islanders eagerly bartered their lands, their copra and their pearls.

These two—Louis Golding and Primrose Codrington—contrived to travel in Soviet Russia as freely and in much the same way as the *wandervögel* did in Europe. But they were exceptional. No one following the customary technique stood a chance of escaping from official scrutiny.

As I said, I arrived in Moscow with letters of introduction; anywhere else those letters would have insured that within a fortnight I should have been on sufficiently friendly relations with a sufficient number of people in different walks of life to have formed some idea of the life of the average citizen. In Moscow that was not enough. I did, through persistence and good fortune, manage to contact unofficially one Russian family and the extent of my efforts showed how difficult it was for the average visitor to form any idea of the realities of average Russian life. This particular home is worth describing. Its owner was a member of the white collar class. He was not a party member. He was unpolitical. He had never got into trouble with authority. He was the Russian opposite number of junior manager in an insurance office who would expect before retirement to be earning an eight hundred a year salary. He was thirty-five, married, with two young children. In London he would have been living in a semi-detached villa in the suburbs, and the foreign visitor would have learnt more about the English way of life from spending half an hour in his home than from the study of the most accurate statistics.

In Moscow this man lived in an apartment building designed in Tzarist days to contain eight flats. He shared one of these flats with five other families. A narrow hallway passage had been converted into a communal kitchen, or rather, a long shelf had been set up, along which kerosene lamps and pots had been arranged. At the end of the passage the original hall served as a nursery for half a dozen children. His private residence measured twelve feet by six. It contained a wardrobe, a narrow single iron bedstead, and a cot. The bedstead was for the wife, a bed for the elder child was kept in the passage. The man slept on the floor. They had done their best to make it cosy. They had disguised the bedstead with a rug. There were a couple of good pictures, a book or two; a shelf in a corner had been set with knicknacks. It was not until I noticed a rack of tooth-brushes that I realized that the shelf had to support the family's ablutions.

Intourist did not include such homes in its itinerary. In an article that I wrote on my return, I summed it up by saying: "The average foreign visitor is shown so much that he does not realize how little he has really seen."

And that, the critic may well retort, is a very inadequate return for three weeks' travel.

I anticipate his protest. "Was there any need," I can hear him arguing, "to have travelled all those miles, merely to confirm for your own satisfaction the conclusions that Robert Byron had reached and published, wittily and effectively, several months before? Surely it would have been easier to have taken his word for it." It might have been, if I were the kind of person to accept another traveller's testimony unexamined. But I am not. And in point of fact two things did happen in connection with that visit to convince me in a way that nothing written by anyone else could have done that life in the U.S.S.R. is a form of existence completely foreign to our own, that Soviet citizens are a different order of human beings, that it is useless to try to interpret their behaviour and reactions in terms of how we behave ourselves.

The first incident took place while I was still in Moscow. Normally Intourist clients were taken round to the various exhibits, hospitals, factories and crèches, in parties of four and five. One day we were joined by a fellow tourist whom we had not met before. She was thirtyish, well dressed, pretty, speaking good English with a foreign accent. She was a girl who could be expected not only to inspire but to welcome masculine enterprise. There were just the three of us and under normal conditions, I imagine that my companion and I, travelling as we were *en garçon*, would have tossed to see who should make the running for the first three days. We did not though, and it was the last we saw of her.

She was, it must be admitted, a lady whom in spite of her announcement that she was Polish and a tourist, we found it difficult to place. Beyond a certain point, she was uninformative. We suspected at the time, since then we have felt almost sure, she was a "plant," the authorities having felt it worth their while to know a little more about us. It was not however the fear that she was a Marie Louise bent on inveigling us into treason that made us cautious. Caution did not come in. We were not in the mood. There was too much on hand. Surrounded by that tremendous and terrifying experiment, by that raucous attempt to reconstruct society on a basis that gave different incentives for ambition, with every hoarding announcing the progress of the latest Five Year Plan—the amount of steel produced, the number of cars manufactured, the acres of wheat harvested—with the progress of this Plan presented in terms of a war effort, as battlefields in the proletariat's struggle, we could not, in all that din, concentrate on simple gallantry. I had heard the apologists of the system maintaining that sex in the Soviet Union was relegated to its proper place; that there was no such thing as prostitution; that books and films and the advertisers of cosmetics did not create and titillate an artificial appetite; that the Soviet worker could find better employment for his energy and leisure. I had heard that, but I had not believed it. I now knew how effective an anaphrodisiac are the radios of the communistic regime.

That was the first incident; the second, though it fructified when I was back in England, came as a corollary to the same high pressure atmosphere of conflict. Within a month of my return I was no longer on speaking terms with my travelling companion. We are both, as I said, Liberals at heart. I am indeed so unpolitical that I have in my whole life only voted twice. But because I am more to the right than my companion, I found myself in all our discussions of what we were seeing, presenting myself as the assailant of the Soviet experiment while he became its advocate. We were both using arguments in which we did not altogether believe because neutrality in that atmosphere was impossible. You had to be one thing or the other, so we ranged ourselves in opposition. During our three weeks, the strain of not quarrelling became so great, that the moment we were back in England and the necessity for restraint had gone, we began a ridiculous quarrel on the telephone. That is one of the things that the Soviet world does to you; it presents every issue in black and white; there are no half tones. Who is not with me is against me. Against your will it forces you to make a choice, and when you have made that choice—very probably because you have made it against your will you find yourself at enmity with those in the other camp. I had read that this was so, but I should not have believed it unless I had actually been to Russia.

The quarrel did not last long, but the fact that there ever was one, taught me more about Soviet Russia than anything that I have read in any book. I got no "fresh copy" out of Russia, but my personal curiosity was appeased. I got what I went there for.

Copy indeed, has never been as regards travel a first consideration in my calculations. Unlikelihood of finding it has never deterred me from visiting a place that I was curious to see. Actually my travels have not supplied me with much material, or shall I say with particularly profitable material. The travelogue is an unremunerative branch of authorship. Until *Holiday* was sponsored by the Curtis Publishing Corporation, there was no market for it except in prestige papers; and though "the slicks" clamoured for stories with an exotic background, they refused to touch any story that dealt realistically with the colour problem—one of the most insistent problems in the tropics and the chief social issue in the Caribbean. So strong is this taboo, that personally I have not placed in the larger magazines a single short story with a tropical background. I have spent far more money on travelling than I have earned by writing about far places. Had I thought of travel in terms of a profit and loss account, of a balanced budget, I should not have begun travelling again when the war was over. But it is not on that basis that I travel.

"Studies teach not their own use." And it would be hard to overrate the value of travel to an author. One of the chief deficiencies of contemporary European writing is a direct outcome of the difficulties and obstacles that passport and currency controls have placed in the way of travel. European writing has become parochial. A writer may not need fresh settings, but he does need to see from a different angle the familiar landscape of his home. It may be true that no Englishman can ever really understand the working of an Arab's mind, but after living for a little among Arabs, he is, back in London, better fitted to assess the relative importance of contemporary issues. He has a new perspective. A classical education by forcing the mind to dwell among and consider important, events that took place two thousand years ago, provides an admirable corrective against too ready and complete an absorption in what is here and now. In the same way the traveller who has in the background of his mind the beaches and peaks of the Pacific, the sandstorms of the desert, the gold domes and minarets of the Holy Cities is able to read his morning paper with a sense, if not of history, at least of distance. Mr. Somerset Maugham's travel scholarships may not produce a single work of travel, but they will add very certainly to the stature of several writers. Travel is an end in itself.

Before the war I travelled, whenever I could, in cargo boats, preferably in foreign ones. I loved the sea and the leisure of long journeys, the sense of freedom and escape; of being away from everything. But when I began to prepare the trip to Ceylon that I had foreseen as the inevitable sideline to my undertaking a biography of Lipton, it was a stack of airline folders that I amassed.

Travel by boat is at this moment of writing an unpracticable proposition for those who cannot make long term plans. There are very few ships, and many applicants; families are anxious to emigrate; families are anxious to get home; there are queues and waiting lists. You can book an Atlantic passage in mid-winter at short notice but that is about all you can do. For the traveller who makes last minute decisions, who needs to be independent, hours spent in steamship offices are a waste of time. I never considered any alternative means of getting to Ceylon.

I cannot say that I looked forward to my journey, to the actual trip, that is to say. The airline companies may advertise attractive hostesses tucking blankets round your knees and serving "delicious complimentary meals"; but the meals even on a transatlantic crossing are usually tepid and though the ladies who wrap you up for slumber are courteous and agreeable, your sleep is fitful. Your head-rest is unlikely to fit your height; as there are some men who can order a suit off the peg and look right in it from the start, so there are certain men for whose frame the charabanc and aircraft seat has been commodiously designed. I am not one of them; I rely on luminol. I am resigned to air-travel, but I don't enjoy it: it is not comfortable; aircraft are capricious, and something usually goes wrong. The betting is evens against your arriving at the scheduled time. It is a wise rule never to make a date within a day of the estimated hour of arrival. You are given little warning when plans are changed. In Calcutta, for instance, I was only told that a flying-boat from Hong-Kong would be three days late on the morning before she was due to fly; a type of negligence that can prove very inconvenient to the traveller—and I am one—who operates on a shoe string and arrives at his final destination with barely enough pennies to pay his bus fare home.

No one, I fancy, would travel by air for the mere enjoyment of the trip in the way that I once booked myself a trip to Kenya simply for the restorative effect of nineteen days at sea. But that is not to say that air travel does not offer moments of excitement, personal and peculiar to itself.

Sometimes it is a kind of dramatic irony, the drama of understatement. You are travelling light—a handbag and a suitcase. No taxi is in sight. Fifty yards from your front door there is a bus stop. A No. 30 will deposit you at the top of Knightsbridge, a few yards from the A.O.A. terminal. As you join the queue, you look at the people round you, smugly, selfcomplacently. There they are, bent on their prosaic pursuits, bound by their trivial routine. Tomorrow they will be queueing here, just the same, when you are sauntering down Park Avenue. Yesterday you were one of them; today you look like one of them. There is nothing to distinguish you from them. You are not alone in carrying a suitcase. You are with them; but you are no longer of them. The sense of your apartness gives you a rich feeling of superiority.

There is that moment. There are others. Two hours later you are in the airport. Now everyone is a passenger. There they sit, well dressed nearly all of them, indistinguishable, standardized, wearing on their faces that frown of vaguely annoyed detachment, as though they were somewhere else, "spirits concerned about departure," waiting for the loudspeakers to announce their flight. They all look the same. Yet how different they are in fact, as diverse as the contents of a mailbag. Of all nationalities, ages, callings, bound for such different ports, some near at hand, Irish or Scottish, others to the extremities of the globe, some on short trips, others on short holidays, some are going to freedom, some to bondage. Yet they all look the same as they sit there tidy and abstracted in their neat modernistic chairs. It gives you a tingling sense of the variety, the multiplicity of life.

Then there are the ports of call—the large luxury hotels in Malta, Karachi, Port of Spain, where passengers converge from many thousand miles to eat at the same tables under orders from the same loudspeaker, falling into talk at the same bar, then within a few hours scattering to their separate latitudes, unlikely ever again in their whole lives to be within a hundred miles of one another. It is impossible for a storyteller not to find himself devising plots out of the situations that must arise from these haphazard meetings for a few hours in strange anonymous hotels: of the curious affinities that spring between people arriving from different points, bound for different goals, knowing that what they have to share must be set within the framework of half a day. No liner gave you an equivalent sensation.

Nor does a liner give you that sense of kinship with your fellow passengers that an aircraft does, at any rate no large liner. When I travelled to Tahiti, a six weeks' journey from Marseilles, by French intermediate class, I gradually came to think of every sailor and passenger in the ship as someone to whom I was bound by shared experience. The Pacific is very wide; the great gates of the Panama Canal close behind you with an air of inexorable finality. The old world closes and a new world opens. Land is three weeks away. A seven thousand ton steamship is very much alone in that great waste of water. But that is a rare experience. I have had that same feeling on every air passage that has involved an all night stop-over.

You get to know people quickly in the air. You are so few, in so confined a space. The fate of one must be the fate of all; no one can act independently. The fact that you are all making the same trip presupposes a similarity of circumstance. Your landings in each foreign airport—Cairo or Karachi, San Juan or Nicosia, maintain your sense of unity. You are the same self-contained unit now as when you were being rushed through the air at a height of ten thousand feet. You have no links with this foreign city whose traditional daily life is continuing around you. You are goods in transit. You are driven from the airport to a hotel. A little card informs you of meal hours and starting time. You take a stroll to stretch your limbs, then settle down together to a session of martinis. The English are cautious socially. We hestitate to enter upon new friendships. Our island is too small. We live in such proximity to one another that we are on our guard against committing ourselves to a relationship that may prove awkward. We are reluctant to "drop a friend." We consider that we have assumed obligations to anyone whom we have invited to our house. In consequence of the reserve we impose on ourselves in our own country, we are the readier to be expansive when we are abroad.

Air travel, moreover, pays a dividend in this, that you see more from the air than you do by sea. Most of the time you are above the clouds, or high over water, but during the few circling minutes of arrival and departure you are given a vivid insight into the nature of the country you are visiting. How clearly you can recognize, for instance, after a day over the Arabian desert, how the green valley of the Nile enriches Egypt. Before World War II I had paid four visits to Antigua; I had covered it pretty thoroughly. But six minutes in the air, showing me the proportions of cane fields to mountain area, taught me more about its resources than many motor rides.

It is hard admittedly from an aeroplane to get a good impression of very mountainous country. The mountains of Dominica for instance are so high and so close together that you imagine yourself to be flying over a green forest, but on the other hand no one who has not circled over it can appreciate

Malta. Stone walls protect its fields against the wind, walls that are too high for the pedestrian to see over. He thinks of it all in terms of grey, sombre and unrelieved. But from the air you get a charming patchwork impression of green and brown.

We shall never, I suppose, see zeppelins again. In 1936 I crossed to America by the *Hindenburg*. It was a boring journey. Three nights and two days with the change of time making each day twenty-six hours long; but the zeppelin with its slow speed, low altitude and built-out windows so that you could lean over and look down on to what was immediately beneath you, gave a panoramic sense of landscape impossible to any other form of transport. I shall never forget my looking down upon the Scilly Islands and on the bays and harbours of the New England coast.

There are no lack of good times during a long air passage, but then one had good times in the trenches, and though I would not stigmatize the pleasure of air travel as "the good hours of an ague," they are very definitely of the "in spite of," not "because of" variety. Before the war you could misquote Stevenson and say that "to travel pleasantly was better than to arrive." You cannot now.

One travels by air because one has to, because one is in a hurry. It is the end not the means that matters. I used to enjoy an ocean voyage so much that I wondered sometimes whether my interest in distant places was not merely an excuse for the purchase of a steamship ticket. I know better now. Anyone who is travelling today has the answer to that kind of question. At this moment of writing, I have in the top drawer of my desk a boat trip ticket to the Seychelles Islands, which will mean the prelude of fifty hours in a plane. Curiosity alone could have driven me to accept, at such high cost, so dreary an expedient.

TO GET AWAY FROM IT ALL

Travel as Escapism

Hilton Brown

MY qualifications to discuss this subject do not lie in my being an escapist traveller because I do not, consciously at least, so regard myself. I claim to be the pure traveller without ulterior motive: I go because I see a name on the map or a picture in the papers which says, "You must come to me," and life becomes unsatisfactory until I have complied. Apart from that, I do not personally feel that in any form of reality, however remote, however outlandish, can refuge be found from other forms of reality. When I take to flight, I remove myself to the regions of the imagination; I invent some non-existent people and write a story about them. Direction by the fictitious creatures of one's own mind, though by no means so negligible as is commonly supposed, is markedly lighter and can be far more readily evaded than the hard control and domination of fact. There are however still a few people in the world who cannot or at least do not write fiction and it is to other resources that these must turn and one of these resources may well be travel. But indeed the resort of the escapist traveller may not be so distant from my own; for, as I hope to show, he nourishes himself on a fiction—and knows it.

How wretchedly our world has been circumscribed! How atrociously the psychologist and the psychiatrist have invaded everything! A century or two ago, the purposes of travel and the reasons why men undertook it—women very rarely undertook it in those days which was another great advantage—were simply and clearly defined. On the one hand, those who sought the backwoods and backblocks of the earth were lured thither by the expectation of discovery; there were still regions, extensive regions, marked enticingly on the map as "Unexplored"; there were rivers whose course was indicated by the dotted lines of conjecture; there were mountains whose figures of altitude were followed by the symbol "(?)". There are few such regions now. The lucky archæologist may hit upon a ruined and deserted city in the middle of the Dasht-i-Margo; but he is much more likely to hit upon nothing but high temperatures, ninety-mile-an-hour sandstorms and thirst—all of which have already been recorded and described by a thousand of his predecessors. Is it worth it? A century or two ago, the traveller could be incited by the wonderful thought, "Mine will be the first foot" . . . (Or the first white foot anyway.) Sometimes he excused himself on the pretext of collecting this or that item of scientific information; but the device was specious or secondary at best. The ambition to be the first that ever burst into— whatever it was, lay at the heart of the old-school traveller; but to be the thousand-and-first that ever burst is another matter.

On the other hand, a century or two ago, the less heroically-minded traveller could indulge in the opposite view; he could undertake the Grand Tour because the Grand Tour was regarded as the essential coping-stone of a gentleman's education. (The idea was no doubt encouraged by tutors and others in charge of young gentlemen; they got a splendid holiday out of it —indeed, if they played their cards well, a lifetime of splendid holidays with a different young gentleman each time.) Instead of aiming at the thing *not* so far done, these travellers meticulously followed the established round, the thing that *was* done; instead of advancing into the remote unknown where no man had preceded them, they concentrated on regions where men had longest and most prolifically assembled. Even this was still an adventure. In parenthesis, however, let me protest against the common assertion that it was infinitely more of an adventure than it is today; it was more, perhaps, but not infinitely. It is an open question whether the Grand Tour presented greater difficulties and dangers in 1750 than in 1950; progress was slower but it was not in the main less comfortable. The roads were bad; the barouche jolted and lurched and rolled; but you had it to yourself, you commanded all its movements, it was your own with all your belongings in it under your hand— including some cases of excellent, and inexpensive, wine and brandy. No Grand-Tourer ever endured the horrors of a second-class compartment between Calais and Geneva in the month of August; or the diesel carriage between Arezzo and

Uberto on the day of the Festival of St. Sepulchre. No Grand-Tourer was told that he must be inoculated against enteric before he could start, or that he must possess a passport with six different visas, each entailing a long long wait in a draughty Consulate. Nor was he restricted to a beggarly allowance of foreign currency, a sudden and unexpected demand on which might strand him; about his person or in one of the capacious pockets of the barouche he carried a bag of good old British gold—sovereigns or guineas—which served as passport, recommendation and *carte d'entrée* anywhere. If he was robbed of some of it, the act was done by a picturesque brigand on whom he could dine out for years to come, not by concièrge, head waiter or dragoman—and the brigand was probably less rapacious to boot. No; it is questionable whether the Grand Tour nowadays is less arduous than it was. . . . But this is all by way of digression; the fact remains that, adventurous or not, the Grand Tour is out of vogue, it is no longer done. The education of a gentleman is more fashionably completed at the London School of Economics—that is to say, if there still exist any such concepts as "gentleman" and "education" at all. And the Grand Tour has become commonplace. To have crossed the St. Bernard, gazed at the ceiling of the Sistine Chapel, floated in a gondola—why, the man who cuts your hair did all three of them last summer; and didn't think much of them either.

I may seem to be wandering from my brief but I am not. What I am trying to say is that, the explorer-urge and the Grand-Tourer-urge having expired with the efflux of time, some other reason for travelling has to be substituted for them. It is a canon of English life that no man does anything without a reason; he does not simply start off on his travels as a leaf starts off that is blown by a sudden gust of wind. Or he may in fact do so, but he dare not admit it; his friends would look on him askance. He has therefore to invent and set up some plausible pretext which he can tell them at the Club; and in this hag-ridden age, he naturally seeks that pretext in terms of the psychiatrist's consulting room. He says therefore, "I am an escapist; my travel is a form of escapism." By this he means or would like to mean much more than is meant by a City friend of mine, an extremely busy executive in his firm, who undertakes a day journey from London to Scotland and back about once a fortnight. I remarked to him that this must involve a terrible amount of wear and tear. "On the contrary," he replied, "it is the only thing that keeps me alive. Once I am into that train and the starting signal drops and the thing pulls out of King's Cross or Euston, I can *not* be got at by anybody for a matter of eight hours. There are no telephones on trains." It was useless to tell him that he could produce the same effect by locking himself into his private office, switching on the red light above his door and tying a handkerchief round his telephone bell; and in fact it could not have produced the same effect; it would have lacked all the delicious sensations of the runaway; it would not, in short, have been an escape. But I doubt if my City friend would have called himself or enjoyed being called an escapist; he would have confused the term with others of a less reputable kind. And I feel, as I have already said, that the traveller who puts forward escapism as his pretext means more by it than this.

Well, then, what *does* he mean by it?

In the first place, let us consider the implications of escaping. Manifestly there must be something to escape *from*; but the gravity and pressure of this something may vary greatly in degree. It may be as serious as prison; it may be as trifling as the Club bore or an overheated room or Mrs. Thingumbob's tea-party. But in some form or another it must exist; it must set up that malaise which becomes, at a given moment, no longer supportable. But the departure from the permanently or temporarily undesirable cannot of itself constitute an escape; if it must be an escape *from*, it must also be an escape *to*. If it has not some goal, some haven, some purpose, it becomes a mere panic flight: it is no better than one of those interminable careers of nightmare in which, for long æons, one is tearing along, sometimes pursued, sometimes pursuing, one is never quite sure which, but mostly just drifting, flying through the air or racing along the surface of the ground, or if the nightmare is a particularly hideous one, the surface of the sea. I have never heard anyone, awaking from a nightmare of this sort, exclaim, "What a relief that was to me! What balm to my soul!" and I never expect to hear it. The sensation of rapt purposeless flight from an undefined horror to what appears to be a vacuum is not one that any sane being would wish to cultivate or repeat; it is certainly not an objective that would commend itself to the purposeful escapist. So while there must be an object or environment *from* which escape is made—or escape could not even begin—there must equally be another object or environment *to* which it is directed. It must be in this sense that the escapist traveller undertakes his voyage if he is to have any hope of benefit; he escapes *from* X *to* Y.

Let us consider first X, the object or environment *from* which he seeks to escape. This may in the initial stages be no more than his daily duties and obligations, when he will be in much the same case as my City friend with his train journeys to Scotland. That the moment occasionally arrives when the office desk, the workshop or the consulting-room begins to exert a pressure which can no longer be endured is a commonplace of human experience. To many of us such a moment arrives every Monday morning; to some of us, perhaps, every morning. The best way of treating this recurring disorder is to pay no attention to it; if it is resolutely ignored for a time, it may disappear; just as, on a long walk, a blister on the sole of the foot may be tramped into insensibility and forgotten—so long as one does not stop. Your Spartan will adopt this method of dealing with the too-oppressive daily toil; but your escapist by nature will do otherwise. He will run from it, he will enlist some diversion for his mind, as the walker with the blister might endeavour to dismiss it from his consciousness by counting his footsteps or reciting *Gunga Din*. And one form of diversion which will readily appeal to him is a change of scene. Provided he has a sufficiently adaptable mind and a sufficiently easy conscience, he can, by the mere process of placing himself at a physical distance from it, forget that file about the development of satellite cities, or those calculations relative to steel castings, or that annoying woman Mrs. So-and-so with her everlasting symptoms of incurable valetudinarianism. He may also—indeed probably will—compound with his conscience by assuring himself that on his return to duty he will fall upon his disagreeable tasks "like a giant refreshed" (he will use that very phrase) so that his sojourn in other parts will be made to appear as in itself a duty which he is obliged in the interests of his work to perform. He may even succeed in working up a very creditable air of martyrdom over it all. But note in passing those words "on his return to duty"; that is a point to which we shall have to come back.

Secondly, the escapist traveller may be endeavouring to rid himself of his acquaintance. And since no man with a happy home (if there is such a thing) need vex himself about his external friends, this will, in the last resort, mean his family. It is a question whether, in this age of freedom and the Welfare State, the family shibboleth has not outlived its vitality. Is the family idea in decay, and indeed in that decay which is the natural prelude to dissolution? A learned friend of mine contends that this is so. The family principle and system, he argues, has had a long run; it has failed and should now be scrapped in favour of something else. The weakness of my friend's position lies in the fact that, when asked what this "something else" should be, he can give no satisfactory answer; told that it is pointless to retreat from any situation unless you can see an alternative, he is forced to retort unconvincingly that if the retreat is vigorously taken in hand, an alternative must and therefore will be found; a doctrine which the best tactical authorities do not support. The strength of his position, on the other hand, is founded on the statistics he has collected—or professes to have collected—from among families within his observation and knowledge. These, as analysed by my friend, present a lamentable picture. Out of seven and twenty families which he has closely examined, he has found only one in which anything approaching the ideal or even the theoretical standard of family contentment and love can be said to prevail. In this family—not, unfortunately, distinguished by a high level of intelligence—a complete sympathy exists; parents and children, brothers and sisters, would never contemplate performing any activity separately which could be performed in unison; they dote upon each other and will at all times form a common front against aggression upon any individual member. This family, says my friend, is a freak; and he supports this by pointing to the other twenty-six concerned in his investigations. In about a third of these a mild unstable toleration may be said to prevail, they can jog along on a precarious balance so long as no great or sudden demand is made. In the remainder the relations vary from indifference to downright hate. My friend says that as the whole family system is an artificial concept based on considerations which no longer operate—defence against enemies, the protection and marketing of the family virgins, the joint managements of the family flocks and herds—its continuance under modern conditions can only be irksome and infuriating and it must therefore go.

Again I may appear to be wandering from my point; again I am not. I wish to observe that if the present state of family life is as my friend makes out—and his statistics are formidable—then these innumerable and artificially-formed nuclei of discordant individuals must represent for those concerned so many cells of incarceration. The need to break away, if only for a time—note again those words "if only for a time"—from the wrangles and maladjustments of the average home must be one of the primary stimuli that hurl escapist travellers about the surface of our globe. If so, these may well bless the name of the racial benefactor who first laid down the principle of "separate holidays." There was a time when the escapist traveller, be his home life never so desperate, could not have cast loose from his family; the weight of public opinion would have pressed too heavily against him. It was the understood thing that the family *never* separated (the under-lying theory being, of course, that it never wanted to). If a journey to Margate were proposed or Mozambique, all went or none. This has been greatly and mercifully modified. It is now possible for Father, to enjoy a ramble through the Bernese passes while Mother and the children explore Northern Ireland; it is possible, for that matter, to dump the children wherever they can be dumped while Mother goes off to Connecticut and Father to Siam. Those who insist that our civilization is declining may well pause to consider this remarkable and liberal advance. Its originator must remain for ever nameless with such bold and beneficent spirits as the man who ate the first oyster; but there can be no doubt as to who seized on the idea and developed it; it was the escapist traveller, whose Magna Charta it has always been.

The escapist traveller then may be trying to free himself from his routine environment—the eight-fifteen to town, the office desk, lunch at the Club, the five-forty-five home again. Or he may seek to break loose from that lady of his choice with whom he has discussed a thousand times every discussable subject, whose every mood is as familiar to him as is his every mood to her, whose every chamber he has explored, whose every alcove importuned—or at least he complacently believes that he has done this which comes to the same thing. He may long for release from the unanswerable interrogations, the deafening disturbance or the cold contempt of his children. But his plight may be more desperate than any of this; he may be trying to escape from himself.

How far, if at all, is it possible to achieve this? It being out of the question to discard the actual corporeal envelope in which his existence is bound up, the escapist must restrict his endeavours to altering the self's externals; and in no way can this be better done than by the process of travel. "I," the escapist traveller will reason, "am a figure dressed in a black coat, greyish trousers and what is called an Anthony Eden hat; this figure proceeds daily from Purley to London Bridge, walks along a certain street, ascends in the lift through a certain building, sits down in a certain room, performs a number of complicated but essentially similar and repetitive evolutions, gets up at last and goes home again. A colourless figure oscillating in dingy surroundings, that is the thing, the self, I call 'I.' But if I can make myself into a figure clad in a bright yellow shirt and terra-cotta leather shorts, sitting on the summit of the Bella Tola or the Albristhorn—rewarding but not exacting peaks—looking out, not upon the suburbs or streetways of London but upon a blinding panorama of snow-topped and crag-studded mountains, then a new 'I' altogether comes into being. Or if I dress myself in white ducks, an open-neck shirt and sandals and sit under a coco-palm drinking rum and playing a marimba, then once again I have successfully altered the 'I.' I have escaped definitely from that black, purposeful, shuttling automaton. It is incredible that these two characters, the exalted mountaineer halfway up the ascent to Paradise or the gay beachcomber sodden with blue seas and golden sun (to say nothing of the rum) can be identical or indeed can exhibit any affinity with that drab metropolitan ant. And if I can go further and yet further afield; if I can stand upon Aorangi, swim in Titicaca, muse upon mortality at La Ferrière; then surely I must further and further escape. More and more exotic and therefore more and more liberating 'I's must be called into being."

The escapist traveller is obliged to say all this in order to

shout down that objectionably persistent voice which keeps reminding him that his premises are false. Your self, the "I"
you are endeavouring to discard—so this voice will implacably
warn him—does not consist in an Anthony Eden hat on the one
hand or terra-cotta shorts on the other; it does not matter
whether it is playing the marimba or playing the markets; it is
immaterial whether its bodily manifestation is seated on Mount
Kenya or on the lunar crater of Pythagoras. This is a thing with
which you are so deeply and inextricably involved that no
change of dress, scenery, food, drink, habits, height, depth or
any living accessory can materially affect it. From your "self"
you can escape only by the really drastic step of death—and we
are not even very sure about that. The objectionably persistent
voice is platitudinous because such voices have been repeating
themselves throughout recorded history; and on this ground the
escapist traveller may for a time pooh-pooh its representations.
He may engage it in complicated arguments on Pragmatism,
Free Will and the Reality of the External Universe; or he may
say to it more simply, "I know all that perfectly well; shut up!"
But he will not be able to succeed indefinitely in suppressing it.
If he is striving to escape from that bag of worries, ambitions,
frustrations, loves, hates, hopes and despairs that goes marching
from Purley to Threadneedle Street and back five days a week,
he is striving for the impossible. It cannot be done. The bag
indeed may be altered in shape, hue and material; but the contents remain and will eventually, seething and boiling, burst
through any envelope whatsoever. The most the escapist
traveller can really do is to stave off to the last possible moment
his realization and admission of this hideous fact. If, however,
he can cultivate a suitable sequence of moods, if he can go far
and fast and keep ringing the changes in all sorts of agreeable
ways—or even disagreeable—he may contrive to postpone the
moment for a very serviceable interval. As long, perhaps, as
may be necessary.

Again in parenthesis, a plea must be advanced in favour of
the disagreeables of travel which I have just mentioned. What
part do these play in the escape—the missed connection at the
most intolerable railway junction in Spain, the hotel crammed
to bedlessness by a conference of Italian viticulturists, the flea
that should never have succeeded in entering an establishment

so heavily starred in Michelin, the sudden tropical downpour that caught one on the open beach road from the Casino—of course, with no overcoat or umbrella? The answer is that, so far as escapism is concerned, they play exactly the same part a the Battle of Flowers, the view from the Gornergrat or the *caneton à la presse* at Luigi's. They divert. Indeed, it is possible that by the acerbity and vigour with which they impinge upon the sensations, they may assist the escapist even more forcefully. Whether our traveller is taking refuge from the tedium of his daily round, the savage antipathies of his family circle or the dark half-guessed horrors of his self, he will be the more rather than the less likely to succeed if he is suddenly soaked in his best suit, stranded bedless in an unknown and unprepossessing township or murderously assailed by a revolting type of insect. No, the escapist should not disparage or discount the undesirables of his travel; like many other unpleasantnesses—perhaps they can be turned to good.

We have now delineated with some precision the objects from which the traveller is attempting to escape—his environment, his acquaintance and his self. But I hope it has all along been borne in mind that escape into vacuum is inconceivable, that "escape" is a mere chimæra unless it is directed towards some comprehended goal. What then will this be? The answer will depend upon which of two alternative lines the escapist adopts —escape into space or escape into time. The former is by far the more common but the latter may be, by an equal margin, the more satisfactory.

As all travel must involve movement in space, the question of travel in space hardly arises in any form worth discussing; it becomes merely a matter of going on and on and on. But there may be more to be said on the aspect of escape into time. Indeed, this is in a sense the fundamental aspect from which all escape should be regarded; because all those other stimuli to flight which we have already recognized—work, the family, the self—can be lumped together under a single heading in terms of time; the present. It is from the present that all escape must eventually be made. Now, it is no use saying that escape from the present is an impossibility because the present is constant and advances continually with us; we all know perfectly well that three in the afternoon becomes in due course *now*, that tomorrow is really today and so on. We must for our present purpose forget these metaphysical refinements and treat the present —as the escapist traveller does treat it—as if it were static; an enclosure, like the office in the City or Mrs. Thingumbob's drawing-room, which can be got out of and left behind. This is not so; but if the escapist traveller cannot persuade himself to the contrary, he may as well go and hang himself forthwith.

From the present, escape can be made only in two directions —backward or forward, to the past or to the future. Or in other words, escape must be either towards the old or the new, towards repetition of an already enjoyed experience or towards realization of one so far only projected as a possibility. Let us take the latter first. The escapist traveller heading for the future may say to himself, "I greatly admire and would wish to emulate the ruthlessness of the painter Gauguin; if my family go on being as tiresome as they have been of late, I will do just what he did and remove myself to the South Sea Islands. I will now carry out a reconnaissance and see what it would be like." He accordingly arranges to transport himself to Fiji or Raratonga or Tahiti. He probably finds on arrival that the conditions for Gauguinism are such as he could not possibly endure, and so he comes back; but for a time he has moved into the future, for an interval he has made himself Gauguin. Or, in another mood, he may say, "I will capitalize all that I possess, hand it over to my offspring and become a *sanyasi* on the Tirupathi Hills. But first let us have a look at Tirupathi." So he travels to South India—with the same eventual result; he finds that Europeans are not permitted to enter upon the Tirupathi Hills and that a diet of temple rice and coconut milk gives him the most infernal indigestion. Yet again, for a time, he has advanced into the future; just for the nonce, he has been in some sort a *sanyasi*. Into the future—as he has chosen to envisage it—he has fled.

The unsatisfactory feature of this escaping into the future is obvious and should need no elaboration. Your escapist is *ex hypothesi* a coward, if only because he is for the time being actuated by the operative impulse of cowards—the desire for flight. But it is of the essence of the coward's flight that it should be to safety, to something known to be secure ; to Mother's lap, or under the bed, or into the only room in the house whose door can be locked without exciting officious comment. The future, the new and untried, holds out no such promise of comfort; as we have seen in the Gauguin and *sanyasi* examples, the odds are that it will disappoint and it will certainly call for courage, resolution, endurance. These are qualities which the escapist will view with distaste, because clearly if he possessed them, he would not be needing to escape at all. He will therefore in most cases be much better advised to direct himself towards the old and the known—to escape into the past.

One of the advantages of the uneasy yearning popularly called nostalgia is that it can often be gratified. It is true that the escapist into the past cannot this evening take a ticket for the Oxford Music Hall and hear Marie Lloyd, but he can now and then listen to a programme on the wireless which will evoke a great deal of that forgotten and cherished atmosphere. He cannot transform himself into a boy and ascend Cairngorm with those other two boys Peter X and John Y who are now men of sixty, if indeed they survive at all; but he can—taking it slowly and easily—ascend Cairngorm and he will find it radically unchanged so that he has a fair chance to recapture the vanished mood he seeks. And it is this—the unchanging place, the setting that defines the ravages of time—that affords the escapist traveller perhaps his very best and most hopeful opportunity.

Let me illustrate by a personal example. There was in South India a certain district where, during a brief official sojourn I was in my younger days unusually contented and happy. Years later, in quite another part of the country, I reached that state of mind which is essentially that of the escapist traveller; I could not endure my present environment a moment longer. I said, "I will go back to that old district and see if it will soothe my heart." The experiment was completely successful. The suns and moons of that now almost deified region were as resplendent as of yore; its forests were as cool and inviting; its mountains as lovely at sunrise and sunset; its beaches as warm, its sea as diamond-bright; its people as simple, agreeable and kind. I knew the district like the palm of my hand; it could show me no novelty; it could have sprung no surprise but the surprise of disappointment, which it emphatically did not do. Never in all the history of escapist travel was there a more successful venture made. And it was made not into the future but

into the past, not to the new but to the old, not to discovery but
to recapitulation. It is a commonplace, of course, that all proverbs are wrong; by this instance I demonstrate the falsity of
that which enunciates, "You cannot put back the clock." It is
a lie; you can.

And putting the clock back is the first thing the escapist
traveller should try. But though it may appeal to his cowardly
instincts as a much safer bid than escape into the future, it still
contains—let me make this clear—an appalling element of risk.
Not the risk normally associated with the ventures of travel—
that the place will not be as the travel agency represented it,
that it will not live up to its maps or its pictures in the *Geographical Magazine*; the voyager backward knows what is before
him—with exactitude. Yet he must be a brave man who will
take a chance with his most treasured memories. *If* the adventure comes off, good and well; but it may not. It may deceive,
disappoint, betray. And if that happens, the last state of that
escapist is infinitely worse than the first. For not only has his
immediate escape failed, so that he is hurled back into the old
environment with neither refreshment nor release; but he has
also ruined and defaced that bright picture of memory which—
if he had only had the sense to let it alone—would have carried
him, as it so often did, through exhausting days, sleepless nights
and all the infinite tedium of affairs. Now whether or not this
will happen; whether the old familiar scene will evoke the old
familiar happiness or whether it will appear faded shrunk
desiccated and meagre so that he asks himself that most tragic
of all questions, "Whatever did I see in *this*?"; this can only be
resolved by the test of actual experiment and until it is so resolved remains hideously open. The one alternative is *primâ
facie* as likely as the other. The escapist who determines on going back to the past, on clock back-putting, must regard himself as the most desperate of gamblers, staking on a single throw
far more than he can afford. But if he can accept an enormous
risk in the hope of an enormous win, then, of all the forms of
escapist travel, that of flight into a known and cherished past
holds out the brightest hope.

Another parenthesis; I apologize for their number but I have
a parenthetical and tangential mind. And there is a word of
warning that must be uttered. The thing must be done by one-

self, relying on oneself and without associate. To attempt to carry back with one into the past a companion however sympathetic is to involve oneself in the incongruity and discomfort of the one man in a dinner-jacket at a fancy dress ball. For any companion drawn from the present must drag the present fatally in his wake. Even if a companion should offer who did in fact share that long-lost Arcady, that Sicilian Age in *the* Place, the temptation to include him (and *a fortiori* her) in the expedition must be resisted. There are risks enough already. As in the cases of Gehenna and the Throne, so the escapist travels fastest and fairest and with the best hope of succeeding who travels —alone.

I said a little while ago that the proverb anent the putting back of clocks was among the more conspicuously false and misleading; this requires some qualification. For the clock can be *put* back, but it cannot be *kept* back. Clocks on which this reversing operation has been performed have an objectionable habit of returning sharply to the present, as the needle of a balance returns sharply to zero immediately the weight in the pan is removed. This, if he is not sufficiently prepared for it, may be for the escapist traveller a horrible experience. He should therefore be prepared for it so that, if the worst comes to the worst— as it *will*, he may transform that swing-back of the pendulum into a gentle glide and not a neck-breaking jerk. And he will most easily do this by considering and reconciling himself to the fallacy which underlies his whole illusion on the subject of what he calls escape.

When Casanova sat musing in his cell below the waters of Venice and planning his escape from the Doge's prison, he meant any such escape—as every sane gaol-breaker always has done—to be permanent. He did not contemplate the possibility that after a time he would come back. Now, if the word "escape" is to be used in its proper sense, this is how it must be understood—as a clear and final cut-away and release without thought or expectation of return. But the escapist traveller cannot and does not understand the word in this unequivocal sense. No doubt this circumstance has advantages for him as well as disadvantages; if it renders his "escape" verbally a convention and ideally an illusion, it is at the same time the source of all the sweetness and vitality of his venture. If it renders the whole proceeding something of a pretence, it also provides him with those pleasing sensations enjoyed by the schoolboy whose truancy would lose half its value to him did he not know that it could not indefinitely continue, that school lay ahead and must be resumed. So obvious a conception requires no elaboration to those who have been taught from their copybook days that Stolen Fruits are Sweetest and that All Good Things Come to an End. Yet the whole of the escapist traveller's argument is based on the contrary assumption—that Good Things will never end, that he can really break away into freedom. He deceives himself; as a little reflection will show.

In the first place, it is necessary to emphasize once more that "escape," to be escape at all, must have a recognized and postulated goal. For Casanova "escape" was a simple concept because completely restricted; his was to be escape *from* confinement *to* freedom, the exchange between the straightforward alternatives, incarceration or liberty. But for the escapist traveller the problem is not so reduced; he must ask himself "where shall I go?" and he is at once confronted with an almost infinite series of exchanges among which he must exercise choice. Casanova said "I escape to freedom"; but the escapist traveller cannot say, with the same significance, "I escape to Tibet." The moment he says the word "Tibet" he begins to think "But would Tahiti perhaps be better?" and so he is at once debarred from any permanent escape at the outset because he cannot make up his mind where to go. His situation is that of the soldier in the old First War Bruce Bairnsfather illustration—"if y' knows of a better 'ole, go to it." So he would; but his misfortune is that he knows of so many better 'oles and he cannot go to them all. He therefore cannot go—as an "escape"—to any.

Let me illustrate again by a personal experience. I ask myself "If I desert my established environment for another which will then become equally established, where is it to be? Where is my better 'ole?" And I cannot answer. To thin the possibles down to the shortest list I can compass, I should like to live permanently in (a) the Nilgiri Hills of South India, (b) the island of Barbados, (c) the Frutigen area of Switzerland, (d) Rome, (e) Maracay in Venezuela. If inexorable fate should say to me, "You *shall* live now in"—any one of these, I would gladly up sticks and away. But I am totally incapable of picking out one of them for myself. If I think of the suns and the song-birds and the rolling grass downs of the Nilgiris, I immediately have a countering vision of the Grosse Lohner and the Hahnemoos; if I fix my mind on Sam Lord's Castle and the Windward rollers, I swerve away to the Parque Carabobo and *dolce far niente* of Maracay. And the result is that I do not transfer myself and all my effects to Ootacamund or Adelboden, Bridgetown or Caraccas; at most I visit these places and return home. I do not escape to them. With the usual process of false analogy, I am persuaded that this experience of mine is universal; and that all escapist travellers must fail at the outset from mere profusion of alternatives. The escapist traveller is like the schoolboy who must go back to the school—nay, in his heart cherishes the school—because it is the one thing *there* and permanent. He goes chasing from one possible to another, as the victim of a nightmare is now in the Amazonian jungles and now in the Albert Hall. And this is not, in any intelligible sense, "escape."

Must the escapist traveller then admit that his "escape" depends not only on something to escape *from* but on something to escape from and *come back to?* It would really seem so. And must he confess to himself that not only is his "escape" merely temporary but that, if put to it and brought down to rock bottom, he would not have it otherwise?

Let us consider once again those objects *from* which we supposed the traveller to be escaping. They were his daily routine, his family and friends, his self. Now so much of life is based upon routine that escape from it is a very doubtful advantage. The human body is a mechanism unfortunately only partially adaptable; there is no doubt, however humiliating the thought may be, that it thrives on coddling, that the organisms of most of us get along most smoothly under a fixed regime and a system of regular attention. Nobody really understands our teeth except that fellow So-and-so in Grosvenor Street; while the ludicrous notions of that doctor in Miami on our occasional tendency to biliousness were as fantastic as those of the Kurhaus at Gimmelsee about our twinges of lumbago. Suppose, just suppose, we had to have our appendix out; *could* anybody do it except old Jones down home at Cheltenham? By his entrails— and still more by those who have habitually ministered to them —man is bound down as by mediæval chain and ball. . . . And again—the office desk. Few men are so miserable as to be without some function, essential to their enjoyment, which can best —indeed can only—be practised with profit in a certain area. Will Smith the publisher, Robinson the editor, come winging to colloque with me on the summit of the Aberdares? They will not; they will prefer to forego my contributions. Man is a rut-dwelling animal. Routine—the routine of health, the routine of profitable occupation for gain—is something beyond a mere bore; it is something without which man cannot subsist. This is a terrible thought, but it is true.

Then the family. Suppose one were told, "You shall *never* see Eleanor, young Skittles and little Buster again?" Could we endure it? Gauguin could; but then Gauguin was a Titan among escapists; we cannot all be of his calibre. And besides, there is the intolerable thought—a mere suspicion to be suppressed as soon as conceived that Eleanor, young Skittles and little Buster could get on as well—better?—without us; an idea so repellant that they must be deprived at all costs of any opportunity to think of it for themselves. Men have seen such a suspicion turned into certainty and lived on thereafter; but they have never been the same men again. . . . And the blank, the hopeless blank there would be in our existence! A woman whose congenital stupidities one can always be kindly pointing out; a child whose activities one can as kindly direct, control and guide—at any rate until it becomes old enough to warn us to desist; these are essential ingredients in any tolerable life.

As to the self, we have already agreed that escape from it is impossible; so there is no use talking any further about that.

So how can the traveller call himself an "escapist"? How dare he use the word? If escape must mean, as it meant to Casanova, an everlasting deliverance from the present, he cannot have it and he does not even want it. And since this is the only sense in which the word can properly be used, then—properly speaking—there can be no such thing as an "escapist," traveller or otherwise, in the sense in which he is trying to use it. The man is not "escaping" at all. He is no rocket, attaining a critical velocity and freeing itself from the earth's attraction; he is a cheap firework sputtering along the ground, a captive balloon, a menagerie chimpanzee allowed to posture to the limit of its chain and then jerked back. The traveller who insists that his motive in travelling is "escapism" is as deeply deluded and immersed in as dense a fog as any sensible man who has misguidedly landed himself in a psychologist's chamber.

There is, however, one consoling thought with which we may well close this investigation. If running away only means in the end running back again, it *is* always running. Either way, going or coming, it is movement; and movement, any movement, is good. When my City friend got into his Edinburgh express at King's Cross, he was in a constant state of stimulated excitement till the locomotive pulled him into Waverley; he had the pleasurable sensation of whizzing past a number of static objects and persons who, he thought, must envy him his mobility. Moreover he could do nothing to control the forces that moved him—short of course of pulling the communication cord, a gesture which, as a business man, he would discount as unremunerative at the cost of a five pound fine. Even if he knew that there awaited him in Edinburgh a recalcitrant Directorate or a raging mob of shareholders, still, so long as he was moving, he was well off. For that brief interval, for the time being—and we have seen that it can never be more than for the time being —he achieved what Casanova aimed at, freedom. He *moved*; and while he moved, he did in some sense "escape."

It was recently my misfortune to be one of a Brains Trust (so called) which submitted itself to the interrogations of a number of young people. I was asked by one of these whether, now that all religious significance had left it, Christmas was still worth while. I replied—without conceding his premises—that I thought it was; on the ground that anything is worth while that carries man out of that all too seductive rut of his, that induces him for once in a way to let himself go. If the young gentleman had phrased his question otherwise and had asked me "now that there's nothing left to see in the world, is travel worth while?" I should have offered him—again without concession of his premise—the same answer; for so much—and no more— can be said for the escapist traveller. Change is after all an essential detonator in life. Man hopes and despairs; yet throughout all his alternations between hilarity and gloom, he clings resolutely to his fantastic belief that change will be for the better. "I need," he says, "a change": and then he starts talking about escapism. Surely there can be no more striking instance of the invincibility of human optimism, the triumph against all odds of human hope.

And it is seen every time one of us gets into a railway carriage, walks up a ship's gangway, or buckles his safety belt at the bidding of an air hostess.

ETERNAL TRAVELLERS

Walter Starkie

ONE of the great charms of the Gypsies is that they are elusive. If you go out gypsying with the intention of discovering a camp, it is ten to one against your finding them. When you follow the Romany patteran you may find only a few smouldering ashes; the birds have fled. To discover Gypsies one must have a Romany nose, which leads you towards these primitive folk whom the author of *Don Quixote* called the "Kings of Nature." In all of us there are two selves. As our first, conventional self we go through life mechanically, paying meticulous attention to what our neighbours say of us; our second self is always clamouring to be released from the prison of everyday mediocrity to which we are condemned. I am convinced that our second personality is affected by the moon, and this was Byron's opinion when he wrote—"the sun set and uprose the yellow moon: the devil's in the moon for mischief." As long as the sun shines I feel tranquil and contented, but as soon as the moonbeams begin to steal into my room I feel the restless desire to escape over the wall. I am becoming a Moonman again and as Dekker said in the sixteenth century, "Moonman means madman, because the moon has greatest domination over the bodies of frantic persons; and just as she is never in one shape two nights together, but wanders up and down Heaven like an antic, so the Moonman never tarries one day in a place but is the only base runagate upon earth." No wonder that the Gypsies were called the Minions of the Moon by Dekker, who had seen them forage restlessly up and down England four, five, or six in a company. During my wanderings in the south of Italy in 1919 I came upon a Gypsy tribe gathered outside their brown tents. Around the fires they clustered and the women were stirring the cauldrons, while naked children darted here and there amidst the mules and donkeys. Night advanced silently. Then suddenly a voice lost itself in the void. The song of the wanderer. "Here today, there tomorrow, for ever wandering on our way through the desert of the world. Who knows whence we come? Who knows the secret of our origin? The Destiny that drove us inexorably since the beginning of history will not disclose." After the music had died away, all was hushed again, save for the tinkle of the mule bells. Then rose the moon as a ghost and cast the paleness of death upon the scene. Voices arose again in songs chanting the hymn of Diana, the mother of Gypsy witchcraft. In the silver night men, women, and children worshipped the full moon, for her daughter Aradia was the greatest witch in the world and the peerless teacher of the lonely wanderer. In accordance with the teaching of Aradia it was their duty once a month, when the moon was full, to assemble in some desert place, or in a forest, and there to join in adoration of the potent spirit of the great mother Diana.

The Gypsies, as Arthur Symons said, are changeless and the world has no power over them. They live by rote and by faith and by tradition, which is part of their blood. Can the world repress this race which is so evasive and slips through its gross fingers like wind? "Like one on a secret errand," they pass through the world. They are the symbol of our aspirations and we do not know it.[1] One word echoes through my mind when I think of the Gypsies: the word Freedom; nowadays it is, indeed, a difficult matter to break one's chains and escape for a moment into a life of Freedom. It is necessary to perform a potent ritual and throw off our well-worn mask of everyday, if we would escape. Nobody who possesses a vagabond second self should ever put on his Gypsy clothes before the sun has set on the last day of term; they should, in fact, be locked in the lumber-room with seven keys, otherwise they might behave like the magic shoes in the fairy tale and lead you a dance over the hills and far away.

On the eve of the holidays we should escort our conventional first self with all pomp and circumstance to the lumber-room and lock him up in the chest, but taking good care to pour a bottle of sparkling wine over him in order to lay his ghost. Then, with light heart and lighter purse, we should depart like the good sons in Grimm's fairy stories who set out at random from their father's door to conquer the world.

On one occasion when I was wandering along the roads in

[1] Arthur Symons: *In Praise of Gypsies.* Gypsy Lore Society. N.S.I. 295-7.

Transylvania with a Gypsy, he described for me how the wandering tribes set out every year in the spring. They have a feast of rejoicing called the *"Kakkava,"* a "feast of the copper pans," on the day of St. George, April 23. "For three days," said he, "every Gypsy man, woman and child goes daft: they drink, they sing, they play, they romp: they drag out their tents into the plain, they harness their horses to the carts; they sacrifice lambs and they wreathe the wine jars in flowers." For the feast of St. George is the beginning of the Gypsy wandering and the rebirth of the year. On that day no man is allowed to curse or quarrel, and woe to the policeman who tries to set foot within the flowering meadow where the tribes are collected together around their beribboned carts and tents. After that day the tribes will scatter in the plain and when the shadows fall the carts will be drawn up beneath the trees, and fiddles and "cobzas" will sound in the night, creating the wild, untutored harmony which inspires the frantic dance of the Bacchantes. There is a Serbian proverb which says, "a Tzigane woman suckled me: that is why I have wings." When the nomadic Gypsies enter their frenzy they give wings to us who listen, for they bring all Eastern romance in their wildness.

Such is the Gypsy spell which leads sane, prosaic men on a wild chase, as though they were following the Firebird. Roaming with Gypsies may become a passion which it is dangerous to deny, for it springs from the wild, eccentric second self. Whenever I set off on the Gypsy trail it takes some time before I can free my wandering personality. At first I am attached to my life of ease and indulgence. I find the roads long, I am conscious of my obesity, my shortness of breath. Then gradually I become inured to hardship and I enjoy the simple meals of raw ham and a few sprigs of raw garlic washed down by rough red wine that tastes of the leather. The sense of adventure rises in me: I long to escape out into the wild country and sleep in caves.

As I have said before, it is not easy to come across Gypsies, for they are the most elusive people on earth and love to lead the prying travellers on a wild-goose chase. They always fear that the *busnó*—the non-Gypsy—will reveal them to the world, and that is why the Romany language, the tabus, the patterans, are all protections against the hated white man. A peasant whom I once questioned on the disappearance of the tribe told me that when the Gypsies leave a place where they have been staying, they go in a certain direction at random and then turn right about and go half a league that way before they finally depart on their right road. "You won't find them," said he, "for they go like hares in the undergrowth, and sometimes they seem to fade into thin air." The Gypsies know that modern life is so hedged in with rules and regulations that it is impossible for a man to escape unless he performs at least a private ritual for himself in order that the gods may give him the courage of the lion, the astuteness of the fox, the hide of the rhinoceros to fight for his independence and liberty. There is a prayer which Rumanian Gypsies recite, in which they offer to God one candle if He lets them steal a hen, goose, or sheep; two candles if the "gorgios" enter the Gypsy tent to discover the stolen property and find nothing; three candles if the police enter the tent, and, after having searched it and found nothing, depart in peace. I have always been ready to offer three, if I could disappear from my niche in everyday society without anybody being the wiser.

Nowadays the only life for the individual lover of freedom is to develop subtle methods of escape. It is useless to be an out-and-out revolutionary, because as soon as you stick out your jaw and contradict the will of the majority you become a victim and spend the rest of your life fighting unsuccessfully for principles which the majority will not accept. Far better is it to wear lightly the mask of society, outwardly following the rules so that you do not awaken the suspicions of the interfering busy-bodies. Then, when the whisperers and Nosy-Parkers think you are obeying the rules, get up on your hobby-horse and amble stealthily away like Don Quixote when he sallied out of the private door of his backyard into the fields, wonderfully pleased to see with what ease he had succeeded in the beginning of his enterprise.

As soon as we have escaped from the city boundary we must adapt ourselves to a new and Gypsy conception of Time. In England we have the odious proverb, "Time is money" to sting and harness us into activity. The hours keep ticking like a meter of an expensive taxi. "Never waste your time, my boy," says the old-fashioned schoolmaster: "every moment of the day must be filled, for every hour you lose is thriftless." In Spain, where they possess a diametrically opposite conception of Time, the national proverb is: "El tiempo es fiesta," (Time is the fiesta), and a Spanish fiesta is an epitome of all the activities of the folk. The true freedom only comes to the wanderer when he ceases to measure time, save by the heavenly bodies. It does not matter when he arrives at the next stage in a journey, that depends on the whim of his capricious hobby-horse. Whenever I went out on the Gypsy trail I took the precaution of leaving my watch at home, more, I must say, as a precaution against Gypsy-thieving, but never once did I feel its want, because there was no need to do anything on time. When you wander on foot from Guadix to Madrid and Madrid to Badajoz it does not matter when you arrive. If night falls and you are far from a town you have only to knock at a farm-house and, if you are lucky, you will get a corner in the barn to sleep in, otherwise you can wrap yourself up in your cloak and sleep under the stars.

Little by little as the wanderer pursues his way through the country he becomes attuned to the many voices of nature. He loses all his city complexes and learns how to endure with equanimity the discomforts of nomadic life and the sordidness of poverty. It is worth enduring many a fatiguing hour of sweltering heat when at the end you are able to prolong a siesta in shady patios or dingy taverns reeking of wine skins. Out on the roads you soon enter into brotherhood with tramps, minstrels, pedlars and vagabonds of all kinds. To join the brotherhood of the road all you need is a tiny spark of individual talent. I spent many days envying a road companion of mine in South Italy who could win fame and money in the villages of Calabria by his mimicry of animal sounds. It is personality that counts and a dash of Gypsy wiles. Fiddling, singing and fortune-telling are welcomed in any village circle when the folk find that time hangs heavily on their hands in the evenings. The landlord of the village inn is no easy fellow to win over: he is loud-voiced and red-faced: he would chase you away with foul oaths if you asked him for charity and he would put the local policeman on your track. But if you win the applause of the villagers by your little performance, you will soon earn a few glasses of wine from him and perhaps a fine meal into the bargain.

Then there is the strange joy of leaving the village behind you with its snarling, snapping dogs, its noisy children, and following the lonely road in search of adventure. A lonely wanderer

gives the name adventure to any chance incident on the road.
For me the great adventure was to come suddenly upon some
Gypsy tribe camped in a deserted nook within earshot of the
road.

To enter the society of Gypsies was to enter into the closest
communion with Nature.

The Gypsy is a most unaccountable human being; you never
know what he may do. When meeting Gypsies in the lonely
countryside I always call to mind the words of warning of an
old Romany Rye, a friend of mine: "whenever you meet a tribe
of gypsies in deserted country don't trust the younger members,
for they might pick a quarrel with you and even tear the
clothes off your back, and leave you stripped in a ditch with a
wound in the head. The best course is to enquire at once for the
'*puro rom*,' or old man of the tribe, for he is the '*Crayi*' or
king, and his word is law. Once you have told him the pass-
word you will be as safe as in a church."

The old man of the tribe is the grandfather. He leads an
enviable existence, for all the men, women and children serve
him and he is a dictator. You will find him generally lying
asleep in the grass, with his black hat pulled over his face and
his "*chuquel*," or hound, beside him. He is not in reality
asleep; although his black hat is over his eyes, he knows all that
is going around him and he lets the younger members of the
tribe make first contact with the stranger.

From all sides they gather round, the naked children, the
naked-breasted women, dogs and villainous men. The
stranger is a luscious object to prey upon and they feel him all
over and thrust their hands into his pockets, push him about and
act generally like a pack of mangy dogs smelling a juicy bone.
The stranger is helpless. All the Borrow, the Leland, the
Wlislocki he has read is of no use to him. When the old man
sees the stranger is hard pressed he rises nonchalantly, shouts a
few oaths to the rabble and welcomes the stranger. It is best
for the stranger to have some coins in his pocket specially if a
tavern is nearby, for the word "mol," or wine, has a magic ring
about it. When the Romany Rye pays a first visit to a Gypsy
camp he should double the wine ration whenever he can and add
in from time to time a dose of "*repañí*," or brandy. Nothing
loosens the tongue of the Gypsies like brandy, for it whips the

sluggish up to vigour; hence the picturesque Spanish for having a drink, *"darle un palo al burro"*—"give the mule the stick." As the wine-skin passes from man to man and warms up the hearts of these wanderers they soon begin to call the stranger *"Quiribó,"* or companion, an affectionate word which occurs in many Romany dialects under different forms and means the same as *"compadre."* The scene is a fantastic one, especially at sundown when the tribe gathers around the fires outside the tents. The women who are not busy stirring the evening stew which is cooking in big pots over the fires, sit basket-making, and as they work they sing songs in a lilting rhythm in the fitful glare of the fire. I see old wrinkled crones, buxom women suckling their babes, amber-skinned maidens with golden earrings and bracelets on their arms, swarthy bearded men with long black hair and wild looks, mangy and lean dogs skulking in the background; then is the time to hazard a few timid phrases in Romany and become a word taster and add to my store.

The old woman of the tribe was the first to test the Gypsy scholar, but the words she used would not be found in the school book, for the Gypsies like to shock the Romany Rye in case he might have some remnants of gentile modesty. She fired obscenity after obscenity, the coarse words bespattered me like a fusillade of dung pellets, and between each shot the hag cackled with mirth and the other women swayed to and fro with laughter. It was better to have a rich Picaresque vocabulary and to answer back in spirited dialogue; for the men cracked their fingers like castanets, the naked children squealed and the dogs barked. Then the scholar's opportunity came as he listened to the strange lilting tones of the language and began to catch the fleeting words as the naturalist does butterflies in his net. Many of the words were as nomadic as the Gypsies themselves. They were like a magic patteran leading him back over the Gypsy's trail to the east. Their language is based upon certain fundamental words which express their nomadic existence, there are few words signifying organization, stability, and the steadfastness of the peasant who ploughs and reaps, but a multitude of synonyms for action, and movement. The Gypsies will say, "God condemned our race to sterility; hence we are for ever fleeing from desert wastes towards the land of plenty. When we discover an oasis for our halting-place we mark it with the Indian Swastika, but we do not tarry there long. As soon as it has given us its fruits, we pack our tents and slip away in the night to fresh pastures."

"Accursed parasites," replies the civilized man, "you sow not neither do you reap, but you prey upon the workers of the soil. For this reason God condemned you to wander like poverty-stricken gleaners over the plains of the world."

The Gypsies have been extraordinarily successful in preserving their secrets, and their origin is wrapped in mystery. Many scholars have racked their brains to solve the problem, but in vain. Dickens used to declare that he rejoiced in the enigma of Shakespeare's life and personality, and he was always afraid of waking up one morning and finding that some scholar had solved it. This is how many a Romany Rye feels concerning the Gypsies when he plods through innumerable theories of scholars, ranging from those who seek for the origin of the Romanies in Homer and Herodotus, to those who make them the descendants of the Jats, Doms, Dards, or Changars of North India. In the eighteenth century by chance a key to the problem of the Gypsy language was discovered by a certain Hungarian student of theology named Stephen Vályi, who in 1763 became acquainted with three Indian students at Leyden. In talking with them he found that their language resembled the speech of the Gypsies he had known on the Puszta near the town of Debrecen, and he quoted the words to his Gypsy friends in Hungary and found that they were able to translate most of them. This was the beginning of philological studies, and, later, Rüdiger and Grellmann in their books prepared the way for the famous work of Pott in 1844 on the Gypsies of Europe and Asia, which analyses the Indian elements of the Gypsy language. Many scholars have carried on the work initiated by Pott, and recently many brilliant discoveries have been made, that have increased the sum total of knowledge, but none have solved the problem of the original home of the Gypsies.

It is probable that the Gypsies were already a nomad people when they were in India. Most of the scholars who have made a deep study of the language agree that the Gypsies could not have left India before A.D. 1000 when the modern Aryan languages evolved, but we meet here and there references in Persian, Arabic and Greek authors which suggest that they had left long before that date. The Persian poet Firdausi in his epic poem the *Sháhnáma*, describes how the monarch Bahrám Gúr imported into Persia ten thousand Gypsy musicians of both sexes from India in the hope that they would turn into good husbandmen. To each he gave an ox and ass for work, and to them all a thousand asses' load of wheat as seed for raising crops, and he added that they should beside make music for the poor and render them this service free of cost. The Gypsies, however, according to the poem, ate the wheat and oxen and after a year came with pallid cheeks to the Shah, who said to them;

> "Was it not your task to plough,
> To sow, and reap? Your asses yet remain,
> So load them up, prepare your harps, and stretch
> The silken chords."
> > And so the Gypsies now,
> According to Bahrám's just ordinance,
> Live by their wits; they have for company
> The dog and wolf, and tramp unceasingly."[1]

In the fourteenth century we find references to the wandering tribes in the *Itinerarium* of the Irish Franciscan monk Symon Simeonis who made a pilgrimage to the Holy Land in 1322. Near Candia in Crete he describes how he saw a race outside the city, following the Greek rite and asserting themselves to be of the family of Ham. "They rarely," he says, "or never stop in one place beyond thirty days and, always wandering and fugitive as though accursed by God, after the thirtieth day, move from field to field with their oblong tents, black and low like the Arab and from cave to cave. For after that period any place in which they have dwelt becomes full of worms and other nastiness with which it is impossible to dwell." In another significant passage of the *Itinerarium* the author describes how these nomads had wounds on their face, and burns made by themselves, as though they wished to be baptized by flames and purged of sin. It was in the fourteenth century, too, that the Empress Catherine de Courtenay-Valois (1301–46) granted to the suzerains of Corfu authority to receive as vassals certain

---

[1] *Sháhnáma.* Trans. A. G. and E. Warner. Vol. VII. Section 39.

"*homines vageniti*," coming from the Greek mainland and using the Greek rite. By the close of the fourteenth century these "*vageniti*" were all subject to a single baron, Gianali de Abitabulo, and formed the nucleus of a fief called the "*feudum Acinganorum*," or Gypsy Fief, which lasted under one chief or another until the abolition of feudal tenures at the beginning of the nineteenth century. Evidently Greece must have been at that time familiar to Gypsies, for we meet with references among Venetian writers to ruins in the Peloponnesus, which were called *Gyphtokastra*, or Gypsy fortresses, and the Egyptians or Acingani were spoken of as one of the seven races inhabiting the Peloponnesus. Arnold von Hauff, who went on a pilgrimage in 1496–99, came across a suburb of "poor, naked people in little reed-thatched houses; they were called Suyginer and were the same as those whom we call Heiden (Heathen) from Egypt and who wander in other lands. They ply all sorts of handiwork, shoe-making, cobbling, smith-craft. The anvil stands on the ground, the man sits in front of it like a tailor: near him sits his wife, also on the ground and spins. Between them is a fire and nearby two little leather bags like bagpipes, half in the ground and pointing towards the fire. And the wife as she sits and spins, from time to time lifts up one of the bags and then presses it down again, with the result that the wind is sent through the earth into the fire and the man can get on with his tinkering."

This description written in the fifteenth century is an accurate account of the coppersmiths with their portable anvil and bellows, who still roam through the east of Europe. Hauff says that these nomads came from a region called Gyppe, forty miles from Modone in the Peloponnesus. Their territory was seized by the Turks, whereupon some counts and lords fled to Rome to the Pope to demand his comfort and succour. He gave them letters to the Holy Roman Emperor urging him to give them assistance in the name of the Christian Faith. They did not find help and they died in great misfortune, but they passed on the letters to their children who "roam through our lands and call themselves men of Little Egypt. But that is a lie, for their parents came from the territory of Gyppe, which is not so far from Cologne as it is from Egypt." This passage is of great interest when we come to consider the great trek of the Gypsies through Europe towards the West.

the speed with which the Gypsies travelled from one country to another. Already in 1418 they appear at Leipzig and Frankfurt-am-Main and later in the year at Zurich, Basle and Berne. In 1419 we hear of them at Hamburg and in the south at Sis-- teron in Provence, where the inhabitants, who were terror- struck by their appearance, called them Saracens. From there they travelled through Provence into Italy and reached Bologna on July 15, 1422. In the archives of Bologna we find a full description of our eternal wanderers.[1] A hundred of them arrived under Duke Andrew of Egypt. This duke, according to his statement, had denied the Christian faith and the king of Hungary had seized his lands and person, but he told the king that he wished to return to the Christian faith and the latter after having re-baptized him and his followers, commanded them to travel the world for seven years, to go to Rome to see the Pope, and afterwards to return to their own country.

The Gypsies soon became notorious in Bologna and many people came to see them mainly on account of the Duke's wife who, it was said, was able to foretell the future; how many years a man would live, how many children a woman would bear. And the witches walked about the city in bands of six and eight, ferreting in corners, touching everything, robbing, tricking with the most arrant insolence. They visited the shops pre- tending that they wished to buy something, but in reality their object was to steal. Then a great outcry arose against them and a proclamation was made threatening those who visited them with a fine of fifty pounds and excommunication, for they were the most cunning thieves in Christendom. It was even allowed to those who had been robbed by them to rob them in return to the amount of their losses. In consequence of this some of the men one night broke into a stable where some of their horses were tethered and stole the finest of them. When the Gypsies saw what had happened they agreed to restore many of the stolen articles and finding that there was no more chance of looting they set off on their way to Rome. The chronicler, wishing to impress on his readers how sinister these wanderers were, makes the following additional comment: "Mark my words: these were the ugliest brood ever seen in these parts. They were thin and black and ate like swine; their women were

---

[1] *Historia miscella baroniensis.* Quoted in Colocci: *Gli Zingari.* p. 55.

dressed in smocks and wore a pilgrim's cloak across the shoulder, rings in their ears and a long veil on their head. One of them gave birth to a child in the market place, and at the end of three days she went on to join her folk."

After Bologna they reached Forlí, where, according to the chronicler Brother Jerome, they roamed through the town like raging wild beasts, and he adds the important comment that they said they had come from India.

At Rome Duke Andrew was received in audience by the Pope Martin V (though no record can be found in the archives of the Vatican) and their cause was supported by Baldassarre Cossa (Pope John XXIII) who had been deposed by the Council of Constance. The audience with the Pope marked an epoch in their wandering, for after this we note how they systematically visit the great shrines of Europe, and later on, in 1496, there are documents stating that Pope Alexander VI had ordained that Count Martin Gyöngy the Gypsy and his family should go on a a pilgrimage to Rome, St. James of Compostela, and other holy places.

The next place where we meet the Gypsy wanderers is in Paris, on August 17, 1427, and a very lively description is given of them by Pasquier in his *Recherches Historiques de la France* (IV. 19). They repeated the story of their apostasy and their penance and their pilgrimage from the East to Rome, but now they added that the Pope, when he had heard the general confession of their sins, had ordered them as penance to roam for seven years through the world, without sleeping in a bed, but in order to comfort them in their affliction he had furthermore ordained that every bishop or mitred abbot should give them the sum of ten livres tournois for expenses.

The band arrived on the day of St. John the Beheaded, but they were not allowed to enter Paris and were lodged in La Chapelle-Saint-Denis; and they were in all about a hundred or a hundred and twenty. The chronicler adds that when they had left their country they were a thousand or twelve hundred, but the remainder had died on the way, including their king and queen.

Whilst they were at Chapelle-Saint-Denis they aroused great interest among the inhabitants, though by common accord they were considered the poorest creatures ever seen in France in the memory of man. The children, boys and girls, were surprisingly precocious and intelligent. And nearly all had both ears pierced and in each ear a silver ring, worn, they said, as a sign of nobility in their country. The men were very black and their hair was fuzzy; the women were the ugliest and the blackest that could be imagined, hair as black as a horse's tail; for dress just an old blanket fastened on the shoulder by a cord or rag, and underneath a wretched shift as sole covering. Nevertheless, in spite of their poverty, there were among them fortune-tellers who looked into people's hands and told what had happened to them, or would happen, and sowed discord in the families; for they said to the husband: "Your wife has cuckolded you," or to the wife: "Your husband has played you false," and what was worse, while they were speaking to folks, by magic art, by the enemy in Hell, or by dexterity, they would empty the people's purses and fill their own. The Bourgeois of Paris, for that was how the chronicler described himself, then adds that though he himself visited them three or four times and spoke to them, he never noticed that he lost a coin, nor did he ever see them look into a hand, but the people said so everywhere, so that the news came to the ears of the Bishop of Paris, Jean de la Roche-Taillade. He straightway went to see them accompanied by a Friar of the Minors, Little Jacobin by name, who at the bequest of the bishop preached a fine sermon, excommunicating all those who had believed such imposture and showed their hands. And so it was decided that they should move on, and they departed on the day of Our Lady of September and made for Pontoise. In many of the towns in France in the seven years after 1427 we find records of the Great Band, and there is always the same story to tell. Then in 1438–40 thousands of Gypsies began to pour into Western Europe from the East and they began to become a serious problem for the authorities in each country.

It was their reputation for witchcraft which made them feared and even respected in Europe. Being oriental they mingled with their witchcraft strange incantations; every one of these incantations was rhythmic and its significance sprang from constant repetition of the chanted phrase. The witch would use all her powers of suggestion in weaving her spells. Her magic cell was often in some subterranean cavern, or else in a deserted churchyard near some dolmen or fairy ring. Here lords and ladies, peasants and outlaws would come to hear her chants. With oriental cunning she would dazzle their imaginations, showing them the strange tarot cards of the Egyptians with their twenty-one keys; she would arrange them fanwise and in reading the prophecy from them she would murmur in a monotonous singsong voice like a pythoness mesmerized by the god.

Gradually her listeners would become hypnotized by the rhythm and the ceaseless repetition of the chant. Their minds would become released from everyday reality and float away in a dreamland under the spell of the sorceress with her matted, raven tresses, her tawny complexion and her eyes flashing in the candle-light of the cavern. Seeing the power that incantations possessed over credulous humanity the Gypsies began to extend their knowledge of music. In the countryside they would not do the heavy manual work of the husbandman, for they preferred to prey upon his credulity. Music offered them great possibilities of extending their sway, because it could be associated with their Shamanism. In every country the people had songs and poems springing from the earth, songs reminding them of the vicissitudes of fortune, of battles, of heroes, of demigods. These songs had passed down from mouth to mouth and they were hallowed by association with the genius of their race.

The Gypsies in their wanderings from village to village learnt those tunes and began to play them for the peasant to win his favour. And when they sang their strange, exotic voices transformed these folk-tunes into wizardry. The peasant recognized the melodies his grandfather had sung by the fire in the winter evenings, but when yonder brown-faced Gypsy played them they seemed to have caught up magic qualities. The slow song would meander on in endless melancholy, bringing tears to his eyes, for it made him think of the dull torment of life; then the quick rhythm of the dance would lash him into the fury of the pursuit; the repetitions of the tempestuous theme would be a call to arms. It was ever thus; the Gypsy vagabonds with their fiddles or their guitars became a necessity for the peasant after the daily toil, and thus they became the national minstrels in the various countries, inheriting the old traditions of the "*jongleurs*" and "*juglares.*" They could play on the whole gamut of emotions from melancholy despair up to delirium and Dervish ecstasy. The powers that served them as a race in their fortune-telling and spell-weaving became of still greater significance in their music-making. Here they could work authentic magic and waken the Dionysiac spirit in their audience. That is why even today the Gypsy fiddler in Hungary singles out a woman's face in the hall and fixes his gaze upon her as he plays his passionate lament. In this way the Gypsy in the café wins his way into the lady's heart and into her cavalier's pocket. The Gypsy, too, never loses sight of the element of external suggestion that enters into his art. This playing or singing follows always the same ritual, for he wishes to lull his audience into sympathy, then gradually work his magic and raise them up to the required pitch of excitement. Aristotle would call it "Katharsis," a purging of the emotions. He needs thus a great many stimulants to assist him in weaving his spells over the "gorgio." The Dionysiac spirit is not produced simply by the swaying music, but by lights, movements, perfumes, wines. Above all it is the nomadic personality of the Gypsy who has come into the lives of these people from the land of the Arabian Nights.

In the early morning, when the peasants or workers pass that Gypsy fiddler in the street, they pour scorn upon him and treat him as a pariah, but in the evening when he plays his melody to them they fling their arms around him, toast him in wine and stuff his pockets full of banknotes. The Gypsy fiddler, meanwhile, stands like a statue in his passivity; his copper face shows no emotion, his strange dark Hindu sorcerer's eye hypnotizes the fat peasant to whose face he is playing and reduces him to submission. Soon that peasant pulls out the bulging purse and the Tzigan's eye gleams, for he knows that before the end of the evening most of those coins will find their way to the Gypsy camp out there on the plain.

Such has been the story of the Gypsy wanderers since they entered Europe on their eternal trek from East to the far West. They knocked at the gates of Europe saying that they were pilgrims, and the simple folk believed their stories of the penance imposed upon them for sins committed by their ancestors, the seven years as expiation, after which period they would return to their country. Making use of such subtle stratagems they were able to penetrate deeper and deeper into Europe, and they carried their trickery to still further lengths by creating the belief among the rulers of Europe that they should only be judged by their own standards, that is to say by Romany law. This right was recognized in 1423 by the Emperor Sigismund in a letter which he granted to Ladislas, Governor of the Tziganes, in which it was stated that should trouble arise among the Romanichals Count Ladislas had power to condemn or acquit.

Aventinus, who lived in the early sixteenth century and who wrote the history of Bavaria, describes the Gypsies as being highly privileged. Robbing and stealing that were prohibited to others under pain of hanging or beheading were allowed to these people.[1] The Kings of France, too, gave them privileges.

In 1500, however, at the Diet of Augsburg all ranks in the Empire were strictly forbidden to permit Gypsies to pass through their countries or to give them protection and convoy as they had done before. In the preceding year in Spain the first real decree of persecution was promulgated against them: within sixty days the Gypsies must settle down under masters and no longer wander through the kingdom, or within sixty days they must leave Spain never to return. If after the sixty days they should be discovered workless or without a master, they would be given each a hundred stripes the first time they were caught, the second time they would have their ears cut off and would spend sixty days in chains before being banished; the third time they would become the slave of those who captured them for all their life. This decree, furthermore, was to cancel all other letters of safe-conduct. One country after another followed the example of Spain and the Holy Roman Empire, and the terrible era of persecutions began which was not to cease for centuries. The Romanichals were from the first associated with music and witchcraft; Colocci calls them the commercial travellers of the occult sciences, for they spread notions of astronomy, chemistry, alchemy, and tarot cards for divination among the peoples of the West. This knowledge of the occult was to be their undoing, for it brought down upon them the enmity of church and state. Even their traditional metal-

[1] Grellmann: *Dissertation on the Gypsies*. Eng. Trans. by Raper. pp. 72 *seq.* London. 1807.

lurgical work which Arnold von Hauff described in the Morea
was a perpetual testimony to the curse, which, it was believed,
rested upon their race. For there was a widely spread superstition that a Gypsy smith had forged the nails for the Crucifixion and that henceforth his race has been accursed of heaven.
The superstition is mentioned in the seventeenth century in the
"Glossary" by Ducange who quotes references to the writers of
the Byzantine age.[1] In many parts of Europe we may meet this
superstition.

In the island of Lesbos a very beautiful song to Our Lady is
sung on Good Friday which describes the Passion of Our Lord.
Our Lady who is praying in a grotto hears the rolling thunder
and sees the lightning flash in the sky. All the heavens are black
and the stars are veiled. St. John then comes to her in tears
crying out: "The miserable Jews have arrested my master like
a thief and are leading him away like a murderer." Our Lady
when she heard it fell and swooned. When she recovered, she
went with Martha, Magdalen and Mary to the forge where she
saw the nail worker hard at work. "Good day, workman," says
Our Lady, "what art thou making there?" And he replies:
"The Jews have ordered nails of me; they have ordered four of
me, but I am making them five." Then Our Lady faints again
and is revived by three bottles of musk and four of rose. Then
she says to the Gypsy smith;

> "Be accursed O Tzigans!
> May there never be cinder in your forges,
> May there never be bread in your pans,
> Nor buttons to your shirts."[2]

The poem ends with the hurried departure of the Gypsy and all
his tribe. They henceforth, like Juan Espera Dios, the wandering Jew, will become the eternal wanderers through the world.
Georgeakis in a footnote says that the Gypsies in the island of Mity-
lene are all smiths. Groome, who quotes this song from Mity-
lene, also refers to the tradition among the tinkers in Scotland,
who consider themselves the descendants of those who made
the nails of the Cross and are condemned to wander continually

[1] Ducange: *Glossarium ad Scriptores Mediae et Infimae Graecitatis.* Quoted in
Groome: *Gypsy Folk Tales.* Introduction, p. xxiv. Paris, 1685. London, 1899.
[2] G. Georgeakis and Léon Pineau: *Le Folklore de Lesbos*, pp. 273–278. Paris, 1891.

without rest.[1] The tradition is also found in Alsace where the celebrated scholar Bataillard heard it described by an old Gypsy witch who was trying to persuade him to intercede with the police on behalf of one of her relations who had been put in gaol for theft. "The Manush (Gypsies)," she said, "are not wicked; they do not murder." She paused and then continued, "Ah, Rye, stealing; it is in the blood. Besides you must know that they have leave to steal once every seven years. It's a story. They were going to crucify Jesus. One of our Gypsy women passed by and she whipped up one of the nails they were going to use. She would have liked to steal all four nails but couldn't do so. It was just one she stole and that's why Jesus was crucified with only three nails, a single nail for both feet. And that's why Jesus gave the Gypsies leave to steal once every seven years."

I have heard the story of the four nails of the Cross from Gypsy coppersmiths in Spain and in America; and it has become like the song of the Bridge and the seven years' penance, part of the stock in trade of these eternal travellers. As Toma Cristo, one of my sardonic copper-working friends, remarked drily: "Why did the Gypsy 'romni' try to steal the four nails? I'll tell you, Rye, because all the Jews gave the smith for forging the nails was thirty pieces of copper. Why they even gave Judas Iscariot thirty pieces of silver."

The coppersmiths often add that the nail which the Gypsies stole may still be seen where the Gypsy hides it, that is to say, "*en la rabidilla*," or secreted in the coccyx at the base of his spine. After 1499 for the next hundred years the Gypsies were bandied about Europe from one nation to another, with the result that they are spread equally all over the nations which rejected them. Their persecutions lasted for centuries, in fact, the world has never ceased persecuting them. From the earliest to the present times the common people have regarded them with mixed feelings, enjoying their entertainments, fascinated by their mystery and their magic, and exasperated by their swindles. The upper classes adopted a different attitude; less superstitious, they suffered less from Gypsy fraud.[2]

In the West their reception was such as might have been ex-

[1] Groome: *op. cit.* p. xxviii.
[2] R. A. Scott Macfie: "Gypsy Persecutions." *Journal of Gypsy Lore Society*. July–Oct. 1943.

pected. After the first feelings of surprise people began to find these pilgrims a burden; their magic made them suspect with the church, and even their stories and the legends they told of oriental mystery were tainted with heresy. They travelled widely and very rapidly, and almost every ruler in the west found at practically the same time that they were undesirable visitors; and so they began by banishing them. Then they were associated with various crimes; we find them accused in Germany of even cannibalism, as in 1782, when there was the judicial murder of about forty Gypsies on this charge. The accusation of cannibalism has arisen on many occasions. In Spain, according to one of the contemporary writers, Quiñones, in the seventeenth century, a band of Gypsies at the village of Jaraicejo in Extremadura confessed under torture that they had killed a friar and eaten him. In the days of famine after 1918 nomad Gypsies in Transylvania were accused of cannibalism.

In England even in Henry VIII's reign we find edicts against Gypsies, but the Romanichals were a familiar sight in the countryside and there is the famous poem of Skelton describing the Gypsy girl, Elynor Rummynge (the name itself is Romany) with her kyrtel of Bristow red and her clothes wrythen after the Sarasyns gyse. In Scotland they became acclimatized more completely than in most countries and we even find a treaty made between the King of Scotland and the Gypsy chieftain in 1505. King James IV wrote to his uncle, the King of Denmark, commending to him Antony Gagino, Lord of Little Egypt, who had reached Scotland a few months earlier during a pilgrimage to the Christian world undertaken at the command of the Apostolic See. The Gypsies found Scotland a pleasant place for their roaming, because the clan life in those days resembled the Gypsy tribal life. James V, who was called "The Gaberlunzie Man" used to roam with the Gypsies, and it was only after he was ill-treated by them that he published the edicts against them. In Scotland there were some famous Gypsy families such as the Faws and the Baillies whose exploits are celebrated.

In the eighteenth century the attitude towards the Gypsies of the Christian world softened somewhat, and we find attempts made to settle them and allow them to mix with ordinary citizens, but the law has always been severe against the Romany race and we remember the words of the edict of Frankfurt of

1722 which pointed out that "even the Gypsies can neither live in the sky like birds nor underground like worms."

In 1767 the Empress Maria Theresa published a decree prohibiting them from dwelling in tents, from wandering about the land, dealing in horses, from eating "*mulo mas*" or meat killed by the hand of God, from electing their own *voyvodes*, or chiefs, and from using the Romany language. They were given some months to settle in villages or towns, where they were to pass under the name of New Boors or New Peasants, and to practise trades. Yet how could these wandering people suddenly choose and practise a trade from one day to the next? They were unable to do so and so they took no notice of the edict. Then new inducements were given them, and when these were unsuccessful, harsher edicts were made. No Gypsy was allowed to marry unless he could prove his ability to provide for his children; and married Gypsies were to have their children taken away from them to be educated. When the families resisted, the Gypsy children were dragged by ropes to school.

The lack of success of Maria Theresa's measure encouraged the Emperor Joseph II to frame a similar law for Transylvania, and in 1783 it was declared that they must settle and give up their native language and their particular costume. They had also to discard their cloaks because they were too effective a cover for their thieving. The Gypsies refused to be bound by the edict. When they were given cottages, they placed the cattle in them and cooked the corn they were given to sow. In the end, however, the result was satisfactory up to a point because they were no longer outside the law; so they gradually passed from nomadism and began to adapt themselves to sedentary life.

The same laws were passed in Spain by King Charles III. The Gypsies were called New Castilians and settled on the land. But in Spain, too, the measures were unsuccessful, though we find colonies of sedentary Gypsies settled in the South in the towns and villages.

In the nineteenth century an interesting experiment was carried out in Hungary by the Archduke Josef who was a true Romany Rye. He spent a great deal of his fortune in establishing Gypsy colonies on the plain of Hungary outside various towns, such as Hatvan and a large colony on his estate at Alcsuth. He gave them houses, cattle and work, and opened a special school for children. Yet after years of experimenting he had to admit that his experiment was an utter failure. The Gypsies led a settled life as long as the royal protector's eyes were upon them, but when he departed, they dispersed and went back to their nomadic life.

The Gypsies used to settle during the winter in the parishes, but in the summer they wandered about earning their living nomadically. Whenever the people were kind to them, they tended to give up their nomadic tendencies and merge their life with that of the towns, though, at certain intervals, they would for a time give way to their wandering instincts.

In the nineteenth century we come upon an era of greater enlightenment and humanity all over Europe. In England the whole attitude towards the Gypsies changed, and we find sects like the Quakers establishing schools and hospices for them. In Rumania in 1856 came the final liberation of the Gypsies from slavery, and henceforth they became established as real subjects of the kingdom.

When we look back over the centuries of persecution we find that most of the anti-Gypsy laws by denying them food and shelter contrived to make honest living impossible for them. They were compelled to rely more and more upon criminal activity and, when driven in desperation, to add violence to their theft, and even to commit murders when resisted. That is why records and police orders give a false picture of Gypsy life, for they only noticed Gypsies who had made themselves conspicuous by their criminal behaviour. We should thus, never forget as Scott Macfie, the Romany Rye, says, that for every Gypsy pilloried in the records or in the "*Zigeunerlisten*" for his crimes, there were a thousand leading a more or less honest, or at any rate, unobtrusive, life; and when we talk of persecutions we must not imagine that the persecutions of the past were worse than those of our own days. In the eighteenth century even the German conscience began to prick German writers. Rüdiger refers to the inhumanity of burying alive old, helpless and probably quite innocent Gypsy women, but it has been left to the year of grace 1942 to supply the answer as to what was the worst persecution the Gypsy race has ever had to suffer. For in that year there came to the Gypsy Lore Society from the Belgian Review *Message* of November 13, 1942, the following report of the wholesale massacre of Gypsies in Serbia, a crime far more horrible than any committed in the three centuries of anti-Gypsy legislation:

> "L'un des derniers crimes des Allemands en date nous paraît dé-passer de loin tous les autres parce qu'en plus de la souffrance qu'il a créé, il a detruit de la douceur et de la beauté: tous les tziganes de Serbie ont été massacrés! Les tziganes—ces derniers libéraux, comme les appelle mon ami Motz—ne sont plus. Ces marchands de poésie, de pronostics, de mensonges et de chansons ont été traqués le long des routes où s'enfuyaient au galop de leurs haridelles leurs baraques roulantes pleines de cris, de couleur, et de mystère.
>
> Ils ont tué tziganes, brulé les roulottes, éteint les feux de branches où grimaçaient les yeux noirs. Ils ont tué ceux qui allaient où va le vent, n'importe où, plus loin . . . malheur à eux."[1]

But persecution has never subdued the Gypsy race, and still we find the Gypsies wandering towards the West on their eternal quest.

In recent years during my wanderings along the Mediterranean coast of Spain I have met many of the Gypsy nomads not only from Catalonia, but also from Greece and Serbia and other countries. I have been struck by the dignity and sense of honour of these Gypsies. A few years ago, when I was in the town of Lorca in Murcia, I made friends with the Gypsy cattle dealers of the fair there and I organized a big *zambra* or musical performance to which all the Gypsies, old and young, contributed; all I did was to act the part of the "*padrino*" according to the usual ritual in Spain, namely I ordered two barrels of red wine and that was all there was to it. For hours the Romanichals, old and young, danced as though inspired. They danced collective and tribal dances; they danced secret dances, of the "*romanó pando*" type, and the individual hypnotic dances, in the intervals of singing "*Cante Jondo*."

At a certain moment the chief of the tribe came up to me. He was an unusually tall bearded Romany of bronzed complexion and flaming eyes. He stood before me with his long horse whip in his hand, wearing his black "*faja*" and his deep crimson muffler. "Erai," said he, "I hope that my companions have been to your liking." "I should think so," I answered. "Let us

[1] R. A. Scott Macfie: *op. cit.*, p. 77.

give the Gypsy toast, 'Grease for the body,' '*manteca pal cuerpo*,' as they say among the Gypsies." As soon as they had drunk the toast, at a sign from the chief, they all departed without a word. They would not accept any payment whatsoever, and there were no belated farewells and no protests. All ended in complete calm, and though I thought I had been the giver of the feast, it was they who had entertained me. The chivalrous dignity of their behaviour is characteristic of the "calés" of Spain.

I had a similar experience at the famous fair at the tiny village of Verdú in Catalonia. Every year for centuries past the Gypsy tribes camp in tents there. They come not only from Spain but also from France, Italy and Belgium, and all of them are cattle dealers. They pitch their tents around the castle of Verdú which dates from the twelfth century. Verdú is also celebrated as the birthplace of the saint so beloved by the negro people, Saint Peter Claver. These Gypsies by their lives are a continual warning and reproach to our modern way of life which is becoming daily more mechanical. In my life in the city I am a second or third-rate machine of futile efficiency, dinning into my ears the belief in the progress of humanity, in civilization, uttering great hallowed words to prevent myself from thinking. What is human progress but a huge titanic struggle between those who protect life and those who destroy it? One group of scientists say they have discovered a remedy for the plague which would save millions of lives. The other answer, "We have discovered a new type of poisonous gas or a bomb which will kill not only human beings, but every living thing, within a large radius." To both these groups the Gypsy says, "Become a vagabond, a nomad. Steal out of the city like a thief at dead of night. Follow the Gypsy patteran on the road and soon you will catch up with the Minions of the Moon. What of poverty, you will forget poverty in the tents which are the Gypsies' moving palaces."

In Provence, in the little town of Les Saintes Maries de la Mer, every year on the 24th and 25th of May these eternal travellers hold the famous pilgrimage of the Gypsies. Over the plain of the Camargue roam the nomadic tribes, towards the church of the Sea Marys, not only from France, but from Spain, Italy, even Germany. They worship their patron, Sarah, the Egyptian servant of the three Marys, who came from the Holy Land after the Crucifixion of Our Lord. Above, in the church, the faithful pray all night around the relics of the saints. Down below in the dark unconsecrated crypt the Gypsy tribes sleep on the ground around the altar on which stands a little shrine containing the remains of the Gypsy Sarah. The Gypsies who take part in this pilgrimage every year are unconsciously renewing a very old tradition going back to Greek times; for here there had been an altar to Diana which afterwards the Romans transformed into an altar to the Sun god, Mithras, and his bull victim. The Gypsies do not know that they are perpetuating this ancient tradition, but it is because of this unconscious perpetuation of prehistoric rites that the Gypsy race so fascinates the Romany Rye who sees in these wanderers an eternal reminder of the past.

In that pilgrimage to Provence when the religious ceremony is over and St. Sarah has been carried by the Romanies into the sea, then come the bull-fights which are Mithraistic in character. The *"gardians"* of the Camargue follow the wild bulls and the white horses that have sprung from the sea foam, from Neptune. Theirs is a mediæval life. Their great chief was the famous troubadour, descendant of mediæval troubadours, the Marquis Folco de Baroncelli-Javon. He was the great follower of Mistral, Aubel and Roumanille, and perhaps the greatest Félibre of them all. All his life he was considered the high priest of all the Gypsies that came annually to the shrine of Les Saintes Maries.

When roaming through this lonely land of the Camargue, the land of the Fata Morgana, or as Mistral calls it, *"La Viéio Danso,"* I have seen him ride over the plain at sunset after his bulls, dressed like a "Gitano," with his blue faded shirt and his chamois breeches. He was the father, the protector of the *"faraones."* Many times by the camp-fires of the Gypsies in the evening he would talk to me of the origins of the Gypsy race. He always considered that there were two races of Gypsies, completely different one from the other. To one race belonged those whom we call Spanish, French or Italian Gypsies, those that meet at Les Saintes Maries de la Mer and deal in horses. They are the Gypsies we see all over Spain at the fairs in Andalusia, Catalonia and Murcia. They have nothing in com-

mon with the other race of Gypsies who are copperworkers and
have since the earliest times carried on their metal working and
are called in Spain *"Húngaros."* The coppersmiths are tall,
muscular, and walk with their feet turned outwards. They
have a big skeleton and are as bronzed as mahogany. Their
eyes are slightly oblique with the white of the eye bluish and
they have curly hair. Such are the copperworkers. But they
rarely stray near the Saintes Maries de la Mer.

The Southern Gypsies of Spain and France are different.
They are lithe and agile, with small limbs. Their wrists and
ankles are slender, and they walk with the toe leaving a mark on
the sand. They are not hairy like the copperworkers, and their
skin is reddish-brown. Their nose is aquiline, their eyes almond-
shaped. They have slender waists, long legs and they walk like
panthers. These *"Gitanos"* are by nature attracted to the horse
and the bull. By nature, too, they are antagonistic to the
copperworkers.

Baroncelli's theories have always fascinated me because, in
addition to knowing the Gypsy race, he has been a great follower of the Red Indians, and once a Red Indian chief came to
visit him at his little *"mas"* or farmhouse in the Camargue.
This chief, who was a great friend of his, was called Philip
Blue-Shield, Chief of the Sioux Indians. Philip Blue-Shield
used always to say to Baroncelli that his race came from the
land where the sun rises. And Baroncelli then told me that the
"Gitanos" always used to tell him that their race came from
where the sun sets. Here was the explanation of the eternal
trek towards the West to the end of the world, the scene of their
beginning.

Baroncelli was convinced of the truth of the Atlantis legend,
so marvellously described by Plato: the same Atlantis that has
been sung by Verdaguer and set to music by Falla—a mighty
continent linking Europe and America. When the cataclysm
came and the continent was submerged in the waters of the
Atlantic the original race was sundered in twain, becoming the
Red-skins in America and the *"Gitanos"* in Europe. Philip
Blue-Shield in describing to Baroncelli the origin of his race,
would say, "My race always follows the instincts of hunting and
wandering. They came from where the sun rises, that is to say,
they came from over here in the East."

Baroncelli also would speak of the similarity between the architectural remains in Mexico and in Egypt. The pyramidal structures in the West were called "*teocalis*." The Aztecs believed that they came from the land of Aztlan, the land of the herons, and that they came from it in order to conquer the Anahuac, the land of the water.

There is no doubt that the Gypsies we meet in our wanderings again and again refer to their wandering towards the West, and there seems to be some strange urge in them to reach the end of the world, which they imagine lies in the West in the land of the setting sun. It is curious to note how this obsession comes again and again into their conversation, especially among the older men of the tribes when they are crouching by their tent fires at dusk.

They believe that at the end of the world there is a hole through which they can descend to the underworld, but this can only be reached if they follow the direction taken by the setting sun. According to some Gypsy tribes the world of the dead is situated on a mountain. A cavernous passage leads into the interior which is guarded by nine white dogs. The nomads in East Europe, when one of their number is dying, make a white dog lick his legs to ease the agony of death. The souls of children born dead are borne to this mountain in a sack by an old woman. To this kingdom of the spirits of his ancestors every Gypsy wends his way after death, and on his journey thither during this life he never omits to do all in his power to placate these spirits of the dead, for they have power over his life, and their vengeance would ceaselessly threaten him and his tribe. That is why Gypsies consider the oath sworn by the dead (*ap i mulende*, as they say in Romany) as the most sacred bond of all. And all over the world we have met Gypsies who refer to the long journey after death over lands full of thorns and furze, when they will need a good pair of strong shoes. Hence the custom of burying a new pair of shoes with the dead Romanichal. The shoe is for the Gypsies the symbol of life and fertility. Hence our custom of throwing an old shoe after the bride on her wedding day with the wish that she may have many children, and we celebrate the symbolism in the old nursery-rhyme:

There was an old woman who lived in a shoe;
She had so many children she did not know what to do."

Thus even in death there is life and the Gypsies passing on to the undiscovered country from whose bourn no traveller returns will continue their eternal wandering. Can we wonder that Thomas Coryat, that inveterate traveller of the sixteenth century, before starting on his journey to the Holy Land, hung up as a votive offering in his parish church at Odcombe the shoes in which he had walked from Venice?

Ever since the time of the Persian Monarch Báhram Gúr attempts have been made to settle the Gypsies but none have ever really succeeded. The longing which many people have for roaming in the country and seeing new places amounts to a mania in Gypsies. I have known countless cases in England, Spain and America where Gypsies, after settling down with their families in one place and becoming sedentaries, will one day suddenly, without warning, disappear mysteriously and take to roads. Their nomadic craze is instinctive and it attacks them periodically in their lives. Anthropologists have pointed out how this nomadism becomes a kind of rite even in the lives of the Gypsies, whose wandering is confined to a certain region of a country. When their instinct urges them to set out, they do so secretly, and they always follow the same circular course with certain variations in their path from year to year. It is in the spring that the urge to wander comes upon them with special force and, willy-nilly, they must follow the spell of over the hills and far away. All the centuries of persecution, torture, burning at the stake; all the crass brutality of law and police; all the misdirected charity of the philanthropists have not extinguished this "wanderlust," for travel is their way of life, and when they abandon it they do so merely temporarily out of expediency. They have watched our civilization growing almost from its infancy. When I visit my friend, Cagachin, the Gypsy blacksmith in his cave in Granada today I realize that his Romany ancestors helped Ferdinand and Isabella to forge the artillery that broke down the walls of the Alhambra in 1492. All that the Gypsies have seen of our civilization has not made them wish to imitate it except outwardly and hypocritically in order that we may cease persecuting them, and leave them to their own devices.

Their long wandering for centuries has given them a philosophy of travel which Borrow and his Gypsy "*pral*" Petulengro sum up in the following words:

"Life is very sweet, brother; who would wish to die?
    "I would wish to die—"
"You talk like a gorgio—which is the same as talking like a fool. Were you a Romanichal you would talk wiser. A Romanichal would wish to live for ever!"
"In sickness, Jasper?"
"There's the sun and stars, brother."
"In blindness, Jasper?"
"There's the wind on the heath, brother: if I could only feel that, I would gladly live forever."

And again there come to my mind the words of the English Gypsy Alma Boswell, which I read in an article by Arthur Symons; "Well you've heard of the man called Cain. Now, don't the Old Book say that he went away and married a black-eyed compergel, one of our roving folks? I reckon we springs from them. We was the first people that the dear Lord made, and mebbe we shall be the last. When all the rest is worn out, there'll still be a few of our folks travelling with tents and waggons."

And when I ask myself what is the quest of these eternal travellers I have only to recall one scene, which I have experienced again and again throughout my life among Gypsies, whether in Hungary, Rumania, Greece or Western Arizona and New Mexico. . . . The fair is over and the peasants and rich farmers jingle the coins in their pockets; fat bargains have been made, purses are bulging. Now for the tavern and the spree. I see them walk arm in arm with their doxies into the courtyard of the café and call for wine. Huddled in a corner lurk some Gypsies—a collection of ragged scarecrows—caressing their fiddles. When the peasants begin to drink, one of them, the leader, comes up to the table and starts to play. The wine flows, the peasants sing, the Gypsies play. The leader stands, holding his violin a few inches away from the face of a fat peasant sitting at the head of the table, gazing into his eyes, searching for the tune which will establish the bond of sympathy. Gradually the fat man sinks into a dreamy state as the elegiac sadness of the harmony envelops his senses. But not for long, for suddenly the Gypsy quickens the pace, the music becomes martial in rhythm, and an inexorable force draws the peasants after the Gypsy band as if they had been following the Piper of Hamelin. The Gypsy leader now knows he has awakened the slumbering magic, and he leads his musical tribe over hill, over dale of harmony with the peasants tumbling blindly after them. The ragged minstrel now wields the power of a god and his bow is a wizard's wand, which will transform for a brief moment those peasants from brute slaves of daily toil into heroes who draw strength from the traditions of their race. As that great composer and noblest of Romany Ryes Ferencz Liszt once said; "The Gypsy does not create, he perpetuates." He is the chief actor in a drama in which the gorgio or non-Gypsy is the chorus. The chorus stimulates the Indian Gypsy by clapping and stamping in time to the rhythm, by drinking Tokay or manzanilla in the hope of reaching the moment when the tension of life is relaxed and emotions need purifying. Aristotle called it "katharsis." These Gypsy minstrels, eternal travellers, minister to this need of humanity, and that is why the poet loves them and makes them say:—

> "The wild air bloweth in our lungs
> The keen stars twinkle in our eyes,
> The birds gave us our wily tongues,
> The panther in our dances flies."